50 Memorable and Unusual QPR Matches

Ray Eaton

To Evelyn,

Thank you for encouraging me to continue to keep on
writing.

.

CONTENTS

Acknowledgments   i

1   The Loneliness of The Long-Distance Hooligan   1

2   Collins Ahead of The Game   10

3   Kelly Blooded Against Poole   16

4   Brother Beyond   21

5   Amateur Hour   27

6   A 'Roy Of the Rovers' Performance   32

7   The Poisoned Challis   37

8   Afternoon Delight   41

9   Parkes Loses Out   46

10   A Topsy-Turvey Goalless Draw   51

11   The Fastest Goal Mystery   56

12   Madness at Millmoor   61

13   Surprise Lucky Shirts   68

14   Stanchion Deliver   72

15   Perfect Ten   76

16   A Red and Black Love Affair   81

17   Mullery's Last Stand   85

18	Here's to You, Mister Robinson	92
19	Goal of The Season Afternoon	98
20	Astroturf Finale	103
21	The Gray Show	109
22	Parker Scores Sixth	116
23	Most Vital Draw	124
24	Another Giant Slayed	131
25	The Summit of English Football	136
26	Spot-Kick Legend	142
27	Same Again, Please	149
28	Les Bids Loft Farewell	154
29	Macca's Bizarre Return	160
30	Pollock Saves Rangers	164
31	End of Away Day Misery	169
32	Kiwomya's Mystery Goal	174
33	New Faces	179
34	The Curse of Nine	184
35	Langley Makes Bittersweet History	190
36	The Astonishing Ainsworth	196

37	Home Supremacy	200
38	The Hand of Bean	206
39	The Petrified Forest	210
40	One Size, Two Goals, No Hat trick	215
41	Nineteen and Counting	221
42	The International Brigade	226
43	Another Hitchcock Cameo Appearance	231
44	Record Shutout	235
45	The Second Coming of Zamora	240
46	A Win Away	247
47	The Gift Outright	254
48	35th Time Lucky	258
49	When Rangers Declared War on Wales	262
50	A Fair Wind	268

ACKNOWLEDGMENTS

I would not have been able to compile this book without the help of others, so I am delighted to take this opportunity to show my gratitude. First of all, I would like to extend my thanks to my great friend, lifelong supporter and long-time fanzine contributor John O'Mahony. Without the time he spent freely helping me with the research needed, as well as offering his own views and personal memories, this publication would never have happened.

I would also like to thank other long-standing and highly-respected supporters, like Chris Guy, Steve Russell and Alan Barnes. At least one chapter of the book was proving to be hard work, to the point that it was almost being dubbed as 'the lost game', because of the difficulty in finding out any information about it. But they were all happy to share their memories and knowledge, and I am especially grateful to Chris for going out of his way to dig up information where it was needed. In among some fellow QPR followers, I was also delighted to call on the help of my friend, Tranmere Rovers supporter and sometimes teammate in my quiz team, Rudy Noriega. Rudy had the experience of publishing a book himself, and was more than happy to share his own memories of what it takes to go through that process.

I am also grateful to Ron Phillips, the former Club Secretary and programme editor, and Michael Wale, who was a long-serving columnist from the same era. Their respective writings were also a big help when delving into the past. Their regular columns in the programmes from many years ago, remain a wonderful source of reference from a different age and were most helpful when trying to learn about particular matches in the past. And speaking of sources of reference, I was also lucky enough to be able to refer to the work of the late Gordon Macey. Gordon was a wonderful club historian and his book was a most reliable guide, whenever I had to check dates, goal scorers, results, league standings, or any number of other details.

My thanks must also go to my friend and former work colleague Karol Malcolm. A very talented artist whom I have known for over 20 years, I was most grateful when she kindly agreed to illustrate the cover of this book. I would also like to extend my gratitude to all of my family, friends and work colleagues who expressed an interest in the book and encouraged me to see this project through to its conclusion. Most notably my sister Karen, who helped me enormously, with the publishing process. I was delighted to get messages of support for this book, from as far afield as the Philippines and the Gambia. And finally, thanks to all of you who went to the trouble of buying my book as well as reading it. I hope that you will enjoy it.

INTRODUCTION

As we celebrated the start of the new decade, around the time QPR destroyed Cardiff City in a 6-1 home win, the thought never entered my head that I was about to embark on an extensive writing project that would look at football matches from a period of seven different decades. However, there were two reasons why I developed an interest in this venture. First of all, in the away league fixture at Nottingham Forest in February 2020, something unusual happened in a Queens Park Rangers game, that I had never seen before. When I spoke to a couple of fellow supporters about the incident in question, they also had no recollection of any similar occurrence from the past. That gave me the idea to explore taking a detailed look at memorable and unusual Rangers matches, over the years. Secondly, the global lockdown meant that I was able to devote time towards delving into the past, rather that feel disappointed about the absence of any football for over three months.

There are numerous reasons why certain QPR matches could be described as being either memorable or unusual. Some are as a result of club records or a unique occurrence. Meanwhile, others are notable for a particular 'first' or 'last', in relation to all of the games the club have been involved in over so many years. Whilst many of those achievements are as a result of team efforts, some are also down to a particular individual. For example, a couple of chapters look at players who were not popular with Rangers supporters, yet would win over hearts and minds with their endeavours in key matches.

Whilst writing this book, it was interesting to note there were a number of recurring themes throughout. Often when a player left Queens Park Rangers for a new challenge, they often found themselves facing their former club, in double-quick time. Also, in this collection of memorable games, there have been numerous spectacular goals that fans will recall with great clarity. Yet at the same time, there were also many examples of own goals and a long list of blunders from opposing players, that lead to Rangers goals. Which was the cause of some of those matches being memorable in the first place. Another recurring theme was the number of strange or appalling decisions from referees in these games. Although in the interest of being fair to match officials, plenty of them were in QPR's favour, as well as a number of which that went against the club.

I am not the first person to write a book featuring matches involving Queens Park Rangers. In 2013, journalist Mike Donovan wrote his own account of 50 of the greatest games that Rangers took part in. A most enjoyable book that I was delighted to add to my collection, when it came out. Out of respect for Mr Donovan and in the interest of not going over the same ground he covered, I have not featured any of the matches he did in his book. Though I have looked at some of the games that would have been worthy of inclusion, otherwise.

As a long-standing supporter, I have on a few occasions heard fans of other teams, claim that Rangers "don't have much of a history" because of a perceived lack of silverware. Whilst it would have been nice had QPR picked up a few more trophies in the past, it is wrong to say that the club doesn't have a history. It has a rich and colourful one, with so many memorable moments, players, teams, managers, and of course, matches. Even while researching this book, it was at times a learning process for myself, finding out about some of the games that I would actually write about.

In an attempt to compile a publication of notable Queens

Park Rangers games, naturally the focus is on numerous high points. But occasionally, matches will be noteworthy for the wrong reasons. They also deserve inclusion. Though with 34 wins, ten draws and six loses, the emphasis is definitely on the more positive aspects of this football club. If you are reading this as a supporter of QPR, I hope that this book has brought back some great memories, or introduced you to a few interesting moments from our colourful and fascinating history. And if you are reading this from a non-Rangers background, it will be gratifying to know that you have learned something about the club's history.

Ray Eaton
August 2020

1. *The Loneliness of The Long-Distance Hooligan*
Queens Park Rangers 1 Northampton Town 3
1962/63

Many supporters making their way to a home match, via either White City or Wood Lane tube stations, may not realise that their walk from the Underground to the Kiyan Prince Foundation Stadium takes them past a site that was once used to stage the Olympics. Completed just months before the 1908 Games, White City Stadium originally had a capacity of 93,000. During its heyday, it hosted concerts and a number of different sports including athletics, greyhound racing, boxing, speedway, stock car racing, and of course, football. It was aside from Wembley Stadium, the only other venue in the London area, used for the 1966 World Cup tournament. Doing so when in staged the group match between Uruguay and France. QPR also had an association with this famous old stadium. They played there for the period from 1931 to 1933, and returned to White City during the 62/63 season. But in what proved to be the first of many strokes of bad luck, Alec Stock's side couldn't move into their new venue in time for the start of the new campaign.

Rangers had to wait until the athletics season was over, before they could make the short journey along South Africa Road. For the visit of Hull City for an evening game on Monday 1 October 1962, their new home could finally be used. The lead-up to the match was accompanied by a blaze of publicity. Celebrities like television and radio presenter Judith Chalmers and disc jockey Alan "fluff" Freeman had turned up to see what was by the club's standards, a showpiece event. Unfortunately, just prior to the game, the heavens opened and West London experienced some of the worst rain it had seen in many years. Conditions had become so bad, referee Tommy Dawes from Norwich, had no choice but to call the match off. This after most fans were already at the game. Although the same could not be said for the visiting team. The coach taking the Hull team to the White City Stadium was held up in traffic and only turned up at the ground, 20 minutes after the scheduled kick-off time. Unaware that the match had already been abandoned, Tigers manager Cliff Britton admitted that his players had actually changed into their playing kits, whilst the coach was making its way to the game. An estimated 20,000 fans went home very disappointed.

This particular season coincided with the infamous big freeze, when Britain was almost brought to a standstill, owing to the adverse weather that continued for weeks on end. This meant that on more than one occasion, the entire weekend programme of football matches, was wiped out. By the time Rangers hosted Northampton Town on 9 February 1963, it was the first home league game at White City since 22 December. Although an FA Cup tie against Swindon Town did take place in the intervening period, on a surface that bore a greater resemblance to an ice rink, than a football pitch. Curiously, there was already a track record of bad feeling between the two teams. At Loftus Road in April 1962, Peter Angell was the victim of a bad foul committed by Northampton's Cliff Holton. Before Angell could be stretchered off, a Rangers fan invaded the pitch, seemingly intent on getting hold of Holton. Thankfully, Queens Park Rangers captain Roy Bentley, escorted the man from the field of play. Almost immediately, another supporter also got on the pitch, only to be grabbed by the police. Taking the gloss off of what was actually an excellent 2-0 win for Alec Stock's men, at the final whistle, around twenty further R's followers got on the field of play and shouted abuse at the visiting team. For the start of the following season, the first couple of home programmes featured an Official Warning, under the instruction of the FA, against carrying out any further misdemeanours at home matches. Clearly, a certain supporter did not heed that advice.

As one of the few matches in the country not called off as a result of the weather, QPR's game against Northampton Town the following February, attracted more attention than would normally have been the case for this Third Division fixture. Rangers started the game the brighter of the two sides, and enjoyed a number of good goalscoring chances. Inside-forward John Collins was unlucky when he hit the post early in the game. Queens Park Rangers took the lead after 18 minutes, when Mark Lazarus crossed to Stuart Leary and his header presented Brian Bedford with a straight forward chance which he duly converted. Nine minutes later, Northampton equalised when Billy Hails crossed from the right and with the ball getting stuck in the mud, fell kindly for Barry Lines who swept home.

In the second half, QPR had a great opportunity to take the lead. The unusually named 38-year-old referee and schoolmaster Reg Spittle awarded a penalty following a foul in the area from Town's centre half Terry Branston and up stepped the regular spot kick taker Peter Angell. Unfortunately, the man who remains to this day, second only to Tony Ingham in terms of league appearances for Rangers, shot tamely at goalkeeper Chic Brodie who didn't even have to move to make the save. A rare failure for Angell, who actually had a fine reputation when it came to spot kicks. The match was about to turn in Northampton's favour.

Within minutes of that wasted opportunity, the visitors went ahead as Lines seized on a loose ball after teammate Alec Ashworth had bored his way through the middle of the pitch. With that, Barry Lines struck a shot from outside the area, which was too good for Ray Drinkwater, who was in goal for Queens Park Rangers, that afternoon. Shortly afterwards, came the moment that would make national news. A collision between Bedford and defender Theo Foley, left the Rangers striker lying on the pitch in agony, after Foley's studs caught him in the face. An incident that even Brian Bedford later admitted was an accident rather than anything malicious. Some of the home fans however, were furious. One in particular took it upon himself to dispense his own brand of justice.

Tearing his way onto the pitch came 24-year-old Queens Park Rangers supporter John Kennedy. Somehow, he managed to get to Theo Foley and promptly clouted the visiting defender. In the aftermath of this shocking incident, Foley was left with two black eyes and a cut lip. During the same brawl, teammate Terry Branston was left with a bruised cheekbone. In the process of defending his colleagues, goalkeeper Brodie managed to land a punch on John Kennedy, before the police removed the unwanted fan from the pitch. All this while Brian Bedford was being treated for the challenge that caused the ill-feeling in the first place. Chic Brodie would incidentally, develop a track record of his own when it came to both unexpected injuries and unwanted visitors on a football pitch. Whilst playing for Brentford in 1970, his career ended when in an away match at Colchester, a dog somehow got on the pitch and collided with him, while he collected a routine back pass.

In the final minute of the game, a defensive mix-up between Mike Keen and Drinkwater, gave Ashworth an unexpected opportunity. He promptly rounded the QPR keeper and sealed both points with Northampton Town's third goal of the game. Regardless of the fact that the final score line did not go in the home side's favour, it had almost become an irrelevance, as a result of incident involving Theo Foley. Exasperated manager Stock declared "We don't mind having lost this match, but our crowd have given us a bad name in the past mainly through small incidents that have been magnified".

The behaviour of Kennedy can never be condoned, regardless of what happened in the lead up to his pitch invasion. Yet it must be said that it was an incredible feat of athleticism on his part to carry out that act of hooliganism in the first place. He had to jump over the barbed-wire fence in front of the stand from where he was watching the match. After that, he had to negotiate the dog track, followed by another fence that separated the dog track from the lanes used during the athletics season. And once he dealt with those, ran half the length of the pitch to attack Foley. Although you could probably have filled this famous old stadium with all of the people who have caused trouble at English football matches over the years, it is doubtful that any of them ever had to go so far inside a ground to carry out the said wanton act.

Kennedy immediately appeared in a number of national newspapers and was quick to give his own side of the story. The 24-year-old from North Kensington admitted that prior to the game, he and some friends had been celebrating the upcoming birth of his first child and he would not have behaved in that manner, were it not for the fact he was "wetting the baby's head". The repentant fan added "I hope everyone will understand why I did what I did. I lost my temper and I am very sorry for what I did. Ever since my dad took me to see Rangers when I was four, I have been a keen fan. On Saturday I was the second man through the gate-and the first to leave". He also mentioned that a foul from Theo Foley on Lazarus earlier in the game, was also the cause of anger on his part, which spilled over, with the later incident involving the same visiting player.

The view of his father Joseph, who was also at the game and tried to stop his son from going on the pitch was "This would never have happened if Rangers had been winning". The sharp-eyed among you may have noticed that not only did the fan who carried out the assault share his first name and surname with the US President who would be assassinated later that year, his father also had the same name as JFK's father who was patriarch of the Kennedy family, as well as being a famous businessman, politician and ambassador, in his own right. When he wasn't fielding interviews from the media, John Kennedy had time to hone his writing skills by composing four letters of apology. The recipients being QPR and Northampton Town Football Clubs, respectively, along with Theo Foley and Terry Branston. The visitors were unmoved and decided to prosecute the supporter who had attacked Foley.

In April 1963, he appeared at the West London Magistrate's Court, facing charges of attacking the two Northampton players. Kennedy pleaded guilty to assaulting Foley, but not guilty of striking Branston. In court, prosecuting QC Mr Robin Dunn said that Kennedy had been in the three-shilling enclosure before negotiating the aforementioned obstacles, prior to carrying out the assault. "You may think this was a most deliberate and savage assault with irresponsible exhibitionism", Mr Dunn told the magistrate, Mr E.R. Guest. "It happened in front of a crowd of 20,000 people. It was on television that evening and must have been seen by millions". Mr Dunn added that at White City, every possible precaution was taken to control the ground and prosecutions of this kind were not brought lightly and was authorised to say that this prosecution had been brought with the full knowledge and consent of the FA.

When giving evidence, John Kennedy said that he was a lifelong supporter and that in his defence "Brian Bedford was my idol. When he was kicked i just saw red, jumped across the fence and struck Foley". He also claimed that he never saw Branston, let alone even lay a finger on him. The magistrate said that he was not satisfied beyond doubt that Kennedy had assaulted the second defender and dismissed the summons. The resulting court case saw John Kennedy fined £5 and he was also ordered to pay £15- and 15-shillings cost. A not inconsiderable amount of money back in 1963. He was also warned that any repeat of that behaviour would result in a six-week prison sentence.

As was mentioned in the court case, there was television footage of this match. Reiterating the point made by the prosecuting QC, it would indeed have been seen by a large proportion of the British public, as this was the age of just two television channels. But like so many episodes of famous BBC TV shows from the same decade, the film from this match has long since being wiped from existence. The outcome of the case would have been as much as a relief to Queens Park Rangers, as it was to Kennedy. There was a possibility that the Football

Association could have ordered the closure of White City-a sanction that had in the past being carried out, elsewhere.

In the aftermath of that notorious game, Rangers had to play catch up, with regards to the backlog of fixtures. At one stage, QPR hosted three home league games during a period of just five days. Likewise, did so with three more successive home matches in nine days at the end of the season. The campaign itself, fizzled out in a disappointing manner, as Alec Stock's team finished fourteen points worse off, compared to the 61/62 season. By the start of 1963/64, Queens Park Rangers had returned to Loftus Road. A decision that was met with the approval of the overwhelming majority of supporters. White City Stadium closed its doors for the final time in 1984 and was ripped down, a year later. Incidentally, Manchester, Liverpool, Glasgow, Nottingham, Cardiff and Newcastle, all had their own White City Stadiums that hosted greyhound racing. The one in West London, was the last of them to disappear.

The White City experiment was not a success, and fans never warmed to being there, mainly for the fact that they were so far from the pitch. This of course was in stark contrast to the closeness between the stands and the pitch that Loftus Road offers. Attendances plummeted too, which looked all the more disappointing given the vast size of White City Stadium. Yet despite the late arrival there, the opening night washout, big freeze, ridiculous backlog of fixtures and that infamous incident during the Northampton game, the move was not without its merits.

As a bold plan, it probably came a few years too early. Had it taken place in the 1966/67 season, it would have played host to a team on the verge of the winning the Third Division title, along with its run to League Cup glory. This would have been followed by another promotion and then top flight football for the first time in the history of QPR. This would inevitably have meant larger attendances, which would have justified the move to the famous old venue. By the early 1970's, athletics had found a new spiritual home in the form of Crystal Palace Stadium. And with the slow demise of the sport of greyhound racing, Rangers would have had White City all to themselves in the long term. It could in time, have been developed to become more 'football friendly'. The irony is that for well over 20 years, respective Queens Park Rangers owners Chris Wright and Tony Fernandes have both spoken of, and explored numerous potential opportunities to move elsewhere. Discussions regarding moving from Loftus Road usually divides opinion, among supporters. Especially if that means moving miles away from W12.

Yet a permanent move to White City would have meant staying in the same area. And by definition, the same walk to the ground, or bus or train ride to the game. And supporters would still have met up with friends at the same pubs, cafes and restaurants before home matches, as they would have done otherwise, because White City Stadium was so close to Loftus Road. With the universal view that the Kiyan Prince Foundation Stadium is nowhere near big enough should it host Premiership football at some point in the near future, that would never have been a problem with White City. With its vast size, the capacity while well short of its original 93,000, would still have given the club scope to play in front of crowds much higher than the current figure of 18,439. And enjoy much better legroom, to boot. We can but wonder how different the history of QPR might have looked, had the move to the White City Stadium come later in the 1960's, or had not been burdened with such bad luck, during their ill-fated season there.

2 *Collins Ahead of The Game*
Queens Park Rangers 3 Hull City 3
1965/66

The first league match of the 1960's, saw Rangers' prolific frontman Brian Bedford score a hat trick in an away win at Newport County. In what turned out to be a golden age for QPR hat tricks, this was the first of 32 of them in that particular decade. In comparison, the drought-like 2010's, saw just the one. That came when Charlie Austin scored all three goals when Rangers memorably came from behind, in a 3-2 win over West Bromwich Albion in the 2014/15 Premiership season. Not surprisingly, the list of those hat tricks in the sixties, is dominated by Bedford and Rodney Marsh. But others got in on the act as well. One such example came in the middle of that decade and was probably the most remarkable of the lot. Because of the unusual nature of the occurrence in question, it is a feat that has not been repeated since.

When Hull City arrived at Loftus Road on 19 February 1966, they were top of the table and looked like a pretty safe bet for promotion. But Rangers came into this fixture off the back of some fine form of their own. The preceding six matches for Alec Stock's team had seen them hammer York City in a 7-2 win and also beat Swansea City with an almost-as-impressive 6-2 victory. In what turned out to be the penultimate home match before the arrival of Marsh, this QPR side still contained a fine combination of youth and experience. Among them were Jim Langley and Frank Sibley. The age gap between the hugely experienced Langley and the promising young Sibley was just under 19 years. This would surely have been a club record that stood for 30 years. When player-manager Ray Wilkins (then aged 39) and Nigel Quashie (17) played together in a 1-0 home defeat against Blackburn Rovers in the 95/96 season, the two midfielders took ownership of that feat, boasting an age difference that came in at slightly shy of 22 years. One of those club records that may never be broken.

Also, on the Queens Park Rangers team for the visit of Hull City, was John Collins. Hailing from Chiswick, local lad Collins was born in 1942. He came through the junior ranks before signing professional terms in August 1959, and made his debut the following April. Over the next few years, he would be a key figure in the team, in terms of both appearances and goals, from his position of inside-left. He was about to put in a star-turn, in what was one of QPR's best performances of the season.

Whilst Hull were undoubtedly the best team in the Third Division, Rangers were competing well which was no surprise given that they had recently racked up two great wins of their own. Jim Langley was looking sharp despite being the oldest player on the pitch, and Mark Lazarus caused the City defence plenty of problems with his attacking play on the wing. On 35 minutes, QPR deservedly took the lead. From a Keith Sanderson cross,

Collins was able to head home from close range. The Rangers players did not have much time to dwell on being in the lead, as the Tigers immediately put the home side under pressure. The class act in a very good Hull team was forward Ken Wagstaff, who would score at a rate of almost a goal every other game, in twelve years with Hull City. On 43 minutes, his solo goal took him past half of the outfield players in the Queens Park Rangers team before slotting home the equaliser.

Towards the end of the first half, Rangers lost their experienced forward Les Allen with a pulled muscle. Tony Hazell replaced Allen, which actually gave John Collins licence to take up a more attacking role in the team. On 65 minutes, another dangerous run from Lazarus produced a cross that allowed John Collins to head past the visiting keeper Maurice Swan for the second time that afternoon. But once again, Hull fought back. City's other prolific forward Chris Chilton, took advantage of a defensive error to make it 2-2. Following on from Sanderson and Mark Lazarus, defender Ian Watson became the third player to assist Collins. The youngster flighted a high cross into the penalty area and it was met at the far post by yet another header, to give him this most amazing of hat tricks.

In the modern era, the most talked about and remarkable example of the genre, is the 'perfect hat trick', whereby a player scores with his right foot, left foot, and a header. There haven't been too many of them at QPR over the last few decades. Just prior to his controversial departure, in his role as player-manager, Trevor Francis achieved that in a 3-1 win at Villa Park. As a bona fide Birmingham City legend, those three goals gave him such satisfaction, Francis admitted in his autobiography that he deliberately substituted himself, just to rub it with the Aston Villa supporters, by walking off the pitch slowly. In a 1996/97 home league game against Barnsley, Scottish forward John

Spencer also ticked all three boxes on his way to a perfect hat trick. Yet as praiseworthy as they both were, in many ways, a hat trick of headers is perhaps as impressive, as well as being an even rarer feat.

Unlike the prolific Bedford who was famed for his excellent ability in the air, John Collins wasn't the most obvious candidate to manage to find the back of the net with his head on three occasions in the same game. At five foot eight inches tall, he was far from being the tallest player on the Queens Park Rangers team. Nor would many people have expected it to come against the best team in the division-Hull City would go on to win the league with an impressive 69 points and had a goal difference of plus 47. But on this particular day, the quality crosses kept coming in his direction and he took all of them.

Unfortunately, this amazing feat from Collins did not win the game, as Ken Houghton netted less than five minutes from time. A memorable afternoon had seen QPR take the lead on three separate occasions, yet got pegged back every time. Both teams were applauded from the pitch at the final whistle. Although there would have been considerable disappointment for the home supporters, it must be said that Hull City more than played their part in what was a hugely entertaining game. Had Peter Springett not shown such good form in goal, Wagstaff would have scored a hat trick of his own. After the game, the Rangers hero couldn't hide his own disappointment, saying "The first time I've ever hit three, and still we can't win". Alec Stock meanwhile, was more than happy to look at the positive aspects of the game, declaring "When we play as well as that with five teenagers in the sides, our future must be bright".

If John Collins was responsible for the best individual performance from a Queens Park Rangers player in that 3-

3 draw, then the same has to be said for Hull's Ken Wagstaff, in that regard. Wagstaff was full of praise for what Collins had done. "A hat trick of headers - that's certainly something I'd never be able to do", was the assessment of the Tigers' striker. Wagstaff incidentally, knew a thing or two about scoring goals, and could boast 266 of them in a league career with Mansfield Town, as well as Hull City. So revered was he at both clubs, Ken Wagstaff has the unique distinction of being voted the "All Time Greatest Player", with two different Football League teams.

Alec Stock was indeed right when he spoke about a bright future, as Rangers stormed to a League and Cup double, little over a year later. Only, that would not happen with John Collins. In October 1966, he was transferred to Oldham Athletic. But in one of those twists of fate that happens so often in football, he would be back at Loftus Road with his new team, just a month later. Coincidentally, Collins wore the number ten shirt for the Latics, and was part of the only team that would win a league game at Loftus Road in the 1966/67 season, when Ian Towers scored the only goal of the game.

With 172 appearances and 46 goals for Queens Park Rangers, John Collins is not near the top of either list, in terms of being among the most prolific performers for the club. But equally, those sorts of numbers are rare in the modern era at Rangers. For example, when it comes to goal scorers for the club in the 21st century, the only QPR players who could match Collins, are Kevin Gallen, Paul Furlong and Charlie Austin. Like Brian Bedford, he was very unlucky to leave Rangers not long before promotion and success in the League Cup. Stock was even on record as saying that it was a shame that John Collins wasn't at the club to enjoy that period with his former teammates, especially as the much-respected manager believed that he was such an important figure in the side, for a few years prior to 1967.

With hat tricks from Queens Park Rangers players being such a rare commodity over the last couple of decades, the achievement of Collins on that day against high-flying Hull City, looks all the more amazing. Most of the managers who have come and gone from Loftus Road over the last 25 years, with the possible exception of Stewart Houston, has favoured the presence of a commanding figure up front, who will win his share of headers. Supporters have seen the good, bad and indifferent among a whole host of names that have come and gone. Yet none of them came close to emulating what happened back in February 1966. Not even Les Ferdinand with his famed dominance in the air, managed this. Yet this one-time trainee from just down the road in Chiswick, managed to score a hat trick, unlike any other for QPR, in well over half a century. With Rangers, we never know what the future holds and perhaps at some point, someone else may replicate that achievement. That being the case, just as a right footer, left footer and a header is known as a 'perfect hat trick', one with three headers, should perhaps be called a 'John Collins hat trick'.

3 *Kelly Blooded Against Poole*
Queens Park Rangers 3 Poole Town 2
1966/67

On the face of it, the draw for the FA Cup First Round that took place in November 1966, looked like a very kind one for QPR. Alec Stock's men faced non-league Poole Town at Loftus Road. Surprising as it may seem, this wasn't the first time that the two teams had faced each other in the competition. At the same stage of the 1946/47 FA Cup, Poole had held Rangers to a surprise 2-2 draw in Dorset, before the Third Division South team easily won 6-0 in the replay. If it was regarded as the easiest possible draw for Queens Park Rangers, that wasn't the message that was conveyed, from those within the club. The programme notes from this match are worth looking at again.

"Today we take on Poole Town in the Football Association Cup - that most glamourous of all competitions. Poole have shown themselves to be very tough Cup campaigners in previous years and will be coming to Loftus Road determined to topple us. For this

reason, we are approaching this match with the greatest caution and will not make the mistake of underestimating the opposition today. For that reason, also we are appealing to our supporters not to look on this match as an easy one. Their support will have to be loud and sustained for Poole are bringing a large band of vociferous followers with them".

A very strong side with the likes of Tony Hazell, Mike Keen, Jim Langley Mark Lazarus and Les Allen, all featured for this cup tie. Alongside them was debutant Mike Kelly who was signed on the March transfer deadline day in the 1965/66 season, for a fee of £1,000 from Wimbledon, with Rangers third choice keeper Eddie Wicks making the opposite journey. Incidentally, the new stopper can always claim that he signed for QPR, on the very same day as Rodney Marsh. At the time, there was a famous photo featuring the pair signing their contracts simultaneously, with Chairman Jim Gregory, proudly looking on.

Prior to coming to Loftus Road, Kelly worked for the GPO as a telephone engineer, before he became a fully-fledged professional footballer. He won an FA Cup Amateur winners medal during his time with the South London side. He also appeared for the England Amateur international team. As a result, it meant that in the future, he would be ineligible to play for the Republic of Ireland. Even though both of his parents hailed from there. Although it was thanks to his Irish roots, that he was able to hone his goalkeeping skills. One of his strengths as a keeper was his knack of accurately throwing the ball out to a teammate who was well up the pitch. A skill he attributed to the many hours he spent as a youngster, throwing a hurling ball against a wall.

Upon joining QPR, Mike Kelly was viewed as being the reserve goalkeeper, with Peter Springett enjoying the status of being the established first choice stopper at the time. There was also another keeper at the club at the time in the form of Johnny Brooks. Unfortunately, Brooks suffered a broken leg, and was effectively out of the picture, no sooner than Kelly had arrived. Prior to this FA Cup First Round tie, Springett had a slight hand injury. He might have played were there no alternatives. But it was decided that this was the perfect opportunity to give the new man his chance. With the League Cup very much in the mind of Stock, the manager chose to miss the FA Cup tie at Loftus Road and watch Millwall play Carlisle, instead. The reason for this being that the Cumbrian side would be our next opponents in the other domestic knock-out competition. As a result, coach Bill Dodgin was acting manager for the FA Cup match.

For the first half hour of the game, the programme notes were looking prophetically accurate as the non-league outfit kept the home side at bay. Then on 35 minutes, Queens Park Rangers took the lead. Les Allen took on members of the Poole defence and found his way to the by-line, before slipping the ball back to Marsh. The QPR number ten then hooked the pass into the net. The combination of these two forwards, was responsible for countless goals during this period. Just after the start of the second half, a Roger Morgan cross found Rodney Marsh to perfection, and he smashed the ball into the top of the net, to double the lead. But rather than being the springboard for an easy home win, the visitors rose to the occasion.

On 65 minutes, Poole got a goal back while there was still enough time for a cup shock. But nine minutes later, Les Allen collected a long through ball from Ian Morgan-who had replaced the injured Tony Hazell at half time-and he sent a low pass to Marsh, who seemed to miskick the ball as it trickled into the net. Though it was not one of his best goals, it was still another hat trick to his name. Just three minutes after Rodney Marsh had earned the right to take home the match ball, the non-league side were back in the game, once more. Poole striker Tony French headed home from Kelly's badly-punched ball from a corner. That as it happened, was the end of the goalscoring, but the controversy was about to begin.

On 80 minutes, Mike Kelly dived forward to collect a ball, and had the misfortune to collide with French, not long after he scored Poole Town's second goal. Many of the 9,534 fans were angry with what they saw and were in no doubt that French had gone into the challenge in a somewhat reckless manner. This incident left Kelly covered in blood, and more worryingly, he was unconscious. Some players have scored on their QPR debuts, whilst a select few, have even been sent off. Mike Kelly's meanwhile, was about to come to a premature end, in somewhat painful circumstances. Having already made their one permitted substitution, there would be no replacement for Kelly, and through no fault of their own, Queens Park Rangers would finish the match with just ten men. With a new keeper, not to mention a clean jersey now required, 37-year-old left-back Jim Langley went in goal for the remaining ten minutes of the game.

Sensing their opportunity, the non-league outfit charged forward and the remaining nine outfield players spent what time was left in the game, trying to protect Langley from any pot-shots that the Poole attackers could muster. From a neutrals point of view, it might have looked like a fairy-tale story for the team from Dorset to pull of an unlikely draw, against a high-flying QPR side. But had it come about courtesy of the goalkeeper going off in such controversial circumstances, which would have been a cruel blow for Rangers. There would be no third goal for the visitors so Jim Langley and his teammates went through to the next round of the competition.

Poole had given the home side a bit of a scare, and it would have been Queens Park Rangers who were happier to hear the final whistle. But in this remarkable season, the cup tie against the non-league outfit saw yet another bit of club history. Rodney Marsh's hat trick meant that he managed this feat in the League, League Cup and FA Cup, all in the same season. Given how rare Rangers hat tricks have been in the last couple of decades, it is not an achievement that is likely to be emulated any time soon.

In four years, Kelly would play 54 games between 1966 and 1970. Having made his first team debut when one Springett brother was left out of the team, he would in the future, compete for first team action against the other. Peter swapped places Ron, as the elder sibling returned from a nine-year spell at Sheffield Wednesday, with Alan Spratley also in the frame during a competitive period on the goalkeeping front. Mike Kelly gained a reputation for being an agile and athletic keeper who pulled off flamboyant, stylish and eye-catching saves. Though it is doubtful that he ever wanted to remember his debut for QPR. Even if he did, the twelve stitches that he needed for that head injury, along with the painful state that he left the pitch in, probably prevented him from doing so in the first place.

4 *Brother Beyond*
Queens Park Rangers 0 Everton 1
1968/69

On 14 November 1946, Roger Morgan and his twin brother Ian, were born in Walthamstow, East London. Both would come through the Queens Park Rangers youth system, and they would make their debuts for the first team, just a week apart from each other. Ian did so at home to Hull City on September 25 1964, before Roger did likewise at Gillingham on 3 October. Both had made the breakthrough before their collective 18th birthdays. By way of a remarkable coincidence, when the Morgan twins played for Rangers together for the first time, they weren't even the only siblings in the team. Ray and Pat Brady (who also happened to be the elder brothers of Irish football legend Liam) were also in the side on this memorable afternoon at the Priestfield Stadium, in which Alec Stock's team drew 2-2.

Whilst Roger enjoyed a regular run in the side which continued for the rest of his time as a Queens Park

Rangers player, Ian was in and out of the side, over the course of the 65/66 and 66/67 seasons, before nailing down a regular place in the side, a year later. For any fan who was too young to remember the 1968/69 season, they could be forgiven for thinking that it was a complete nightmare. QPR finished bottom of the table, amassing just four wins and a miserable total of just 18 points. Which was very low even in the days of two points for a win. Coventry City who just avoided relegation were all of 13 points clear of Rangers. On the basis of that, it would be easy to start drawing comparisons with the miserable relegations of 2013 & 2015. But at the same time, fans understood that the 68/69 season came off the back of two outstanding promotions and the absence of Rodney Marsh for much of the first half of the campaign, was also a massive blow.

While Rangers were not winning many matches, they were earning plenty of praise from fans, the media and even opposing managers, for the way that they played, despite rarely getting the rewards their performances deserved. On their way to the First Division title, Don Revie's Leeds side won 1-0 at Loftus Road. About Queens Park Rangers, he had the following to say about our performance against his side; "I'm completely baffled, the way Rangers played tonight they should be near the top of the league-not bottom". Kind words indeed, but like on so many occasions, QPR went behind in a match, and their attacking football was not rewarded with anything in the way of points. One such example of this, was when Everton visited Loftus Road, at the start of February.

Everton were a force to be reckoned with and would themselves, finish the season in third place, behind Leeds United and Liverpool. On a cold but clear winter afternoon, Rangers dominated for much of the game, but found themselves falling to that now familiar curse of going behind early in the game. On this occasion, striker Jimmy Husband put the visitors ahead. Thereafter, Everton were happy to put all eleven men behind the ball. QPR dominated the midfield, and in particular, the Morgan twins were making life difficult for the visiting full-backs, Sandy Brown and Ray Wilson. Roger incidentally, adopted his usual position on the left-wing, whilst his identical twin operated on the other side of the pitch. Ironically, Everton were the top scorers and as well as being league contenders at the time. But they chose to play in a surprisingly negative manner, against the struggling Rangers side.

Despite their undoubted midfield dominance all afternoon, Queens Park Rangers had nothing to show for 90 minutes of endeavours. "What have Rangers got to do to win"? bemoaned R's striker Frank Clarke at the end of the game. He might as well have been speaking on behalf of every supporter, as well as his teammates. Not for the only time, the media were very sympathetic towards the luckless strugglers. How fans must have wished they could have swapped some of those plaudits for points. As it happened, and even well before a disappointing season would come to its inevitable conclusion, it was about to be the end of an era at Loftus Road. Roger Morgan was sold to Tottenham Hotspur for a club record £110,000.

It would inevitably be a massive disappointment for supporters who regularly chanted their own tribute in the form of the Manfred Mann's 'The Mighty Quinn', that went as follows; *"Come on Without, Come on Within. You've Not Seen Nothing Like the Morgan Twins...."*. In his programme notes, player-manager Les Allen claimed that he was only able to leave after long and careful considerable from the club. Also, that the money that they would receive from the North Londoners, would enable Rangers to build for the following season and that although the talented winger was gone, those who remained had not reconciled themselves to relegation. But perhaps the disappointment was felt greatest by his sibling. In an interview in the programme that was conducted by Michael Wale, Ian made his feelings known;

"When Roger left Rangers, I felt sick that he was going. Choked more than anything, after being your whole life together and you get split up it's a bit of a blow. Plus, the thing inside you which says you want to do as well as him".

In the same interview, he also revealed how he was very close to Roger, both as a brother and a teammate in the same Queens Park Rangers team;

"We always seemed to get on well playing together. You feel very close. There was this time at Ipswich, the season we went up from the 2nd Division. He got injured and had to have a cartilage operation. I was so emotionally involved I raced over to the ambulancemen".

With Roger Morgan no longer a QPR player, the club would have to continue their battle against relegation without him. But football has a habit of throwing up strange coincidences, and there would be one for the twins. As a result of the previous week's fixtures being wiped out as a result of weather, Roger's debut for Spurs would come against his former side, at Loftus Road. On a freezing cold day, Roger got a great reception from the Rangers support before the match started. A photo of the twins was taken before kick-off, and that very image would get a new lease of life many years later, when it appeared on the cover of the critically acclaimed retro football magazine Backpass.

Following a goalless first half, Rangers took the lead in the

48th minute. This after a back-flick from Rodney Marsh found his teammate Allen whose cross was met with a powerful header from Frank Clarke. But just when it looked like QPR would record a first ever win over Tottenham Hotspur, Jimmy Greaves caused controversy when he used his hand to control the ball, before shooting past Mike Kelly. The Rangers players all saw him use his hand, as did many of the journalists, who lead with the incident when doing their match reports. Unfortunately, the referee missed it, and Greaves scored his 30th goal of the season to secure a 1-1 draw. Honours even for the Morgan twins, regardless of the manner in which it came.

Not surprisingly, there were a number of similarities between the talented brothers. The pair were brave, fearless competitors, who despite not being tallest, were both superb in the air, being blessed with excellent timing and a 'good spring'. Roger was a ball-playing winger and an accomplished dribbler. Ian was fast and direct, often making the best use of his pace. Roger made 180 appearances for QPR, scoring 39 goals in the process. While Ian played 173 times, getting 26 goals himself. How fitting it would have been had they made the same number of appearances. Sadly, there was a similarity between them, when it came to injuries. Roger suffered with them for much of his time as a Tottenham player. As a result, he retired from the sport, before his 27th birthday. In 1973 Ian transferred to Watford. But within a year, injuries forced him to quit football as well.

And so that 1-0 home defeat to Everton on 1 February 1969, remains the last time two brothers-never mind identical twins-appeared in the same Queens Park Rangers team. In the decades that have followed, there have been a couple of examples of brothers playing for QPR, but never at the same time. Clive and Bradley Allen being the more famous example. The elder brother last played for Rangers in 1984, whilst the younger sibling did not make his debut until 1989. Likewise, the Graham brothers from Northern Ireland also came through the youth system in the 1990s. Mark made an impressive 20 appearances in his first full season in 1996/97, but hardly featured, thereafter. Richard would make just a couple of appearances for the first team in the 98/99 campaign, before he too, was surplus to requirements.

By its very nature, the chances of seeing two brothers in the same Rangers team, is pretty slim. It might be a record that will stay with the Morgan's, for years to come. Though given that they started their own QPR careers as the second pair of siblings in the same side, the odds on *that* occurrence happening once again, would probably be on a par with picking out jackpot numbers in the National Lottery. Although it is probably a good idea if that is never replicated. That last time that all four Brady and Morgan brothers played in the same team, was away to Mansfield Town in March 1965. Queens Park Rangers lost 8-1 at Field Mill. There are some historic moments that are better not to dwell on.

5 ***Amateur Hour***
Queens Park Rangers 5 Birmingham City 2
1970/71

The television highlights of the 5-2 win over Birmingham
City in October 1970, is amongst the most famous
footage, of any Queens Park Rangers match of that
decade. It is of course, famed for a hat trick from Rodney
Marsh, that is regarded as the best ever from a QPR player.
The first and third goals from Marsh were both a bit
special. The first saw him cleverly controlling a cross from
Ian Gillard, which he then volleyed home from 30 yards.
His hat trick goal consisted of some amazing footwork
that managed to make the entire Birmingham defence look
foolish, before his low shot found the corner of the net.
Even half a century later, both would be among the top 50
Rangers goals ever caught on film. Terry Venables also
scored courtesy of a brilliant pass from Rodney Marsh, and
former R's keeper Mike Kelly had the misfortune of
having to retrieve the ball from the net on no fewer than
five occasions. The highlights from this match are all the
more significant given that there is a limited amount of

such material, featuring Marsh during his years at Loftus Road. In so many ways, this match and the brilliant all-round performance, has always being regarded as the perfect tribute to the talent of Rodney Marsh. Yet despite all that, it was a significantly less known figure who made a bit of Rangers history that afternoon.

Making his debut was 20-year-old Andy McCulloch. The six foot two-inch-tall striker, had a background in non-league football, and scored 27 goals in the previous season with the Surrey outfit Walton & Hersham, before joining QPR. Having spent a couple of years qualifying as a civil engineer after a failed trial as a youngster with Tottenham Hotspur, it looked for a while like his future would lie away from football. McCulloch's debut for the visit of Birmingham City was a surprise for a couple of reasons, none of which were related to the fact that he had failed to score in nine Football Combination appearances for Queens Park Rangers, in the lead up to his first league appearance.

Supporters were stunned when popular striker Barry Bridges, was sold to Millwall in September 1970. In the absence of Bridges, other forwards staked their claim to play alongside Marsh. At the time, Mick Leach played as a striker, but he suffered a broken arm early in the 70/71 campaign, away to Blackburn Rovers. This gave an opportunity to others, and leading up to, and including the visit of Birmingham City, three different players would wear the number nine shirt. First up was seventeen-year-old Martyn Busby, who was pressed into action as an emergency forward. He played in a superb 5-1 win at home to Orient, and although he didn't score, Busby was involved in the build-up of most of the goals. The following weekend, Rangers lost 1-0 at Swindon Town and it was now the turn of Canvey Island-born Frank Saul to partner Rodney Marsh up front. With the visit of the

Midlands outfit to Loftus Road, manager Les Allen sprung a surprise by giving Andy McCulloch his debut. An unexpected move given that at the time he wasn't even a professional footballer. He had to hastily sign professional forms the day before the match, in order to play. But at the time, registration would take a few days so he was to all intents and purposes, still an amateur footballer.

From McCulloch's point of view, he was very much playing second fiddle to Marsh who seemed to be involved in everything, when the home side bore down on the visitor's goal. Though the debutant did force a save from Mike Kelly, with a diving header while the score was 1-0. A good example of how he was brought into the team for his aerial prowess and was putting that to good use. Rodney Marsh had scored twice and set up the other, by the time Rangers were leading 3-2. Andy McCulloch's moment came in the second half. QPR were enjoying a good spell of possession on the left side of the pitch when Mike Ferguson crossed to the far post, where McCulloch headed home from six yards out. It was not the best goal of the afternoon, but it was certainly the bravest. His marker Roger Hynd was right on top of him as Andy McCulloch was closing in on goal. There could easily have been a clash of heads, so close were the two of them. But McCulloch did not back out of the challenge and rose highest to score the fourth Queens Park Rangers goal. When Marsh sealed his hat trick with a brilliant solo goal, it concluded a truly memorable win. Though as a result of his amateur status, the new man wouldn't get paid for turning out for Rangers, despite having scored one of the goals.

When interviewed after the game, Andy McCulloch said that he had been happy to remain as an amateur footballer, whilst trying to qualify as a civil engineer. He also strongly believed that youngsters should not turn their backs on their education, even if they wanted to become a professional footballer. Especially given that only a small percentage of them will actually make the breakthrough. As an out-and-out target man, McCulloch singled out Wales and Southampton forward Ron Davies as being his footballing hero. Not surprising because Davies was another six-footer who was very dominant in the air.

McCulloch remains the last amateur footballer to turn out for the Queens Park Rangers first team. Although it wasn't as if there was a long list of similar such individuals before him. One such example was inside forward Mike Tomkys who played for Rangers in the 1950's. Another amateur at the club was goalkeeper Mike Pinner, who was at Loftus Road between 1959 and 1961. Pinner had the rare distinction of being a QPR player who also took part in the Summer Olympics. Doing so at the 1956 Games in Melbourne and Rome in 1960, making three appearances for the Great Britain football team.

Andy McCulloch's time with the club between 1970 and 1972, spanned the periods when both Les Allen and Gordon Jago were in charge. With ten goals from 41 appearances for Rangers, he was a useful squad player to have around. But with the arrival of Stan Bowles, Don Givens and Dave Thomas during the Jago era, McCulloch's chance of being a major part of the first team set-up, was minimal. Gordon Jago explained after his departure that the striker had been disappointed not to be able to hold down a place in the side and that his move to Cardiff City was as a result of wanting first team football. As it happened, the move suited both parties. In a career that spanned 15 years with seven different league sides, he scored 140 goals in 433 appearances.

Immediately after he left Loftus Road, Andy McCulloch sent telegrams to both the first team and the reserves wishing them luck and signing it 'Lucky 12th'. McCulloch's time at the club coincided with that of some of the best players who ever wore the blue and white hoops. Naturally, he wasn't one of the standout performers in his two years in West London. But importantly, he didn't disgrace himself either. With his departure, the age of amateur footballers playing for the first team came to a close. Sending those telegrams represented the sign of a man who keep the 'Corinthian spirit', that he almost certainly retained from his earlier days as an amateur footballer.

6 *A 'Roy Of the Rovers' Performance*
Queens Park Rangers 3 Orient 1
1972/73

With over 300 league appearances which covered a period of more than a decade, and 61 league goals that makes him QPR's tenth highest post-war goal scorer, Mick Leach is rightly lauded as a wonderful servant of this football club. But for a long time, things were not so easy for him. For a while, both he and Alan Wilks suffered terrible abuse at the hands of home supporters, whenever they wore the number ten shirt, during those periods when fans' idol Rodney Marsh was unavailable. In the case of Wilks, it pretty much ruined his career as a Queens Park Rangers player. This despite the fact that he remains the only player to date to score five goals in a single game for Rangers- doing so in a League Cup tie against Oxford United, in October 1967. At one stage, things got so bad, both manager Les Allen and Club Secretary Ron Phillips attempted to address the matter by raising the issue in both the match programme and the local newspapers. That is not to say that every single QPR supporter was getting on the backs of these players. But there was still a significant and particularly noisy element who were never slow to express their opinions. It would take character and patience to win over this mindless minority. And much of that was achieved on Boxing Day 1972, when Orient made the journey across London to Loftus Road, for this festive derby match.

Rangers were pushing for promotion at the time and made a great start by taking the lead after just five minutes. Stan Bowles had possession and his brilliant vision allowed him to put Leach in the clear, and he finished superbly, to make it 1-0. Midway through the first half, a nasty collision saw Phil Parkes, Dave Clement and Orient's Derrick Downing all go for the same ball. The two Rangers players came out of this incident worse off, and both went down injured. It seemed like it was the end for Parkes and Clement for the duration of the match. Back in the 72/73 season, only one substitute was permitted, so manager Gordon Jago's problems were twofold. Firstly, he had the prospect of playing with just ten men. And secondly, none of them was a recognised goalkeeper. Fate however, was about to intervene.

Ian Watson was the usual emergency keeper, in the event of Phil Parkes having to leave the pitch. But Watson wasn't playing so someone else would have to take up that role. Thankfully, just days earlier in training, Jago told Mick Leach that he would be the new stand-in keeper, if required. And as a result, Leach spent a training session fending off shots from Clement, Bowles and Don Givens. Gordon Jago's preparation for the match, would benefit both QPR and Leach. 18-year-old John Beck was the substitute, but for one brief moment, an announcement over the loudspeaker would have had left most of the crowd somewhat confused, when there was a call for regular reserve keeper Alan Spratley to go to the dressing room. Was this a cunning attempt to unsettle the Orient side? Would Rangers try and sneak him on under the guise of being John Beck? As it happened, there was no such skulduggery. The gloves belonging to the six foot three and a half inches tall Parkes were too big for Mick Leach, so the kit belonging to Spratley who was a more modest five foot nine in height, proved to be a more suitable fit and with that, Beck officially replaced Clement who would be out of action for the next couple of weeks and the game was able to continue.

This was an entirely new role for Leach, but his teammates made a point of giving him as many back passes as they could, so he could get a feel of the ball. This worked very well and the Queens Park Rangers utility man soon gained in confidence. He even made a few good saves. One such notable example was when Orient defender Phil Hoadley floated a fine ball into the penalty area and just when it looked like two different forwards were in a position to nod home, up popped Leach to take the cross. By now, the Loftus Road crowd that had got on his back so many times in the past, were now cheering every time he saved or collected the ball. The forgotten man in that collision earlier in the half was Downing. Having escaped any punishment for that incident which Phil Parkes later admitted was a complete accident, referee Tommy Dawes sent him off after he swore at the match official. Which meant that belatedly, all three players involved in the original collision, would all have to leave the pitch. Later in the game, Ian Bowyer, Peter Allen and Barry Arber were also booked for Orient. When the half-time whistle blew, Mick Leach had not conceded as QPR preserved their one goal lead. As the newest member of the 'goalkeepers union', his opposite number Ray Goddard praised him for his performance as he left the pitch. But Goddard also advised him to remove his wedding ring for the second half, as he would not want to be wearing the said item, were he to damage his finger whilst making a save.

As it happened, Leach did not need to worry about that, as Parkes had sufficiently recovered and was able to return to the pitch. After this game, the giant keeper joked that the manager had told him that he'd better get back on the pitch for the second half as he was in danger of losing his place to the new R's hero. The man of the moment coincidentally, was able to return to the outfield. Only now he was about to take up his third different role of the afternoon, as he slotted into the right-back position. And just to remind you all, QPR went from being in a situation where it was ten versus eleven, to eleven versus ten, with Derrick Downing departing and Phil Parkes returning to the pitch. A very rare occurrence in any match. If Gordon Jago was ever in need of an after-dinner story to regale friends with from his time as manager, this would have been a good one to tell.

Although the first half might have been the more dramatic of the two periods of the game, there would be further goals in the second period. First of all, Don Givens scored from the penalty spot, to make it 2-0. Orient's Terry Brisley scored for the visitors to half the deficit, but Mick Leach would add to his list of telling achievements for this Bank Holiday cracker. Leach executed a superb defence-splitting pass to find new-boy John Beck, and he in turn picked out Givens. A backwards header from the Irish international, allowed Dave Thomas to score his first goal for Queens Park Rangers. The headlines however, were all about one man. A goal, some saves and a role in the build-up to the third strike of the afternoon from the midfielder-turned keeper-turned fullback, helped seal an excellent victory. Rarely if ever, has a Rangers player put in such a varied and all-round outstanding performance, as Mick Leach did that afternoon.

In the aftermath of that game, he met up with journalist, programme columnist and supporter Michael Wale to discuss the events of this memorable London derby. He explained that when not playing football, he loved participating in other sports like golf, tennis, badminton and cricket. In the case of the latter, Leach would probably have been an all-rounder. Another sport that he had taken a keen interest in was volleyball. He took a liking to it, having seen it at the Munich Olympics, during the previous summer and met up with some local teachers to play the occasional game. If his new-found love of volleyball did not help him when he temporarily replaced Parkes, it certainly did him no harm, either.

Mick Leach died from cancer at the tragically young age of 44, in January 1992. By then, he had long since cemented his reputation as one of the finest and most versatile servants, QPR ever saw. A couple of years after Leach passed away, the BBC brought out a video that featured some of the best Queens Park Rangers footage, from their Match of the Day archives over the period between 1967 and 1994. That video featured numerous goals from him. And on so many occasions, he was seen bravely putting his body on the line, in the process of scoring vital goals for the club that he served so well for many years. And from a DVD featuring some of the best Rangers games covered the ITV show The Big Match, Mick Leach scored a quite wonderful goal in a 4-2 win at Wolverhampton Wanderers in October 1973, when he executed a brilliant bicycle kick from just inside the penalty area. Mick Leach won over the doubters in an emphatic manner, and much of that happened thanks to one of the most remarkable all-round displays, Loftus Road has ever seen.

7 *The Poisoned Challis*
Queens Park Rangers 0 West Ham United 0
1973/74

On the face of it, when QPR hosted West Ham in September 1973, everything seemed to go according to plan. A team consisting of Phil Parkes, Dave Clement, Ian Watson, Terry Venables, Terry Mancini, Tony Hazell, Dave Thomas, Gerry Francis, Mick Leach, Stan Bowles and Don Givens, were in outstanding form. They played a brand of football that dazzled neutrals and media, as well as their own supporters. The press was full of praise for the performance of this Rangers team, managed by Gordon Jago as the hosts managed 30 attempts on the visitor's goal, as opposed to a meagre three, from the Hammers. And for good measure, Queens Park Rangers found the back of the net on no fewer than three occasions. The only downside to the events of this midweek match, were the decisions made by the match official for this midweek London derby.

Ron Challis from Tonbridge, took charge and his name

would be remembered for many years to come, by those in attendance. As ever, Stan Bowles was involved in so much of Rangers attacking play and he was at the centre of the drama that night. The first goal to be disallowed came from the man who wore the number ten shirt with such distinction. It was ruled out thanks to a somewhat dubious handball decision. Many of the home supporters-regardless of how biased they might have been-claimed that he had actually used his chest and not his hand to control the ball, before a raking low shot found the bottom corner of the net.

Bowles was also heavily involved with the second goal that was disallowed. QPR's brilliant winger Dave Thomas beat his marker like he did on so many occasions, before getting to the by-line and putting in one of his trademark crosses. With pinpoint accuracy, his ball into the West Ham penalty area, found the head of Stan Bowles. A perfectly legitimate goal on the face of it. That was not the view of Challis, who promptly disallowed a goal for the second time. The reason for this one? Thomas was in the eyes of the match official, in an offside position. It goes without saying that it is unusual for goals to be disallowed because the player who provided the assist with a cross, is immediately deemed to be offside. But then this was fast becoming a very unusual game.

Later on, a third Queens Park Rangers goal was disallowed, leaving the home fans both stunned and angry with the turn of events. Despite the dominance of Gordon Jago's side, they had just a single point to show for it. One moment that summed up how one sided this game was, involved one of the most iconic figures from both the history of English football, and British sport as a whole. Late on in the match, West Ham captain Bobby Moore passed the ball back to his goalkeeper Bobby Ferguson from around the halfway line. This led to a chorus of jeers from the Rangers supporters. With that, Moore turned to the home crowd and spread his arms wide as if to apologise. The gesture was pretty much his way of say "What else can I do?". Soon after that, the match finished 0-0. Almost immediately, it was hailed as perhaps the most one-sided goalless draw that QPR were ever involved in. As well as being one of the most controversial.

There was no shortage of praise for Rangers, in the national media. "Three QPR goals were disallowed on a night when, if there was any justice at all, they would have scored twice that number. Ron Greenwood's West Ham cavalry escaped with the luckiest point of their lives" said the Daily Mail. "Rangers were always the more inventive and imaginative side, playing in a swinging style we have come to accept as a West Ham copyright" said the much-respected Daily Express sportswriter Norman Giller. Whilst in The Sun the view was "A night when West Ham were little more than helpless onlookers. Rangers had a torrent of chances. To say that they dominated Hammers is to say that George Foreman only shaded his victory over Joe Roman". Closer to home, the notes of programme editor Ron Phillips shortly afterwards, stated "Rangers hit a new peak in all-out, full-blooded attacking football. But all they had to show for it were three disallowed goals and the admiration of all sports critics". Plaudits from the national media were as plentiful as the chances Queens Park Rangers created in this match against the Hammers.

In the aftermath of the controversial goalless draw with West Ham, Jago's team settled into life in the flight, in fine style. Which was in stark contrast to the difficult and luckless campaign of 1968/69, when Queens Park Rangers were rarely rewarded for their endeavours in their maiden season in the top flight. Four successive league wins between October and November, over Wolverhampton Wanderers, Arsenal, Derby County and Coventry City, well and truly established Rangers' credentials as a team who were worthy of their place in the First Division. And the brand of football they were playing week in, week out, was winning no shortage of admirers, too.

As the Easter period approached, Queens Park Rangers were still in with an outside chance of earning a historic place in the UEFA Cup. But just when the possibility of European club football was on the horizon, that man Ron Challis was back. On Good Friday, midway through the following April, he took charge of the First Division home game against Ipswich Town. In keeping with the habit of errors occurring when he turned up, the match programme for his second visit to Loftus Road in 73/74, stated that the referee was from Trowbridge which is in Wiltshire, rather than Tonbridge in Kent. Given how unpopular he made himself on his previous visit to West London, there may well have been a school of thought that suggested that perhaps he moved to the west of England, in order to steer clear of Queens Park Rangers supporters, still angry about his previous refereeing performance at W12.

But in the interest of letting bygones be bygones, perhaps the fans who attended might now look forward to a less controversial encounter. With both teams in the hunt a place in the UEFA Cup, there was every reason for looking to the future, rather than the past. As it happened, Bobby Robson's side went home with both points thanks to Trevor Whymark scoring the only goal of the game. With his standing already very low among Rangers supporters, history somehow managed to repeat itself. Challis disallowed another Queens Park Rangers goal that afternoon as well. A long-range shot from Don Givens was ruled out, when like during the controversial referee's previous appearance, it was claimed Givens was in an offside position at the time. The only saving grace of the afternoon was that it was two less disallowed goals against

40

QPR, than the last time Ron Challis came to Loftus Road.

8 *Afternoon Delight*
Queens Park Rangers 1 Chelsea 0
1973/74

The Three-Day Working Week that lasted between January and March 1974, saw the British Government strictly control the use of electricity, owing to the long-running dispute between Prime Minister Ted Heath and the National Union of Mineworkers. Dwindling coal supplies in the country meant that commercial users of electricity were limited to three specified consecutive days' consumption each week during this period and were prohibited from working longer hours on those days. As a direct result of both the upheaval to everyday life and the Miners' Strike that lasted sixteen weeks, the Conservative Party were voted out of office in February of that year, following Heath's ill-fated campaign that used the slogan 'Who Runs Britain'? The BBC and ITV were also required to cease broadcasting at 10.30 pm each evening to conserve electricity. The new measures impacted on so many aspects of people's lives during this period, and English football would not be exempt. The 3rd Round of the FA Cup would be such an example.

On 5th January, QPR were drawn away to Chelsea. At the time, Rangers had never beaten their local rivals in a league or cup game, so there was no shortage of incentive for Gordon Jago's side to change that not insignificant detail. At Stamford Bridge, Rangers put in a superb performance, but Chelsea's stand-in Welsh goalkeeper John Phillips kept his side in the tie with some excellent saves and the match finished goalless. The two local rivals were supposed to meet just three days later but the replay was called off at very late notice because of a waterlogged pitch, by which time many fans of both teams were already on their way to the game. As a result, the tie was rearranged for 15th January 1974, ten days after the team's first met and on a normal working Tuesday to boot. Because of the restrictions on the consumption of power, the match would have to be played at 1.30 pm that afternoon. Bank holidays aside, such an early kick-off during the week, had not happened for a Rangers match since the days of wartime football back in the 1940's. The early kick-off allowed for the possibility that the game could go to extra time.

Nowadays, it would be easy to think that having an important game played at such an unusual time when a fair proportion of the population would still have been at either work or school, would have an effect on the number of people who turned up to watch. Club Secretary Ron Phillips was however, in no doubt that there would be a healthy crowd for this most unusual of kick-off times. In his column that appeared in the match programme for the Chelsea game, he offered the following thoughts; "We shall be surprised if this cup tie does not tempt large numbers away from other duties. West London statisticians are going to be puzzled at the remarkable numbers of grandmothers who expired in the area since

Saturday". As it happened, Phillips almost certainly had a valid point. 28,573 fans were in attendance at Loftus Road. Along no doubt with a fair number of phony bereavements, many long serving QPR fans of a certain age would now freely admit that they simply bunked off of school, to be at this game.

The chances of a historic first Rangers win were helped by the opposition, courtesy of the man who would succeed Jago as manager. Chelsea's talented pair of Peter Osgood and Alan Hudson had a massive falling out with Dave Sexton, and both were dropped for this cup game. Neither would be at Stamford Bridge by the end of 1974, and in many ways, that signalled a downturn in their fortunes for many years after, whilst Queens Park Rangers were in the ascendancy, by comparison. In the absence of Chelsea's two outstanding players, future R's centre half David Webb was played up front as an emergency striker.

Once again, QPR were the dominant team in the tie and were cheered on by the large crowd on a heavy and greasy Loftus Road pitch. This did not go down well with some sections of the visiting support. As was often the case around this period, many Chelsea fans managed to get into the Loft End and in particular, the long-standing enclosure popularly known as the Boys Pen. The Boys Pen had been a fixture of Loftus Road for a number of years and so many youngsters would have stood there, when they first started attending matches. Having so many unwelcome visitors who were just able to pay at the turnstiles and walk in, was always going to be a recipe for disaster. Sure enough, at one stage, they charged forward in great number on the terrace and that caused the wall to collapse and some youngsters were forced to go on the pitch for their own safety. In the aftermath of this game, the club decided not to repair the damage and that signalled the end of the Boys Pen. It was not the easiest afternoon for Stan

Bowles either, having to deal with the constant attention of Chelsea defender Ron 'Chopper' Harris. Harris spent much of the match fouling Bowles and the defender with a fearsome reputation was only booked towards the end of the game.

But the talented Rangers forward would have the last laugh. Over an hour of non-stop pressure from Jago's side was finally rewarded when in the 63rd minute, the outstanding Dave Clement got a cross into the box and Bowles header found the back of the net. The visitors had nothing to offer in terms of a comeback and with that, Queens Park Rangers had at last beaten Chelsea in a competitive match for the first time. And it had been done with an exciting brand of football, despite the fact that the playing surface didn't necessarily lend itself to such a high-class performance.

The win was the springboard for an exciting run in the competition. In the 4th Round, Birmingham City were beaten 2-0, with goals from Mick Leach and Don Givens. Rangers defeated Coventry City 3-2 in a 5th Round home replay, as Givens, Bowles and Thomas all got their names on the scoresheet. Surprisingly, QPR were beaten 2-0 in the quarter-finals of the competition, when hosting Leicester City. The Foxes could boast a number of talented players, including Peter Shilton, Frank Worthington and Keith Weller. But as it happened, their match winner was the comparatively unknown Joe Waters. The Irish midfielder scored twice, yet would make less than 20 appearances for Leicester City, before spending the rest of his career with Grimsby Town, and then a number of years playing indoor football in the USA, with the Tacoma Stars. This FA Cup tie was also notable for the fact that Rangers wore their change colours of red shirts and white shorts, despite the fact that the game was held at home.

The Three-Day Working Week came to an end in March of that year, and things soon went back to normal in the footballing world. But not before Loftus Road staged one more midweek afternoon match, with the kick-off now being 2 pm. A First Division game saw Rangers lose 2-1 to Norwich City, with Stan Bowles getting the consolation goal. Interestingly, only 12,427 people attended, which was by a considerable number, the lowest home crowd all season. All of which suggested that the novelty of going to football matches at such an unusual time, was quickly losing its appeal. As a result, every football club in the country would have breathed a sigh of relief when the Three-Day Working Week came to an end, and welcomed the extra gate money that came with healthier attendances at their more traditional starting times.

With just the two home matches played in this unusual time slots-one of which ended in a win, whilst the other was in a losing cause-there was not enough evidence to suggest that it was either a positive or a negative for the club. Whereas other chapters in this book look at games that had one significant 'first' or 'last', that FA Cup tie, could boast a few of them. Obviously, we had the first daytime kick-off on a working weekday, since World War II. A historic maiden victory over our local rivals, which was yet another achievement in the Queens Park Rangers career of Stan Bowles. And we also saw the end of the Boys Pen in the home end, as a result of hooliganism. An afternoon not short of memorable moments. Certainly, one all those who skipped either school or work, did not regret attending.

9 *Parkes Loses Out*
Queens Park Rangers 4 Leicester City 2
1974/75

On Boxing Day 1974, 17,311 spectators turned up at Loftus Road for a First Division game against Leicester City. It was at that point, the lowest home attendance of the 74/75 season. As it happened, those who stayed away missed an absolute cracker. Among the Foxes line-up was 20-year-old goalkeeper Carl Jayes. Jayes actually started the season as their third-choice keeper, but would soon enjoy a meteoric rise through the ranks. In November 1974, Peter Shilton was sold to Stoke City for a then world record fee for a goalkeeper of £325,000. That record incidentally, would eventually be broken when Phil Parkes left QPR to join West Ham United in 1979. Shilton's understudy prior to departing, was Mark Wallington. He was injured at the time so Carl Jayes found himself thrust into the limelight.

Rangers and Leicester played against a backdrop of strong winds, following some heavy rain prior to the match. Maybe, just maybe, the wind played a part in the proceedings. The home side took the lead after just three minutes when John Beck struck the back of the net following a header from David Webb. That was the only goal of the first half, though it would not take long after the break for Rangers to add to their total. In the 48th minute of the game, Dave Thomas managed the rare feat of scoring direct from a corner kick. And fifteen minutes later, Don Givens appeared to wrap up both points, when he scored from close range to make it 3-0. Then a previously unknown opponent, threatened to single-handedly inspire a stunning comeback for the visitors.

Striker Bob Lee was making his debut for Leicester City and must had thought that league football was a cinch, when he found the net in the 65th and 67th minutes. From cruising to an easy win, QPR were now having to defend a slender lead. Thankfully, the game was made safe when a little-known figure of our own, got his own name on the scoresheet. Danny Westwood enjoyed a highly prolific goalscoring run with non-league Billericay Town, with an astonishing 48 goals in one season, alone. Queens Park Rangers beat Southend United in the battle for his signature in 1974. Westwood made a couple of appearances in the League Cup, but when he came on for Mick Leach at half time, it would be the first time that he would play in a league game for his new club. In the 87th minute, a massive goal kick from Phil Parkes found its way into the opposite penalty area and Danny Westwood was quicker to react than Carl Jayes, to make it 4-2.

Rather than being the start of a successful association with QPR, it would be the first and last time that Westwood appeared in a league game for the club. He was sold to Gillingham in November 1975 for a fee of £17,500. He would incidentally, enjoy a longer and happier association with the Gills, making 211 appearances and scoring 74 league goals in six years with the Kent side. And so those who went to Loftus Road for this match were treated to six goals. Among them, one of which came direct from a corner-kick, as well as a spirited fightback from the visitors, and two youngsters enjoy dream goalscoring league debuts. Yet despite all of those things, many of the fans of both sides would have left the ground talking about a completely different incident.

The surprising assist that came from Parkes for the fourth Rangers goal, was not his only massive punt up the pitch, that afternoon. With the home side attacking the School End just after Lee had scored the second of his two goals, Phil Parkes kicked the ball in the direction of the Leicester City goal. Perhaps helped by the conditions that afternoon, the ball got almost as far as the opposite penalty area. Jayes advanced to collect the ball, but misjudged the kick which promptly sailed over his head and into the net. It seemed like Queens Park Rangers had just added their fourth goal of the day, thanks to the most unlikely goal scorer in the history of the club. Only referee Ray Tinkler, was having none of it. He ruled that it was offside. If Parkes finding the back of the net courtesy of a goal kick wasn't unusual enough, the fact that it was disallowed, seemed even odder.

If you look on YouTube at some modern examples of the phenomena that is goalkeepers scoring with a punt from their own area, you will see that each example of the genre takes between four and six seconds to go from one end of the pitch to the other. Which begs the question, even in the absence of any of his teammates expecting Phil Parkes to boot the ball so far up the pitch, who in that Rangers team was seeking an unfair advantage? During their top flight days in the 1990's, Wimbledon with their turgid brand of football, were notorious for regularly try to catch teams in an offside position, via an opposing goal kick. But otherwise, offside calls from that position do not happen too often. Back in 1974, examples of goalkeepers scoring were even rarer, with Pat Jennings doing so for Tottenham Hotspur against Manchester United during 1967 FA Charity Shield, being the only high-profile example. Even the legendary BBC commentator Kenneth Wolstenholme was somewhat confused when he had the microphone in his hand whilst watching that game. "Oh....it's....yes, a fan....tastic effort", exclaimed the befuddled reporter. Despite having some 20 years' experience as a commentator, Wolstenholme was completely confused as to whether it was a goal or not. We can only guess as to whether this most rare occurrence also caught out the match official, at Loftus Road a few years later.

Goals that come direct from a keeper, are a very rare and unusual type of strike. Nobody ever really expects them happen in the first place. Keepers by nature, concern themselves with clean sheets and can often be found berating their defence, even if they are to blame for a goal in a match that they still run out comfortable winners. There are of course, exceptions to this rule. Paraguayan keeper Jose Luis Chilavert became famous for taking free-kicks and penalties, and finished his career with an unbelievable tally of 59 career goals, for club and country. And aside from all of the trophies he won at Manchester United, Peter Schmeichel was also well known for his late appearances in the opposing penalty area, if his team were seeking a late equaliser or winner. Not as prolific as Chilavert, the big Dane still managed nine career goals of his own. But they are hardly typical of goalkeepers. Indeed, on some of the occasions that a keeper has scored direct from a goal kick, he has been seen putting his hand up to apologize to his opposite number. Because inevitably, they are more concerned with spoiling the afternoon of the opposing forwards, and not make a fool out of their opposite number on the pitch.

The following weekend, those at the club were able to see the humorous side of the goal not being given. A cartoon in the following home programme for the FA Cup Third Round tie against Southend United, by Len Marshall who had replaced Bill Tidy as the regular cartoonist in the matchday magazine, poked fun at that incident. It pictures a scenario in the Leicester City dressing room, after their game against Queens Park Rangers. The Leicester keeper is lying on a couch and being tended to by their club doctor. The medical officer turns to the manager and exclaims "It's some kind of shell-shock! We should keep him away from Phil Parkes and high winds".

To date, there is no example on record of a goalkeeper scoring for Queens Park Rangers. Nor are there any moments caught on television, of one of our own players scoring from inside their own half. With the aid of VAR in the modern game, the likelihood is that the goal would probably have stood. Or it might even have done so had in the mid 1970's, there been more examples of this type of occurrence, so both the match officials and players would have been more aware of just what had happened. It is a shame that Parkes never scored, for a few reasons. As one of the most popular keepers ever to wear the QPR number one shirt, supporters couldn't have imagined anyone they would rather have seen become the first Rangers stopper to pull off this remarkable feat. For Phil Parkes himself, had the goal been given, no doubt he would to this day, still have fans coming up to him to talk about that incident, delighted to tell him that "*they were there*" when it happened. And finally, were it awarded, it would have been historic for being the day that a team scored from both direct from a corner kick and a goalkeeper's clearance in the same match. How often has that happened in world football?

10 *A Topsy-Turvey Goalless Draw*
Queens Park Rangers 0 Derby County 0
1977/78

By the time the 77/78 season got underway, the QPR team was looking significantly different to the one that came within a whisker of winning the title, a mere fifteen months earlier. Frank McLintock and Dave Thomas left Loftus Road and other key individuals would follow. In September 1977, so too did David Webb, who joined McLintock, after the latter was appointed as manager of Leicester City. Don Masson moved to Derby County and as a result of that transfer to the East Midlands, talisman Stan Bowles was deployed in a much deeper role, to give the team some much needed creativity. Dave Sexton had also departed for Manchester United, at the end of the 1976/77 campaign. In Sexton's otherwise brilliant tenure as Queens Park Rangers manager, no prospects came through the youth system, during his three years in charge. And after some initial successes in the transfer market, like Masson, John Hollins and Don Shanks, there was also a lack of significant incoming transfers, thereafter. Under the new management of Frank Sibley, a number of new faces came into the side.

Central defender David Needham looked like an excellent buy from Notts. County and fans were quickly impressed with his all-round performances at the heart of the Rangers defence. Inexplicably, he was sold to Nottingham Forest after just six months. Others like Paul McGee, Ernie Howe and Tommy Cunningham, were simply not in the same class as those who wore the blue and white shirts, less than two years earlier. Another one of the new signings-in the form of winger Brian Williams who was signed from Bury-looked hopelessly out of his depth and departed for Swindon Town, after just one season. By Christmas 1977, Rangers were in a relegation dogfight as Derby County were the visitors on Boxing Day. Sibley's preparation for the visit of Derby was not made any easier, with Phil Parkes and Dave Clement both absent through injury. There was one very familiar face in the visitor's line-up in the form of Don Masson, having joined the Rams in a swap deal that saw winger Leighton James make the opposite journey.

QPR had struggled to get any momentum going against County and it was goalless by half time. But on the hour, the match was thrown into turmoil with one of the most controversial incidents, Loftus Road ever saw from a referee. Derby's Bruce Rioch was about to take a free-kick. The ball was not where official Alan Turvey thought it should have been and promptly ordered a retake from a different position, booking Rioch in the process. Disgusted at what he perceived as harsh treatment, he proceeded to launch a foul-mouth tirade towards Turvey. Off the back of what was a pretty harsh booking in the first place, it was perhaps no surprise that the referee's response to getting that abuse was to send off the Derby County midfielder. That would normally have been an unusual enough incident in its own right. But things were about to get somewhat surreal.

Bruce Rioch's teammates were very unhappy with the decision, none more so than striker Charlie George. In his anger, George picked up the football and promptly booted it over the Ellerslie Road stand and out of the ground. With that, Alan Turvey ordered the him from the pitch too. Both sets of supporters now had to get their heads around the fact that seconds earlier, Derby were about to take a free-kick, and now they were down to nine men, without so much as an innocuous foul being connected to either of the dismissals. It was no surprise that the visitors were furious with the turn of events. Among them, manager Tommy Docherty. After the match, his own assessment of the official was "Mr Topsy-Turvey blew his top and lost control".

Eventually, things settled down and play was ready to continue. Only now, Rangers had the rare luxury of having two extra men on the pitch. The trouble is, the Queens Park Rangers side were if anything, more stunned than the away team, at being two men to the good. Somehow, QPR managed to be just as inept against nine men, as they were against eleven. About the most entertaining thing to happen for the rest of the afternoon was whenever Derby County's Don Masson was on the ball, the home crowd started chanting "Off, off, off...." in the vain hope that the referee would also send off the former Rangers man. The fact that Rangers came into this game struggling so badly in the league, and proved completely inept at making the most of this numerical advantage, showed how bad things had become in such a short space of time.

Referee Alan Turvey certainly made a name for himself, and not for the only time in the 1977/78 season. On three separate occasion during that campaign, Turvey sent off two players in the same match, including West Ham's Derek Hales and Wolverhampton Wanderers Derek Parkin, in a controversial match at Upton Park in March 1978. This being the late 70's, it was very rare for two players to get sent off in the same match. Let alone the same referee being responsible for that happening three times in a single year. At the end of that campaign, Alan Turvey would get his very own marching orders, when he was dropped from the League referee's list. Something of an unprecedented occurrence at the time. But in a bizarre act, Turvey went from 'poacher to gamekeeper' when he was immediately installed as a Referee's assessor. The former police officer would go on to become a highly respected administrator within non-league football, for many years prior to his retirement in 2016. He passed away, two years later.

At the time, it was somewhat unprecedented for Queens Park Rangers to be involved in a competitive match where they were playing against nine men. Even more so for that fact that it came about in such unusual circumstances. A couple of diabolical challenges would at least have made it look like there was some legitimacy for the two dismissals. For many years, it would be the only example of QPR enjoying the luxury of being in an eleven versus nine scenarios. But many years later, Rangers were involved in a whole raft of similar such games. With regards to how those panned out, they will be discussed in a later chapter, though it's fair to say that it hasn't been the lucky horseshoe that supporters might have hoped for.

The failure to take advantage of playing against a severely diminished Derby line-up, was a sign that this Rangers side were in big trouble. Sibley's team was one of a number that were involved in a relegation battle, in which the sides between 15th and 20th, out of 22 teams in the First Division, were separated by just four points. Queens Park

Rangers secured top flight football thanks to a goalless draw in the penultimate match of the season, at home to Leeds United. By a curious twist of fate, that vital point was achieved thanks to future R's hero Tony Currie. A piledriver from the talented Leeds player hit the crossbar, before the ball rolled to safety. Had it finished up in the Rangers goal, Currie would have condemned QPR to relegation. Clearly, he was making vital contributions to the Queens Park Rangers cause, even before he became a one of our own players.

11 *The Fastest Goal Mystery*
Queens Park Rangers 3 Bolton Wanderers 1
1980/81

Tommy Langley joined Queens Park Rangers from
Chelsea for a fee of £400,000, in August 1980. He scored
eight times in 25 appearances for the club, including one
on his debut against his former side. A respectable, if
somewhat unspectacular return during his brief spell at
Loftus Road, before joining Crystal Palace. Little wonder
then that compared to forwards like Clive Allen, Paul
Goddard and Simon Stainrod who also played for the club
in the early 80s, he rarely gets a mention when supporters
discuss strikers from that era. But Langley does have one
claim-to-fame that very few individuals in the history of
QPR can boast. And that is an appearance in a book most
supporters would have owned at some point in their
lifetime.

In the lead-up to Bolton Wanderers coming to Loftus
Road, manager Tommy Docherty was sacked by owner

Jim Gregory. With Terry Venables yet to take over on a permanent basis, Rangers scout Derek Healy was put in charge of the team in a caretaker role. As QPR kicked off, Tony Currie played the ball forward to Steve Burke. He outjumped his marker and, in the process, gave Tommy Langley a scoring opportunity. The Rangers striker duly took his chance and his left-footed shot from a narrow angle found the back of the net. A flying start for Queens Park Rangers, as the goal was timed at six seconds. The visitors equalised thanks to a strike from Brian Kidd after the home defence failed to clear a corner. But a penalty from Burke into the bottom right corner of the net and a third goal from Dean Neal who tapped in from close-range in the 90th minute, ensured the victory for Healy's team. Meaning that perhaps for the only time, Rangers had scored in the first and last minute of the same game. And of particular significance, the swiftness of Langley's strike had earned him a place in the Guinness Book of Records.

His goal was judged to be the fastest ever, in a competitive game. As a result, Tommy Langley took his place in what was regarded as one of the most famous works of reference, in the world. Over the next few years, other goals from around the world would also lay claim to the record of the fastest ever goal, also being timed at six seconds, but the one time Queens Park Rangers forward hung in there for several editions of the much-loved book, ensuring that his name appeared in this annual publication for a good years. But in recent times, there have been a couple of developments on the *fastest goals'* front.

First of all, with so many matches screened from all over the world, the record of scoring in six seconds, has been eclipsed many times over. A visit to YouTube will allow you the chance to see numerous incidents of players from all around the globe to try speculative shots from the kick-off. There is no shortage of keepers getting caught off-guard by inventive players who try their luck as soon as the referee has blown his whistle and score after just three or four seconds. The other development is that Langley is no longer credited as having found the back of the net in just six seconds.

Decades later, that opening goal against Bolton Wanderers in 1980, is now officially ratified as having being scored after twelve seconds. Quick yes, but never enough to earn a place in the Guinness Book of Records. So just how did the situation arise where this mix-up was allowed to happen in the first place? Ironically, footage of this game does exist. In theory, this means that there should never have been any confusion about the time of the goal in the first place. Unfortunately, it does not capture the kick-off and only shows Tommy Langley scoring the goal. Ultimately, the exact timing of the dramatic start to the game, was left open to interpretation. Was the announcement that Tommy Langley's goal was scored in just six seconds an honest error? Or was it a slight exaggeration that ensured that the Queens Park Rangers striker entered the record books? For many years, that has remained a mystery.

Although Langley is now credited with scoring in twelve seconds rather than six, it is still a phenomenally quick strike. Not surprisingly, there are very few examples of a Queens Park Rangers goal being scored anything like as early in a game, as what happened in October 1980. But as achievements go, it has been challenged on a handful of occasions. Gary Bannister had a couple of stabs at the record in the 1986/87 season. In the home league games against Wimbledon and Sheffield Wednesday he managed the unusual feat of scoring in the opening 30 seconds, in two league matches in the same campaign. But neither goal was as quick as Tommy Langley's new confirmed record. But twice from the kick-off, we saw quicker goals than what Bannister managed and for both of them, we must turn our attention to the League Cup.

The 8-1 win over Crewe Alexandra in the first leg of the Second Round of the League Cup in 1983, is the joint biggest QPR win found on film, alongside the 7-0 victory over Burnley in 1979. The rout began from the kick-off, when Simon Stainrod found Ian Stewart on the left side of the pitch. The Northern Irish winger managed to get a cross into the box which was only partially cleared, and quickest to react was Stainrod when his shot from the outside of his left foot, went between four Crewe defenders and beyond the dive of the Crewe keeper to find the bottom corner of the net. As with Langley three years earlier, it took Simon Stainrod just twelve seconds to put Rangers in the lead.

In a 1994 League Cup tie at home to Manchester City, Rangers attacked the School End and just like Stainrod's goal all those years earlier, a cross from the left side of the pitch was delivered into the area and struck home by Kevin Gallen. The timing of this goal? Yes, you've guessed it, twelve seconds of course. This trio of strikes can all claim to be the quickest ever scored by a QPR player. Curiously, there is a fourth goal that was also technically scored after twelve seconds. Although that particular one would not be eligible for a stake of this record.

In the 6-1 win over Middlesbrough in the 1982/83 season that featured on Match of the Day, Gary Micklewhite gave Rangers the lead. Exactly twelve seconds after the visitors restarted the game, the ball was in the net for a second time, as the away defenders were quickly dispossessed and Mike Flanagan scored with a low shot inside the penalty area. Many of the Queens Park Rangers supporters hadn't even retaken their seats from Micklewhite's goal, before the lead was doubled. Discussions about the fastest ever

QPR goal are usually concerned with what happens at the very start of a match so this effort cannot be recognised for record purposes. But perhaps Flanagan's goal is the most impressive of the lot, given that it was the only one scored of the back of the opposition being in possession just seconds earlier. Among QPR club records, this may well be the most debatable of them all, as well as being the one that carries more than a hint of ambiguity about it.

12 *Madness at Millmoor*
Rotherham 1 Queens Park Rangers 0
1981/82

Every club in the country will have its own tales about bad tempered games over the years, and Rangers would be no exception. Each generation of QPR supporters would probably point to one game or another, as to what might be the most notorious example of this select group of matches. But all contenders for the title of 'most bad-tempered Queens Park Rangers match ever', inevitably live in the shadow of the events that took place at Millmoor in March 1982. Off the back of a 4-0 home win over Charlton Athletic, Terry Venables took his side to South Yorkshire during the same time that they were also involved in an FA Cup run that would take them all the way to Wembley. Neither Venables or his team could have imagined just how nasty things would turn that day.

Rotherham had actually come in this game in a great run of form of their own, having picked up 31 points out of a possible 36, in their previous twelve matches, which included a 6-0 win over Chelsea, a week earlier. The game marked the league debut of left-back Ian Dawes, and it also saw the return of Steve Wicks, after a brief spell at Crystal Palace. Just over a minute into the game, The Millers took the lead when a through ball found John Seasman who managed to beat the offside trap. He took the ball past Peter Hucker and found the net, despite Bob Hazell's desperate attempt to clear the ball off the line. Following a late challenge on Rotherham's John Breckin a few minutes later, referee Alan Banks booked QPR midfielder Gary Micklewhite. It would be the first of a number of moments when tempers would get heated. Rangers continued to attack and Simon Stainrod very nearly set up Micklewhite, who shot just wide. Shortly after, a shot from Hazell was cleared off the line, following a corner. Then came the moment that was one of the worst injustices ever inflicted on a Queens Park Rangers player, as well as being the flashpoint that would make this such a bad-tempered affair.

A goal kick from Hucker reached the half-way line and Terry Fenwick and Rotherham player-manager Emlyn Hughes both rose to try and head the ball. A moment later, Hughes collapsed to the ground in agony. This was followed by most of the Rangers players surrounding the referee as Rotherham's Barry Claxton came on the pitch to tend to the former England international. Claxton served in numerous roles at Millmoor, being kitman, trainer, and assistant to Emlyn Hughes. As a result of the bad feeling between the two sides, he would briefly and unexpectedly, take on a starring role of his own, later that afternoon.

After some discussion between referee Banks and Fenwick, everyone was stunned to see him order the Queens Park Rangers captain from the field of play. Fenwick looked absolutely perplexed as he walked off the pitch. And with good reason. The replay of the incident in question revealed that Terry Fenwick wasn't responsible for anything as cynical as elbowing his opponent. The football had simply hit Hughes in the face and he went to ground covering his face in pain. When Claxton helped Emlyn Hughes to his feet, the latter reacted in a manner which suggested he did not know what day of the week it was. But continued playing on. As a result of that appalling decision, there was little chance of this match being played in a good spirit for the rest of the afternoon.

Rotherham very nearly made it 2-0 from an unlikely source, as Gary Micklewhite misjudged a back pass and very nearly chipped the ball over Peter Hucker from 20 yards out. Micklewhite did manage to clean up his own mess when he headed the rebound clear, with Rotherham forwards closing in on him. Later in the first half, a Gerry Forrest shot was saved by the Rangers keeper, though rather than award a corner, a goal-kick was given. It would be one of the few decisions that went QPR's way, but it was far from being the worst decision from the referee. Things would not get another better on that front, in the second half.

Despite being a man light, Rangers still played attacking football where possible, though Rotherham had the first decent opportunity of the second period, when Billy McEwan only had Hucker to beat, but the QPR keeper managed to palm the ball away. Soon after that, a volley on the turn by Clive Allen very nearly bought Venables side level in a spectacular manner. A rare moment of humour came when Millers hardman Gerry Gow attempted a long pass across the pitch, which hit Alan Banks in the head. The referee fell on the floor in a heap, to cheers from both sets of supporters. On came the giant figure of Barry Claxton to check if he was okay, before play continued. You could in his defence say that some of the dubious decisions that followed were as a result of been hit on the back of the head. But truth be told, they were not that brilliant before the said incident.

Seconds after play resumed, the next controversial moment arrived. From a throw-in, Dawes was about to play a pass to Flanagan, when Gow came flying in all studs showing, with a challenge that could have seriously injured the young Rangers debutant. Ian Dawes was furious and so too were his teammates. Whilst Gerry Gow tried to play down the incident, anger extended to the respective dugouts. Among those most angry was Alan Harris, who left no-one in any doubt as to what he thought of that foul from the Rotherham hardman. Charging out of the home dugout, Claxton was having none of that and attempted to shout down the QPR assistant manager and for one moment, has his hands on Harris's shoulders as he and another member of the Millers coaching staff looked like they were personally going to escort him back in the visitors' dugout. But one man wasn't intimidated. The R's burly kitman Jock Skinner pushed Barry Claxton and his pal away from Alan Harris, and both the officials and the police quickly had to intervene. It was hard to tell whether there was more anger regarding that bad foul, on the pitch or off it. Even as the game was about to restart, Skinner and Claxton continued their war of words, but the latter no longer seemed so keen on manhandling anyone from the opposite bench. Gow was eventually booked for the original incident.

After a shot from a narrow angle by Mike Flanagan which was well saved by Ray Mountford, we had another flashpoint. A Rotherham ball forward saw Ronnie Moore and Hazell go for the ball. Moore caught Bob Hazell as his elbow as the pair were airborne. The referee blew up as the traveling fans demanded his dismissal. Instead, the Rotherham forward was only booked. So, we now had a match in which Terry Fenwick was sent off, as ITV commentator John Helm stated was for 'violent conduct' after he spoke to Banks at half time, when in truth, he did nothing wrong. And now there was a genuine use of the elbow, and that only warranted a booking. Perhaps thinking that he could get away with anything, a couple of minutes later, Ronnie Moore came flying in on Peter Hucker, with a challenge that left the keeper injured. After consulting his linesman, Alan Banks sent Moore from the field of play. The striker looked disgusted with the decision and took as much time as he could to leave the pitch, even stopping to take the strapping off of his socks. Eventually, that man Barry Claxton came on the field to tell him to get a move on. Perhaps the only man more annoyed about this red card than Moore, has Emlyn Hughes who continued to argue with any Rangers player who could be bothered to listen to him.

With that drama over, we had another when it became apparent that Hucker was in no fit state to continue. With only one substitute allowed back in the 1981/82 season, there would be no recognised goalkeeper to replace him. Coming off the bench, Steve Burke would replace Peter Hucker in goal. But before that happened, the game looked like it had gone back in time as the barely conscious stopper was carried off by a couple of St John's Ambulance volunteers, who were armed with what looked like an old bedstead that wouldn't have looked out of place on a World War One battlefield. When play did eventually continue, Clive Allen became the latest player to be booked for a late challenge on Gerry Gow. Moments later, popular midfielder Gary Waddock almost scored with a curling shot from 30 yards. In their next attack, Hughes of all people was put in the clear as he ran through on goal, only to be brought down by Gary Micklewhite. Unfortunately, the midfielder was already booked and that would be the end of his afternoon, as he became the third player to be sent off.

Although not a record for the number of players sent off in a match involving Queens Park Rangers, it probably did set another, owing to the fact that there was thirteen and a half minutes of injury time. At the final whistle, Banks blew up in front of the tunnel, and promptly sprinted off the pitch. Even allowing for the fact players wanting to shake hands with him would have been few and far between, it was a gesture that would probably not have pleased either of his linesmen. In is not difficult to imagine that they would have preferred to see a bit more solidarity from their fellow official. With the match finished, the post mortem began, and that role would be taken by Derek Dougan. Dougan had been a pundit, since that role began within English football, when he worked for ITV, during their coverage of the 1970 World Cup. He was in the introduction, very critical of the officials saying that they lost control, but when interviewing Terry Venables, tried to insinuate that the over-enthusiasm on the part of the QPR youngsters keen to play in the FA Cup Semi Final the following weekend might have been the cause of the bad feeling. When Venables directly asked him if he was blaming Rangers for the bad feeling, Derek Dougan quickly backed off. The Rangers manager said that despite all that had gone on, he thought his team played some excellent football.

Then there was Emlyn Hughes. The man who was at the centre of two players getting sent off, won 62 caps for the England team, yet has the unusual distinction of making the most appearances for the national team, without ever playing at either a European Championships or World Cup tournament. He was as well-known for his role as team captain on A Question of Sport for many years, as he was a footballer. But Hughes was not popular with everyone, and it was no secret that some of his teammates actually hated him. Most notably, Tommy Smith at Liverpool. When questioned by Dougan, he still protested that he had been elbowed by Terry Fenwick, despite some camera angles showing that it was the ball that hit him in the face. Emlyn Hughes then tried to make out that there was little in the way of 'dirty play' all afternoon, which was almost as baffling as his view on the non-existent elbow to his face.

With the win over West Bromwich Albion the following weekend confirming a first ever appearance in the FA Cup Final, the events at Millmoor faded from memory as supporters turned their attention towards the trip to Wembley. But many years later, the 'Battle of Millmoor' was given an airing to a new generation of Queens Park Rangers fans. In 1995, a video series for every Premiership club, entitled 'The Pain and the Glory' went on sale, and it featured action accompanied by an assortment of well-known songs. The QPR entry in this series included among other things, great goals, great saves, and a look at the best moments of Les Ferdinand, Ray Wilkins and Trevor Francis. Also featured, was a collection of clips featuring bad tackles, angry exchanges, and sending offs, accompanied by East 17's hit "It's Alright". Although other matches were also featured, the one game that kept turning up in this particular montage, was Rotherham versus Queens Park Rangers from 1982. Its place in R's folklore, was well and truly sealed.

13 *Surprise Lucky Shirts*
Newcastle United 0 Queens Park Rangers 4
1981/82

A midweek trip up to Newcastle's St James' Park is about as demanding as away games get for the keenest of supporters who wish to cheer on QPR. Those hardy souls who made the almost 300-mile-long journey in May 1982, were in for a shock as the game was about to start. The Queens Park Rangers eleven that came running onto the pitch, were wearing unfamiliar yellow shirts, to go with our traditional white shorts. There are two points worth mentioning. First of all, Rangers have worn blue and white hoops on many occasions at Newcastle, just as the opposition have regularly worn their traditional black and white strip, at Loftus Road. And secondly, red shirts and black shorts, was the strip Terry Venables' men would normally have changed into, if the away kit was required. Not foreseeing a problem, only the blue and white hoops were taken up to the North East for the game. Referee Norman Wilson from Morecambe, wasn't happy that one team were wearing hoops whilst the other wore stripes-both of which featured replica shirts that were partially white. With that, QPR were ordered to wear Newcastle

United's away colours.

Fans who made the long journey north, would have been perplexed to see Rangers wearing colours that were completely alien to them. Had the match being played on 1 April, this might at least have been explained as an elaborate wind up. But this was 5 May, making that about five weeks too late for such shenanigans. So somewhat unusually, Queens Park Rangers would play a Second Division match, wearing the colours of their opponents. But if the decision from referee Wilson was a surprise to the players and supporters of QPR, it certainly did not affect them as much as it did their hosts.

John Gregory scored the first goal for Queens Park Rangers from close range. And it was only thanks to photographer Keith Creckendon, that many fans even knew about the club wearing the Geordies strip, in the first place. Creckendon's picture of the midfielder scoring, featured in a programme when Newcastle visited Loftus Road on 15 January 1983. The small matter of some seven months later, incidentally. That photo of Gregory's goal remains just about the only image in existence, of Rangers wearing the yellow shirts. It featured as part of a competition where programme editor Dennis Signy wanted fans to name both the team that QPR were playing and the score that day? The winning entry would bag a pair of tickets for a future match at Loftus Road. As Newcastle were the visitors when this competition was being run, it must be said that their supporters would in all likelihood, have been privy to the answers to both of the questions posed, every bit as much as the home fans. Perhaps even more so. But given the score line of the previous meeting and the prize on offer, not to mention that long journey required when coming to Loftus Road , it is doubtful that the postbag that arrived at Loftus Road in the days that followed, was bulging with entries from the North East.

Before half-time had even arrived, the points were pretty much made safe, thanks to a couple of goals that came in quick succession. On 37 and 38 minutes respectively, Clive Allen and Mike Flanagan got their names on the scoresheet. With the cup final just a couple of weeks away, no doubt Terry Venables would have been delighted with how the team still looked competitive. By the time that Simon Stainrod got the fourth and final goal of the game after 67 minutes, the three sides of the pitch with Newcastle United fans, were already starting to empty.

Although this 4-0 score line represented one of the best wins of the season, the unusual nature of Queens Park Rangers not even wearing their own colours, largely passed the majority of the supporters by. It took place just seventeen days before the FA Cup Final at Wembley. The showpiece match against Tottenham Hotspur was undoubtedly where the priorities of this team lied. With no television footage of this game existing and most fans dreaming of cup success, this odd piece of club history pretty much went unreported, until that picture of Gregory scoring the first goal as part of a competition in the matchday magazine, came to light.

Perhaps the most remarkable aspect of this match, apart from the fact that Rangers wore the Newcastle away strip, was the attendance. 10,670 fans turned up to see this game. Less than four months later, Queens Park Rangers opening day fixture was also away to Newcastle United. This time incidentally, the visitors made sure that they brought their away shirts. For the game up on Tyneside in August 1982, the attendance on this occasion was 36,185. That represented an improvement by the small margin of 25,515 fans. The mind-blowing jump in numbers going along to St James' Park, can be put down to one man, and one man alone. Kevin Keegan was making his debut, and the man who arrived in the North East to a tidal wave of euphoria, scored the only goal of the game. In an on/off association with Newcastle that lasted 26 years, you cannot underestimate the impact Keegan had on that club, and the region as a whole.

Those with even longer memories, might recall a similar occurrence, from the 1974/75 season. Derby County came to Loftus Road and just like when QPR visited St James' Park seven years later, the Rams were prevented from wearing their traditional white shirts and dark coloured shorts. On that occasion, there was not only the sight of Derby wearing the Rangers colours at Loftus Road, it wasn't even the away kit from that season. Instead, they had to wear the change red shirts which featured the letters of 'QPR' where you would expect to see the club crest instead, that was actually used by Queens Park Rangers in the 73/74 campaign. Dave Sexton's Rangers side won 4-1. At the time, it was the club's biggest ever win in the top flight.

In the current era, most football clubs are obsessed with selling replica shirts and often have a choice of three different shirts to choose from. Indeed, usually they will often wear their away kit or alternative shirts, as they are often referred to nowadays, even when they are not required in away games, in order to make them as visible as possible to their supporters. Obviously with the aim of getting them to buy more tops. Subsequently, the days of kit mishaps like the one that happened at Newcastle, have long since passed. Those two matches in which both sides ended up wearing shirts of the same team, remain very rare examples of this most odd occurrence. Given the margin of victory for QPR on each occasion, it is perhaps a pity that it didn't happen more often.

14 *Stanchion Deliver*
Queens Park Rangers 2 Blackburn Rovers 2
1982/83

An entire chapter of this book could be filled with an assortment of different reasons why QPR supporters would have had reason to feel aggrieved about a goal that the R's conceded, over the years. But none would have been more unusual than what happened during a home match that took place against Blackburn Rovers in November 1982. Terry Venables side were going along nicely in the Second Division, and were in the hunt for promotion back to the top flight. It all started off well enough, as Clive Allen scored after his run into the penalty area, gave him the chance to score from close range. As was often the case with Allen, he took the chance that came his way, with a low left-footed drive.

Blackburn's Scottish winger Ian Miller equalised when a cross that deflected off the leg of Bob Hazell fell kindly, and he struck a powerfully hit shot from twelve yards out into the back of the net. This being the side that would go on the win the title the following spring, Rangers went on the attack. Clive Allen who was involved in so much of what happened that afternoon, almost scored his second of the afternoon with a stunning volley from 15 yards out, that shook the crossbar. Tony Sealy got in on the act too, with a shot on the turn, which went just wide.

In the second half, Blackburn Rovers midfielder David Hamilton attempted a cross from the left wing. As crosses went, it didn't seem to cause any problems. Hazell and goalkeeper Peter Hucker looked to have any danger at the near post covered. And when the ball went out of play, logically Hucker would have taken a goal kick just seconds later. Oddly, the ball hit the stanchion of the Rangers goal, and bounced back into play. As the said QPR players waited for the ball to come back to the goalie, Blackburn's Norman Bell nipped in to put the ball into the back of the net. Unbelievably, referee John Deakin signalled that it was goal. For a few seconds, Peter Hucker and Bob Hazell looked on in disbelief at what just happened, before pointing to the stanchion to indicate that the goal should not have been given.

By now, Terry Venables was livid and stormed out of the dugout to remonstrate with the officials. Or at least would have done had there not been so many of his own players blocking his path the referee and linesman who were occupying that half of the pitch. Something resembling a stand-off developed among manager, players and officials. Unfortunately, frustrations reached the stands too, which led to angry fans coming on to the Astroturf. Sure enough, arrests followed. No amount of arguing with referee Deakin would make him change his mind. To add insult to injury, Venables would later be charged with bringing the game into disrepute. Eventually, the game had to restart, but at least one man was still seething.

Queens Park Rangers were unable to kick-off as Clive Allen decided to launch his own one-man tirade against the referee. Needless to say, John Deakin booked him, and it was probably just as well given what happened later in the match, that his teammate Terry Fenwick pushed him away from the match official and gave him an almighty telling-off in the process, which ensured that the Rangers striker didn't land himself in even more trouble. When looking at the footage of the game, it would be easy to say that Allen should not have reacted the way he did, after the initial protests had already died down. But what you have to understand is that he had a bit of history with this sort of thing.

A couple of years earlier when he was playing with Crystal Palace in an away league match at Coventry City, the Eagles got a free kick about 25 yards out. A teammate played a short pass to Clive Allen and his powerfully struck shot gave the keeper no chance and flew into the goal before coming out, as a result of the ball hitting the stanchion. On this occasion, the referee awarded no goal after discussing the incident with the linesman. Once again, Allen and his teammates were furious and protested to no avail that the ball had gone into the net. With that in mind, you can understand why the Rangers striker was so angry. Just about the only two memorable and controversial incidents involving stanchions in English football in the 1980's, happened to be in matches he was playing in, and both times he was on the wrong end of appalling decisions. By way of another strange coincidence, the Crystal Palace manager in that game at Highfield Road, was none other than Terry Venables.

The reason Queens Park Rangers supporters would have been grateful for Fenwick's intervention on Clive Allen's part was that late in that game, the Rangers forward run into the Rovers penalty area saw him brought done. A penalty was awarded and Terry Fenwick duly converted to ensure that QPR got a point. The 2-2 draw meant that Rangers would go to second place in the league, though a win would have taken them to the top of the table. A fitting finale to an afternoon that was not short of controversy.

In the immediate aftermath of the Blackburn Rovers game, the stanchions were removed and an alternative support for the goal nets were used, thereafter. No one around Loftus Road would have been sorry to see the back of them. Regarding those offending artifacts, when Tony Fernandes was touting the idea of a new stadium during the latter part of the 2010's, our owner also expressed enthusiasm for the idea of a Queens Park Rangers Museum. If such a museum ever came into existence, the stanchions would surely have been worth their own spot on display in a glass cabinet. Regardless of the fact that they were the cause of a lot of anger that afternoon, they are still a most fascinating piece of QPR history, which is exactly the type of thing that belongs in a museum in the first place. But even if such a building to commemorate our historical significance came into existence, it is doubtful those stanchions would find their way in. The likelihood is that they finished up in the nearest dustbin, courtesy of either Terry Venables or Clive Allen.

15 *Perfect Ten*
Sheffield Wednesday 0 Queens Park Rangers 1
1982/83

When discussing Terry Venables time as Queens Park Rangers manager, bouquets rather than brickbats, are the order of the day. With one success story after another during his time at Loftus Road, you would be hard pushed to find any criticism of his time in charge. But it you took a closer look, you could at a push, pick out a couple of points. Those in question were that his time as our manager largely coincided with the plastic pitch. Also, it must be said that he enjoyed employing the offside trap, on a regular basis. A tactic that even some of our own fans grew tired of. When QPR visited Hillsborough in April 1983, you could say that criticism of one of those points was justified. But the result, and in particular the historic landmark that was reached, showed that it was unfair to put too much emphasis on the other point raised.

A midweek fixture meant a long trip up to Yorkshire on a Tuesday evening in April 1983, for the Queens Park

Rangers diehards. Just three days earlier, Wednesday were beaten 2-1 by Brighton & Hove Albion, in an FA Cup Semi-Final held at Arsenal's old Highbury ground. With Rangers having more to play for, with the small matter of the Second Division title on the horizon, it looked like a good time to be facing the Owls. Curiously, the front line for Sheffield Wednesday, included one player who was a former QPR striker whilst the other would turn out for us in the future. The men in question being Andy McCulloch and Gary Bannister. Rather than 'biting the hand that used to/would feed them', the Rangers central defensive pairing of Bob Hazell and Steve Wicks was immense and they snuffed out any threat. In a match where the visitors were happy to soak up the pressure, they did not do a great deal of attacking themselves which lead to the unusual sight and sound of the Sheffield Wednesday support booing the visitors. Especially when their own team kept getting caught offside.

And so, we come to the first of the two points that were raised. Playing the offside trap on a regular basis, will not win you too many friends. If you twisted the arms of some Queens Park Rangers supporters at the time, they would have admitted that they were not massive fans of seeing it as often as they did. Even the two next permanent managers in Alan Mullery and Jim Smith, expressed a desire to move away from the reliance on catching teams out so often, courtesy of a well-drilled offside trap. But at the same time, part of the reason that it was so unpopular with opposing fans, and perhaps even managers, was that this side was so well organised by Venables, that it worked so well week after week. Inevitably, with this system being so successful, there was no real need to change anything. In contrast, when this QPR side did have possession of the ball, they regularly played an entertaining brand of football, often at a high tempo, and producing results that had taken them to the top of the Second Division.

In the second half, not many chances came the way of Rangers. One such opportunity did, when Mike Flanagan had a shot saved, and Simon Stainrod's lob went over the bar, as a result of the original effort on goal. Ironically, the home fans screamed for offside for that attack. In the 70th minute, the only goal of the match finally came. A raid down the left flank saw full back Ian Dawes get in a cross which Tony Sealy cleverly dummied. With that, Mike Flanagan's shot beat keeper Bob Bolder, to give QPR the lead. It had the feel of a game in which one goal was always likely to be enough, and that proved to be the case. As a result, Rangers were now in the enviable position of just needing one more point to secure promotion back to the First Division, whilst they still had six league games to acquire this. It was also the day that this side managed by Terry Venables, reached a notable landmark.

That victory was the tenth away league win of the 1982/83 season. From the moment that John Gregory scored the winner at Oldham Athletic in September 1982, Queens Park Rangers enjoyed a great run away from home. It is interesting to note that the first three away victories at Oldham, Leicester City and Barnsley, were all courtesy of single goal. But some of the later wins away from home, came via bigger margins. Such as the 4-1 victory at Cambridge United, 3-1 at Charlton Athletic and 3-0 against Venables former club Crystal Palace. All of which suggested that QPR were growing in confidence, as the season went on. The win at Hillsborough was far from been the best of the bunch. But ten away wins was still a remarkable achievement and it remains one of those *'holy grails'* for Queens Park Rangers. A landmark that is very hard to a reach, but one that becomes imminently possible once the club is involved in a promotion race. Ironically, the 1982/83 team reached ten away wins, despite failing to manage pick up a victory in either of the first two, or last couple of away league fixtures. But they were certainly very productive, in between.

Whilst on the subject of away wins, Terry Venables could boast a very respectable record on that front, throughout his time as Rangers manager. In the 1981/82 season, there were six of them. This of course, was against a backdrop of having to divert much of his and the team's energy towards the run that would take Queens Park Rangers all the way to the FA Cup Final. And following the promotion, the 1983/84 season saw QPR win seven league matches away from home in the First Division. Much was made at the time about teams hating the fact that they had to come to Loftus Road and play on the Astroturf. But they would only have to do so, just once a year back in the first half of the 1980's. In comparison, Rangers had to switch from grass to plastic, all of the time. That cannot have been easy, but under the watchful eye of Venables, it was managed with the minimum of fuss.

Not surprisingly, winning ten away league matches in a single campaign is not a landmark that many Queens Park Rangers sides have gotten close to, in the years that followed. One team that could have done so, was the 1993/94 side. They racked up an impressive eight away wins in the Premiership. Yet against the three relegated sides in the form of Sheffield United, Oldham Athletic and Swindon Town, QPR failed to beat any of them. Fittingly, the 2010/11 side that won the Championship under Neil Warnock, also emulated their 1983 counterparts by winning ten league matches on the road. The last of which was a memorable 2-0 victory over Watford at Vicarage Road.

The Terry Venables era did enjoy the benefit of having the Astroturf at Loftus Road, and at least a small part of their success on the pitch was down to employing that offside trap. But the plastic pitch and the tactics adopted, was only part of the reason for his success at Loftus Road. Given half the chance, many of the teams Queens Park Rangers faced would have been just as quick to employ the same offside tactics. If they had the tactical nous in the first place. And Venables side more than replicated results on the plastic pitch, with those that were achieved away from home. The efforts of his 1982/83 team, remain a benchmark for all future QPR sides that want to excel away from Loftus Road.

16 *A Red and Black Love Affair*
Ipswich Town 0 Queens Park Rangers 2
1983/84

Upon winning promotion to the First Division in 1983, Queens Park Rangers quickly settled well into top flight football with a series of fine victories, after a four-year absence. One such positive result came in the away fixture at Portman Road in October 1983. The home side had the best of the early chances, as Peter Hucker pulled off an outstanding save. Another Ipswich chance came when Hucker sprinted out of his penalty area but failed to connect with the ball. Thankfully for the Rangers keeper, his defence managed to clear the danger before he got back to his goal line. Later in the first-half, Clive Allen did well to dispossess one of the Ipswich defenders. Allen then preceded to pass to Simon Stainrod whose low shot found the bottom corner of the net to give the visitors the lead. The hosts did have a good chance to equalise just after the half-hour mark, when a cross from the right, was headed wide.

In the second period, QPR doubled their lead with a goal not too dissimilar to the first. This time Stainrod beat his opponent on the left, and his cross was met with a shot from John Gregory at the far post. A fine win for Terry Venables team that can still be viewed on YouTube, should you wish to do so. That afternoon was also memorable as it saw the first appearance of a fans favourite that remains popular to this day. It was the very first time Queens Park Rangers wore red and black hoops in a competitive game. From the moment that shirt made its first appearance during that league game at Portman Road, it felt like, for want of a better description, a perfect fit.

The hooped design in the form of the blue and white colours have always been a big part of QPR's identity in home matches. Having red and black hoops feels like an extension of our identity, whenever away matches were played and a change of kit was required. Because of its appearance, that kit has never resembled anything else you would see in English league football. The best-known wearers of red and black hoops in world football is Brazilian side Flamengo. A team that can boast the likes of Zico, Junior and Leandro, among its list of illustrious former players for both club and country. A comparison all of our own supporters could live with, if they were to stop and think about it. And speaking of Brazil, at the 2014 World Cup tournament, Germany ditched their traditional away green shirts in favour of their own variety of the classic red and black hoops. It was famously worn in when they produced one of the greatest performances in the history of the competition, when they beat the hosts 7-1.

Many numerous high points in the club's modern history happened when red and black hoops have been worn by the team, and they will feature in a few of the upcoming chapters. Having blue and white hoops for home games, and red and black colours when a change is needed, also eliminates the need for a third or alternative kit. And to top it all, it is so well loved by the fanbase that they even have a nickname for the colours, referring to it as the 'Dennis the Menace' strip, after the famous character in the children's comic The Beano. When you think about it, how often are supporters so fond of their away kit, they actually have a nickname it?

Yet despite that long list of great and sound reasons for having red and black hoops, the club have continually turned their back on this popular option. Since Bobby Zamora memorably fired Queens Park Rangers back to the Premiership on that sunny afternoon at Wembley Stadium in 2014, when he and his teammates wore the red and black hoops, the famous away kit has only appeared in one season since. The sole example of it returning to favour being the 2015/16 season. Why that famous moment that secured promotion back to the Premiership was never seized upon by the club's marketing department, is a complete mystery.

In recent years, there have been two broad schools of thought, among the QPR fanbase, regarding the introduction of each new away kit. Some supporters cannot get enough of them and are more than happy to add them to their collection at the first available opportunity. It must also be said that each new away kit does seem to sell in large numbers, which in the eyes of many fans, is justification for the club going down this route. But for other Loftus Road regulars, there is also a feeling of alienation on this subject.

There are just as many supporters who find some of the recent away kits little short of being an abomination. Not least because many of the new colours that have turned up on the second and third choice shirts in recent times have no historical connection with Queens Park Rangers, whatsoever. To quote the famous old television presenter Sir Robin Day, many of them could fittingly be described as 'here today, gone tomorrow, replica shirts', given that they will last for just one season, and a couple of years later, many supporters would have forgotten which colours were present in a given year, in the not too distant past.

In comparison, the red and black hoops have a timeless quality about them. So many great players over the past 35 years have worn this shirt, and to this day, it is instantly recognisable as being Queens Park Rangers away colours, even to fans of most other teams. Who knows when it will be used once again? One thing we can all be assured of is that when it will eventually return as QPR's away shirt, it will be both a popular move with the overwhelming majority of our fans, and a great opportunity to reconnect with a great and long-standing symbol of our identity.

17 *Mullery's Last Stand*
Queens Park Rangers 2 Stoke City 0
1984/85

The list of former QPR managers is a very long one, even by the standards of English football. We have seen them all over the years. The good, the bad and the indifferent. Some were awful and it was a relief to see the back of them. While others could feel a bit hard done by, with regards to being dismissed. But when it comes to ill feeling regarding the parting of the ways, no sacking was ever as bitter as that of Alan Mullery. But to look at why Mullery's time at Loftus Road proved to be so acrimonious, you also need to look at the tenure of his predecessor.

Terry Venables became Queens Park Rangers manager in November 1980 and for the next few years, the club went from strength to strength. In the 1980/81 season, Venables oversaw a major turnaround in form and the team finished in eighth place. During the following campaign they would improve their league standing with a fifth-place finish, along with that historic FA Cup Final appearance. That concluded with a heroic defeat to Tottenham Hotspur in the replay, when even those of a Spurs persuasion, freely admitted Rangers had more than matched their London rivals. The 82/83 season saw Terry Venables side storm their way to the Second Division title, finishing the season with 85 points-a full ten points clear of runners-up Wolverhampton Wanderers. The good times continued in the 83/84 campaign with an impressive league campaign seeing QPR finish the season in fifth place, and earn a UEFA Cup spot in the process. The only downside to Rangers going so well under Venables, was that inevitably he would attract the attention of other clubs. So it was that he attracted that of the biggest of them all, in the form of Barcelona. He left for Spain in the summer of 1984, taking his assistant Allan Harris to Spain, with him.

Naturally, there was enormous interest regarding who would succeed Terry Venables. For a very brief period, Gordon Jago was appointed general manager. But he was gone, before the first game of the 1984/85 season even took place. Jim Gregory was keen on bringing Luton Town manager David Pleat, to Loftus Road as successor to Venables. But he was unable to talk him into leaving Kenilworth Road. But if Pleat wasn't so keen on working under Gregory, Alan Mullery most definitely was. In his autobiography that came out in the 1980's, Mullery admitted that he tracked him down to the health club that the Rangers' owner visited regularly, to express his desire for the job of Queens Park Rangers manager. Perhaps off the back of Alan Mullery's eagerness, he replaced Terry Venables before the start of the new campaign. After three and a half great years, a change of manager felt like the start of the new era and at the time. One thing we could be certain of was that Mullery would be a very different personality to his predecessor.

Hailing from Notting Hill, he was a self-confessed QPR fan. This would have done the new man in charge no harm, when pitching his credentials to Jim Gregory. A midfielder for Fulham and Tottenham Hotspur, he played for England on 35 occasions. Although he will always have the unwanted distinction of being the first person ever to be sent off, when representing the national side. As a result of his performances for England, there was an infamous TV debate between himself and Malcolm Allison on ITV's The Big Match, in September 1970, after the latter had been critical of his inclusion in the team at the previous summer's World Cup. Overseen by Jimmy Hill, the pair thrashed out their differences. During the exchange that lasted almost six minutes, Allison came across as calm, confident and knowledgeable, whilst Mullery was confrontational, argumentative and constantly interrupted the well-known pundit with put downs like "How many times have you played for England, Malcolm"? It felt like an insight into the abrasive nature of the man. Alan Mullery became manager of Brighton and Hove Albion in July 1976, a month after Venables took charge of Crystal Palace. And so, began a rivalry between both clubs, and to a certain degree, both men. Especially as years earlier, Mullery was chosen ahead of Terry Venables in the race to become Tottenham captain following on from Dave Mackay.

Things started well enough with two wins and two draws, in the first four league matches of the 1984/85 season. This was followed by a 5-0 defeat at Tottenham Hotspur, which proved to be the first sign that all was not well under the new regime. His few months in charge took in two comebacks that supporters remember to this day. Although only one of them is for the right reasons. The 5-5 draw with Newcastle United, is obviously the good example and remains to this day, one of the most amazing matches in the history of Queens Park Rangers. Having been 4-0 behind at half-time, five goals from the home side in the second period, included a last-minute equaliser from Gary Micklewhite, would almost have sounded too ridiculous were it a plot for film or television. Though interestingly, Alan Mullery was on record as asking the players to go out and show some pride for the people who have paid good money to watch that match. Whilst long-standing physio Dave Butler, memorably encouraged the players by saying that if Newcastle could get four in the first half, then they could do likewise during the second period. Less fondly remembered is the 4-0 defeat away to Partizan Belgrade which remains the only occasion in which an English club side squandered a four-goal lead in European club football. An intimidating atmosphere in front of 45,000 spectators, saw Mullery's team freeze on the big occasion. A defensive mix-up between Peter Hucker and Steve Wicks that lead to a penalty for the second goal, an almighty howler from the Rangers keeper for the third goal, and a couple of missed late chances, all contributed to going out of Europe, having seemingly started the second leg in a dream position. A combination of the result in Belgrade and a bust-up on the flight home with Simon Stainrod in front of some of our own supporters no less, inevitably meant that it was a case of when, rather than if, Alan Mullery was going to get the sack.

A 3-0 loss at Sunderland and a 4-0 defeat at Leicester City, only strengthened the belief that he was on borrowed time. A midweek game at home to Stoke City in December 1984 would be Mullery's swansong. A mere 8,403 people turned up to watch. In many ways, it was a case of history repeating itself. During a previous ill-fated spell as Crystal Palace manager, supporters never took to him, owing to his long association with Brighton & Hove Albion. For a while, Palace fans even boycotted matches, in an effort to get rid of Alan Mullery. That poor attendance for his last match in charge of Queens Park Rangers, suggested some of our own supporters were doing likewise. Those that did turn up were greeted with leaflets declaring "MULLERY MUST GO". Curiously, it was the first time all season that there was no manager's column in the matchday programme. And concluding the gloomy outlook that evening, only three of the floodlights were operational, as the one in the South Africa Road/Loftus Road corner of the ground, was not working. Given what went on in the build-up to this match, it would have been appropriate if that was followed by a couple of vultures flying over the home dugout while the game was going on.

At least the QPR manager had the luxury of playing against what was by far the poorest team in the First Division. Stoke City would finish the 1984/85 season 23 points worse off than fellow relegated side Sunderland. They would win just three times in 42 matches, scoring just 24 times and conceding 91 in the process. A thrashing of the perennial strugglers, might have at least bought Alan Mullery some time. That never happened. After 16 minutes, a long throw from Simon Stainrod was missed by a couple of Stoke defenders, and Gary Bannister struck from 12 yards out. Veteran keeper Joe Corrigan on loan from Manchester City, pulled off a fine save to tip a Steve Wicks header over the bar, to keep the score at 1-0. The visitors even managed a couple of chances of their own, including an effort from Keith Bertschin that hit the crossbar. Although Rangers were winning, it was not the statement of intent Mullery would have wanted, as the team were booed off at half-time.

The football was no better during the second period, and hostility towards the manager grew. One of the few memorable moments of the half came when Stoke's Tony Spearing was sent off in the 74th minute of the game, for arguing with the referee. Two minutes later, John Gregory scored the second goal of the night, when the visitors failed to clear an Ian Stewart cross and the Rangers midfielder struck home with a low volley. Tellingly, hardly any of the home crowd even bothered to celebrate. There was even some booing when the scorer's name was given over the loudspeaker. One of the strangest and most muted reactions to a QPR goal, Loftus Road ever saw. There was a barrage of booing at the final whistle and Alan Mullery was immediately sacked. The club were 16th in the First Division at the time.

In terms of legacy, time has not been kind to him. To this day he is still rated as one of the worst and most unpopular managers, Queens Park Rangers ever had. It was rare for a manager to take charge at Loftus Road when the club was in such a healthy position, yet leave the place in turmoil, just months later. There was no shortage of bitterness on his part either. Mullery is on record as saying that his time at Loftus Road "turned me into a monster" and that the players couldn't overcome their disappointment that Terry Venables was no longer the manager. He also referred to the Rangers playing staff as "the moaning, groaning bunch of players who treated me, themselves and their profession with contempt". In the aforementioned autobiography, he bemoaned the fact that on numerous occasions, he would give instructions in training, and would promptly be told that "Terry used to do it a different way" or "this was how Terry used to things". For all of his faults, it would have been infuriating for Mullery or any manager for that matter, if they kept having that rammed down their throat.

A look at his win ratio while in charge at QPR, is very surprising when you see that Alan Mullery can boast a success rate of 42.3%. Which believe it or not, is higher than, among others, Gerry Francis, Ian Holloway, Neil Warnock and Don Howe. Though it must be said that the list featuring the winning ratios of former managers is a strange and unusually misleading one, especially when you realise who is at the very top of it. Mullery's surprisingly high return is thanks in no small part to the number of wins he oversaw in UEFA and League Cup games. He could actually boast six of them in those two competitions, prior to his sacking. But inevitably, fans largely only remember that defeat in Belgrade. Regardless of what supporters might think of him, it wasn't nice to see the man suffer with financial problems and depression, in the aftermath of his sacking. Which would probably have hurt even more, because of his long-standing fondness for the club. It was not an episode that anyone associated Queens Park Rangers could look back at, with any fondness.

It would have been hard enough for anyone to succeed Terry Venables, who along with being very successful, was so popular with the fans, players, staff, and even the media who worked at the club. Yet with hindsight, the job at Loftus Road was the wrong one for Mullery. His rivalry with Venables goes a long way to explain why he was so desperate for the position of Rangers manager in the first place. Even when he was appointed, Alan Mullery paid tribute to his predecessor, but also spoke of improving on what Venables had achieved before him. Which suggests that he may well have had a bit of one-upmanship in mind towards his old rival, when he took the job. He never stood a chance of topping what Terry Venables achieved, on and off the pitch. Inevitably, resentment creeped in when Mullery attempted to change so many things from a system that had worked perfectly well, until he turned up and tried to make wholesale changes. To this day, no home victory at Loftus Road has been met with such hostility, as when Alan Mullery departed on such unhappy terms.

18 *Here's to You, Mister Robinson*
Chelsea 0 Queens Park Rangers 2
1985/86

Even more than the humiliating FA Cup First Round defeat to Vauxhall Motors in the 2001/02 season, the 1986 Milk Cup Final is the one game that Queens Park Rangers supporters have tried to erase from their memories. It is not difficult to imagine that numerous fans managed this feat on that very evening, thanks to copious amounts of alcohol, as many sorrows were drowned at the first available opportunity. Yet the run to the final itself, is still recalled with great affection by those who are old enough to remember it. And with good reason. With the exception of an easy two-legged victory over a then-lowly Hull City in the early stages of the competition, there wasn't a single easy tie, thereafter. Rangers faced tough opposition in each round, and on three occasions, secured progress in the competition thanks to results away from home. One such example came in the quarter final against Chelsea.

Initially, QPR were drawn at home to their London rivals for this fifth-round tie, who were flying high in the league at the time. Rangers drew first blood when John Byrne found the back of the net with a fine shot from inside the area. The only other goal of the night came from Pat Nevin who equalised from close range. Gary Bannister had what was the best of the remaining chances of the evening to win the game but his shot went well wide. An incident that was covered in some detail by the tabloid media who were pretty critical of him at the time for that missed opportunity. A harsh verdict and rare disappointment for Bannister against Chelsea, given that he scored eight goals in four home league matches against them, including two memorable hat tricks of his own. The two sides would face each other once again just seven days later, and the Chelsea manager was delighted about that.

John Hollins never hid his distaste for QPR's Astroturf pitch, and believing that his team did the hard work by avoiding defeat on the plastic, spoke like he thought that an easy win in the replay was a mere formality. The comments were somewhat of a surprise, coming from a man who would have a fair association with our own club, both as a former player, and around a decade later, coach and caretaker-manager, following the sacking of Stewart Houston. And it should be noted that Hollins is regarded as one of English football's real gentlemen. But back in the 1980's, he was far from being the only manager or player who could not stand the artificial surface that was part of Loftus Road for much of the decade.

The game kicked off on a muddy surface that made a mockery of John Hollins comments, and it would only get worse during the course of the evening. Rangers had the best of the first half opportunities with John Byrne having a couple of shots that went close, and Gary Bannister also forced a save from the Chelsea keeper Eddie Niedzwiecki.

In the second half, the home side started to take control, but could not actually create too many goalscoring opportunities of their own. The best of them being a free header from David Speedie which went wide. With no goals in 90 minutes of football, the tie went into extra time.

Aside from a shot from Michael Robinson which Niedzwiecki needed a second attempt to grab hold of, there was little to suggest that one side was about to make the breakthrough in the first period of extra time. By now, tiredness, the state of the deteriorating pitch and the pressure of the occasion, was starting to take its toll on all of the players. And if the extra 30 minutes couldn't separate the sides, they would have to do it all over again, with a second replay. There was always the possibility that a mistake would open the door for one of the two sides, and sure enough that happened. Whilst clearing his defensive lines, an attempt at some fancy footwork from Mike Hazard went wrong and he conceded a corner. From that set piece, Robbie James swung the ball into the six-yard box and Alan McDonald rose highest to head home, despite having no shortage of Chelsea players around him. McDonald would be a hugely influential figure at Loftus Road for more than a decade thereafter. But he would have few more satisfying moments than this one. Chelsea's chance to equaliser came a couple of minutes later, when a cross into the box was hit first time by Speedie. But continuing his habit of making key saves in the competition, R's keeper Paul Barron turned the ball round the post.

With the game drawing to a close, many of the players had nothing left in the tank, and it seemed that Alan McDonald had won the match for Rangers. But there would be one final twist to the match. For reasons known only to himself, Eddie Niedzwiecki collected a back pass and decided to come charging up the pitch. A poor touch as he ran forward gave Gary Bannister the possibility to rob the Chelsea keeper of the ball, and he had no choice but to try to boot the ball up the pitch to prevent the immediate danger from the Queens Park Rangers forward. He only succeeded in finding Michael Robinson who from just a yard inside the Chelsea half, struck the ball cleanly, and it found its way into the net, without so much as a single home defender within 40 yards of their own goal. Initially there was a lot of confusion as the linesman's flag went up. But after some of the QPR players discussed the incident with the referee, he decided to award the goal. The travelling support would have been happy enough had the McDonald goal won the game. But when Robinson's strike made it 2-0, it sealed a truly great night for Queens Park Rangers.

Michael Robinson's goal at Stamford Bridge was memorable for numerous reasons, among them that fact that it probably remains unique among all Queens Park Rangers goals ever caught on film. Many years after that game, Danny Baker brought out his 'Own Goals and Gaffs' video, which featured some of the most memorable blunders from the archives of English football. Just a few minutes into the video, the Robinson goal made an appearance and Baker was not slow to poke fun at Niedzwiecki for conducting himself like an outfield player. It does beg the question was it a spectacular strike that could have deservedly taken its place on a DVD compilation of great QPR goals, or a blunder worthy of being cannon fodder for Danny Baker?

As it happens, Michael Robinson's goal pulls off the very rare feat of being both. Sure, we had the comical element from Eddie Niedzwiecki. But at the same time, Robinson found the back of the net, from fully 57 yards out. Just for the record, no Queens Park Rangers goal ever seen on the

BBC, ITV or SKY, was from further out than this one. As was mentioned, the pitch was in an appalling state and even John Hollins would have admitted that it would have been easier to execute such a long-range effort on Astroturf, than the quagmire that hosted the replay. And looking at the footage of the game once again, the shot was hit to perfection, landing right in the middle of the goal. It was a great strike, made all the more memorable, because of the opposition and the occasion.

When you look back at Robinson's time as a Queens Park Rangers player, the word 'unremarkable' could easily come to mind. He scored just five goals in 48 appearances and even the keenest of supporters would struggle to remember any of the others. Rather than his favoured position up front, he was usually played on the wing. He didn't particularly enjoy that role and it may well have done much to hasten his departure, early in 1987. But if Michael Robinson could be described as an unremarkable QPR player, then he certainly had a remarkable life, thereafter. He transferred to CA Osasuna. Many players from these shores struggle when they go overseas. They can often find it hard to overcome the language, food, culture or style of football. Robinson had no such problems. He scored 12 goals in 58 appearances for his new side, helping them to fifth place in La Liga the 1987/88 season. A most impressive achievement given that his team have never been among the most fashionable in Spanish football. Thereafter, he enjoyed a long career in the Spanish media, as hugely successful sports broadcaster. By his own admission, when he arrived at Osasuna, he had no idea how long he would stay in Spain. But he found that he loved everything that his new life had to offer, and would remain for the next 33 years until he died in April 2020, aged just 61.

Many a Queens Park Rangers supporter holidaying in Spain, could well have seen Michael Robinson hosting a sports programme or endorsing some product or another, whilst out shopping. I like to think that as a former player, they would have been proud to see how he became so popular in his adopted homeland. His passing saw a memorable photo come to light from that evening at Stamford Bridge. The image in question from Rangers photographer Ariel Friedlander sees Robinson coming out of the tunnel holding a football in his left hand and saluting with his right, as he knows his picture is being taken. There was a swagger about that moment that would be more than matched by the way he doubled QPR's lead towards the end of the cup tie. Sadly, Robinson is no longer with us, but the memory of him scoring from the halfway line at Chelsea of all places, is still very much alive and well.

19 *Goal of The Season Afternoon*
Queens Park Rangers 5 Leicester City 2
1986/87

It has not just been in recent years that the club's record in the FA Cup has been something of an embarrassment. By January 1987, Queens Park Rangers had not won a single tie since Clive Allen scored on that memorable afternoon at Highbury in April 1982, to ensure a first and to date, only appearance in an FA Cup Final. There hadn't even been a goal for QPR in the competition since John Gregory scored a consolation, in a surprise 2-1 defeat away to Huddersfield Town, in the third round of the competition in 1984. Admittedly, this wasn't as bad as the eleven-year winless run in the FA Cup, in the early period of the 21st century. But that five-year barren era in the 1980s, was still disheartening to say the least. Having gone out of the competition at the first time of asking on each of those occasions, fans at least were happy that we would have a home draw with Leicester City coming to Loftus Road in the 1986/87 competition. This was incidentally, also the first time since 1982 that Rangers had a home tie in the FA Cup, so was the perfect opportunity to end what was becoming a wretched run.

It was also the chance for a bit of payback for Jim Smith's side. Earlier in the season, Leicester came to Loftus Road, and the home side dominated from start to finish. Unfortunately for QPR, Foxes keeper Ian Andrews produced a world-class performance, stopping opportunity after opportunity. If a couple of the R's forwards threw a kitchen sink at the visitor's goal, Andrews would probably have prevented that going in, too. Then in the last minute of the match, Alan Smith scored with just about Leicester's only attack of the game. One of the all-time infuriating 'smash and grab' efforts, ever seen from an away team in London W12.

If revenge was in the minds of the Queens Park Rangers players, things did not go to plan in the first half. Just minutes into the game, Alan Smith scored from close range in front of the Loft. For the rest of the first 45 minutes, the home side huffed and puffed looking for an equaliser but despite being in control of the match, couldn't find that moment of inspiration that would bring them level. As the referee blew the whistle for half-time, it already had the feel of being a carbon-copy of what happened in the league match a few months earlier. With the obvious exception being that Smith's goal came much earlier in the proceedings. No-one had any idea about the turnaround in fortune that was about to happen, and in such spectacular fashion, to boot.

Just minutes into the second period, Rangers got a free-kick from around 25 yards out. For much of the mid 1980s, Terry Fenwick was our go-to man, when it came to set pieces. With the entire Leicester City side back to defend the set free-kick, a five-man wall seemed to block Fenwick's path to goal, but with Ian Andrews rooted to the goal line by the left-hand post, the QPR skipper saw a generous gap at the opposite end. Direct from the set-piece, Terry Fenwick curled the ball into the top right-hand corner of the net. A superbly executed effort, but the Leicester City defenders were of a different mind, and had no doubt who was responsible for Rangers drawing level. Three of them gave Andrews a heap of abuse. Clearly his performance earlier in the season earned nothing in the way of goodwill with irate teammates. A short while later, Leicester were awarded a penalty, which was duly despatched by Scottish midfielder Gary McAllister. But Rangers were only getting warmed up with regards to their assault on the Foxes goal.

The resourceful Fenwick and Clive Walker had a discussion as they got another free-kick, this time near the corner flag. With the odds seemingly on Walker flighting a ball into the penalty area, Terry Fenwick started a run into the box, collecting the pass from the Rangers winger in the process. The R's skipper was brought down and the second penalty of the match was awarded. Moments later, Fenwick had his second goal of the afternoon, after he sent Ian Andrews the wrong way. From a match that had the look of a disappointing repeat of an earlier league fixture, we now had a hugely entertaining cup tie on our hands. From a David Seaman goal kick, Rangers launched another attack on the right side. The cross into the Leicester City area, was only cleared some 25 yards out. As the ball came towards Sammy Lee, he hit the sweetest of volleys which stayed low, but was hit with power. Andrews couldn't get his hand to the ball, as Lee scored his only goal for Queens Park Rangers.

If supporters were at this time wondering which was the superior goal out of the two long range shots from Terry Fenwick and Sammy Lee, they would soon see something even better. As with Lee's goal, QPR's fourth of the afternoon started with an attack down the right flank and once again we saw a clearance that would offer a goalscoring chance. This time Clive Walker was able to pick up the clearance and he passed to Robbie James. From fully 35 yards, he smashed the ball with such power, it found the top of the right corner of the net, despite the umpteenth despairing dive of the afternoon from Ian Andrews. With over 850 competitive appearances, James had one of the longest and most prolific careers in the history of the Football League but tragically he died at the tender age of 40. To this day he is revered at Swansea City with whom he made almost 400 appearances and scored over 100 league goals. An astonishing return from a player who spent most of his career in midfield. He was unfortunately nothing like as prolific during his time as a Queens Park Rangers player, with just five goals in comparison. Though the way he found the back of the net in this FA Cup tie, it is something of a mystery why he did not score more times whilst he played at Loftus Road.

Somewhat surprisingly, Rangers were by now 4-2 ahead, yet none of their goals had come from the forward line. John Byrne had other ideas, even after he had an effort of his own disallowed. Byrne knew a thing or two about great goals, having scored what was probably the best of the lot on the Astroturf, in the 6-0 win over Chelsea a year earlier. By now Jim Smith's side were passing the ball around with such confidence, Leicester weren't getting a look in. John Byrne collected the ball just inside their half of the pitch and ran at a couple of retreating defenders who looked too scared to try and tackle him. Then as he got towards the penalty area, cut between the pair and hit a shot into the bottom right corner of the net to seal a perfect comeback.

Not long after that, the match which most home fans wished would go on for another hour, came to a conclusion with the final whistle. A bit of respectability had been brought to our record in the FA Cup and it had been done in such spectacular fashion. And because of that, it raised a very interesting talking point. Whenever Rangers score one of their best goals of the season in any given match, most supporters would have been aware of the fact, and it is something worth talking about on the journey home, or in the pub after the game. If you get two of the best goals over the course of an entire campaign, then it has well and truly been a memorable afternoon. But three of them on the same day is pretty much unheard of. Yet here we were in a cup tie in which QPR were a goal behind at half-time, and had managed four of them on the same day. The Goal of the Season competition might as well have just consisted of their efforts in this one game. It goes without saying, no Queens Park Rangers side has ever come close to repeating the feat of scoring four times with goals of such high quality in the same match, since.

The term 'Magic of the Cup' tends to be an archaic one, in relation to the reputation of the competition, in recent years. And even less so, when it comes to Rangers. But look back over the years, and there have some pretty special goals in the FA Cup. Among them, Trevor Sinclair's overhead kick against Barnsley, which won the 1997 BBC Goal of the Season. And a couple of full backs got in on the act, with David Pizanti and Kenny Sansom, scoring spectacular winning efforts in London derbies against West Ham United(1988) and Arsenal(1990), respectively. All were memorable strikes that really made it feel like sometimes the cup does produce special moments. But for sheer number of great goals on the very same day, it is doubtful anything will ever top what happened when Leicester City came to West London, back in January 1987.

20 *Astroturf Finale*
Queens Park Rangers 1 Sheffield Wednesday 1
1987/88

In the summer of 1981, QPR became the first club to install an artificial pitch. As decisions went, it was not a popular one with the rest of English football. They had been used in both American football and baseball for a number of years, but were an anathema to the beautiful game. The irregular bounce, goalkeepers having to wear tracksuit bottoms to ensure that they didn't suffer carpet burns when diving to make saves, and players bemoaning that it took longer to recover after playing on it, were hardly glowing endorsements of this new innovation. But none of that mattered to Rangers manager Terry Venables. During his time as manager, Venables was positively brimming with ideas about the game. So much so, he almost needed a full-time assistant to write them all down. Playing on a plastic pitch, was among the highest profile of them.

Although Queens Park Rangers lost their first home match 2-1 to Luton Town in August 1981, they soon adapted well to life on the Astroturf and a good record at Loftus Road became a formality in the years that followed. Which usually did not go down very well with almost every team that came to West London. So much so, each visiting manager who left Loftus Road empty-handed, already their reason for losing at hand. Usually it came in the form of something along the lines of "We were beaten because of the plastic pitch". During the 87/88 season, the club decided that it would be their last with the controversial surface, and they would return to playing on grass when the following campaign got underway. If anything, the latter part of the campaign became an even poorer advert for the controversial surface as it was allowed to deteriorate owing to the fact that it was on borrowed time. During the penultimate home match in a 2-0 win over Tottenham Hotspur, keeper Bobby Mimms let a shot from QPR's David Kerslake go between his hands and legs and into the goal. And when I say 'shot', it was hit so tamely, it would barely have reached the goal had Mimms not got in the way in the first place. Some observers would have claimed it was a colossal howler whilst others would put it down to gremlins in the pitch. The reaction of a distraught Mimms, suggested it was the former of those two options.

On 23 April 1988, Queens Park Rangers played their last competitive game on the artificial pitch when Sheffield Wednesday came to town. Wearing replica shirts that could be best described as silvery/lilac, to go with their purple shorts and dark socks. At the time, Loftus Road had probably never seen such a lurid kit from a visiting team. As opposed to such designs that are ´ fairly commonplace in more recent times. For QPR it had been a remarkable season which for the first few weeks saw Jim Smith's side top the table, before Liverpool steamrollered their way to the title. Rangers did in time fall away from the title race, but made huge strides from the lacklustre 1986/87 season which finished with successive defeats to Sheffield Wednesday and Arsenal, by the respective score lines of 7-1 and 4-1, with fans screaming for Smith to go. A remarkable turnaround saw lots of new faces in the team, and a five-man defence which at the time was almost unheard of in the First Division.

In front of a crowd of 12,547, the Owls took the lead in the first half, when a powerful run from David Hirst took him past a couple of defenders, and into the Rangers penalty area. His pass along the box was collected by fellow striker Colin West who had time to control the ball before beating David Seaman with a shot from ten yards out. With no further goals by half-time, it looked like the 'Astroturf era' would be bookended with defeats on the first and very last home matches for QPR. Especially given that Rangers sides under Jim Smith had a notorious habit of finishing seasons, with a couple of very poor results. Thankfully, that would not be the case on this afternoon.

Early in the second period, new signing Trevor Francis showed some great skills down the right side of the pitch before getting a cross in from the by-line. Ian Dawes met the ball just past the far post and a cross of his own, was headed towards goal by Dean Coney. The striker's header was well placed, but a brilliant save from Kevin Pressman, preserved the Owls lead. But shortly after that, Pressman, like Bobby Mimms a couple of weeks earlier, found out that the ageing plastic pitch could be a very unforgiving surface for visiting goalkeepers. A hopeful ball from Alan McDonald was clipped into the box from 35 yards out. Even with Martin Allen trying to get on the end of the ball into the area, the Wednesday keeper should have had the danger covered. Instead, he fumbled his attempt to collect McDonald's pass forward and Dean Coney was on hand to tap-in from 12 yards out. As a result, he would be the last person to score on this pitch before it returned to grass. Although Coney was the club's second highest scorer in his one full season as a Queens Park Rangers player, he struggled to win the fans over. Most of them only remember him for arriving as part of the transfer deal that also brought the brilliant Paul Parker to W12, and a missed goalscoring opportunity at Portsmouth from one yard out, which is regarded as the worst ever, from a Rangers player. There were no further goals in the match between QPR and Sheffield Wednesday, but there was more drama to follow.

Late on, Wednesday striker West and our own Alan McDonald, who had been having a running battle all afternoon finally had enough of each other. One particular scuffle finished up with McDonald clouting Colin West before both sets of teammates intervened. Surely McDonald's afternoon was over, and the best Rangers supporters could hope for was that West would be leaving the pitch at the same time as him. But amazingly, referee Terry Holbrook chose instead to reprimand the pair and just booked them both. The Rangers central defender admitted after the match that he had behaved stupidly and was lucky not to get a red card. Curiously, Holbrook did not miss an opportunity all afternoon to interact with the crowd wherever possible, suggesting that no referee ever came to Loftus Road in such a good mood, as he did.

On the final whistle, and as is often the case for the final home game of the season, hundreds of fans invaded the pitch. Unusually on this occasion, there was no appeal over the loudspeaker for them to leave. Given how what was left of the Astroturf was going to be ripped up, you cannot help but wonder whether the powers-that-be would have been just as happy if the pitch invaders would save them the trouble of having to do it themselves. And with that 1-1 draw against Sheffield Wednesday, QPR's adventure on the Astroturf had come to an end. You would be hard pushed to find a single supporter who liked it or said that they preferred it to natural grass. But even those who were more tolerant of the plastic pitch knew that no matter how well Rangers did with it, we were never going to get any credit for those achievements. Yet you could hardly accuse the period between 1981 and 1988, of being an appalling era in the history of Queens Park Rangers.

Those seven years took in appearances in both the FA Cup and Milk Cup Finals, along with promotion to the First Division. Twice in that period the Astroturf saw QPR finish in fifth place and have the honour of being London's top team. Even during the hugely disappointing 1984/85 campaign which felt like a year-long hangover following the departure of Terry Venables, enough home wins ensured top flight football for the following season. Never once was a match postponed as a result of the weather, though for the 1986 Fifth Round League Cup tie at home to Nottingham Forest, the floodlights proved to be somewhat less reliable than the pitch. Having Astroturf meant that the ground could be used for other events and this meant that one of the most famous sporting occasions of the decade took place at Loftus Road. In 1985, Barry McGuigan defeated Panama's Eusebio Pedroza to become WBA World Featherweight boxing champion. McGuigan finished that year winning the BBC Sports Personality of the Year award. In comparison to the way Rangers squandered money in the late 1990's and 2010's, the artificial pitch years saw the club run a tight ship off the field, as well as progressing well, on it.

Despite all of the criticism it attracted, it did not stop others from following in our footsteps. Luton Town, Oldham Athletic, and Preston North End all installed their own plastic pitches. For Luton and Oldham, it would, like QPR, coincide with golden periods in their history. Of this quartet of League teams, Queens Park Rangers were the first to get rid of the artificial surface. As a result, Coney can only claim to be the last Rangers player to score on our very own version of a plastic pitch. Mark Falco scored at Kenilworth Road in the 1989/90 season and a year later in a 2-1 win at the same ground, Les Ferdinand scored twice including a brilliant last-minute solo goal making him the very last Queens Park Rangers player to score on an artificial pitch. A record that he might not even be aware existed, thanks in no small part to the fact that Ferdinand never actually played on our own version of it.

Of the four clubs that installed a plastic pitch, Loftus Road had the reputation as been the worst to play on. Even when Oldham Athletic installed their own version, manager Joe Royle was quick to point out that it was so much better than the one at QPR. By definition, being the first to go down this route meant that Rangers had to deal with most of the criticism that came with playing on this surface. And as we had a few years head start, technological improvements and the chance for the others to learn from our mistakes, meant that Loftus Road's Astroturf pitch remained the most despised of the bunch. Never that popular with our own fans, words like 'forgotten' and 'unloved' would probably best describe any feelings they still had towards it. Yet perhaps if supporters looked at what was achieved during those years, they may well take a slightly different view of it. And don't forget that an illustrious list of great QPR players appeared during this period. With that in mind, most fans would love to relive everything about the 'plastic pitch' period, except the football they had to watch on it for seven years.

21 *The Gray Show*
Queens Park Rangers 3 Manchester United 2
1988/89

QPR victories over Manchester United, have been even harder to come by, than those that have come against Liverpool. There have only been three of them since the turn of the 1980's. The most famous of that trio is undoubtedly the 4-1 win at Old Trafford on New Year's Day 1992. In front of millions of viewers who tuned in to ITV's live coverage of the game, Rangers went two goals up in a matter of minutes and a brilliant team performance ensured United never came close to getting back in the game. Dennis Bailey had the match of his life, scoring one of the most famous hat tricks in the history of Queens Park Rangers. Although injuries and a loss of form meant that Bailey never hit those heights thereafter, he remains a hugely popular figure who can be assured a welcome fit for a hero, whenever he returns to Loftus Road on any given matchday.

To find the last occasion that QPR beat Manchester United at Loftus Road, you have to go back even further. As with the events of January 1992, one Rangers player got the goals that sealed the victory, only this time, they were of the spectacular variety. And once more, the man in question produced one of the performances of his life, giving United players problems all evening. But in comparison to Dennis Bailey, this former midfielder does not enjoy 'hero status', and even some of the people who attended the game, may well have forgotten who this match winner even was.

Early in 1989, new manager Trevor Francis was given the funds to bolster an injury-hit Queens Park Rangers squad. In came Nigel Spackman from Liverpool for a record £500,000 and Andy Gray for a slightly more modest fee of £425,000 from Aston Villa. Spackman settled in better out of the two. When Rangers played host to champions-elect Arsenal, Spackman was played as an emergency centre-half and completely snuffed out the threat of striker Alan Smith, who at the time was the most prolific goal scorer in English football. In the very same game, a couple of memorable moments summed up how things weren't going so well for Gray. When he took a free-kick facing the away end, he managed to hit the famous old electronic scoreboard, to howls of derision from the travelling Gunners support. In the second half, a brilliant curling shot from substitute Mark Stein beat John Lukic and hit the crossbar. As it bounced down, Andy Gray struck from close range, but breaking QPR hearts, it was disallowed for offside in a game that would finish goalless. Gray couldn't seem to catch a break. And that run of bad luck continued when he was having his best game for Rangers against Luton Town, picked up an injury that appeared to have brought his season to a premature end, as he limped off the field of play.

But by the time Manchester United visited Loftus Road towards the end of the season, Andy Gray was back. The 88/89 season was not a particularly good one for United and at the time, Alex Ferguson's position as their manager was constantly being questioned, whenever they had a bad result. Although they came into this fixture in a poor run of form, Manchester United didn't at any point look like they lacked motivation, which is exactly what you would expect from a team managed by Ferguson. Just minutes into the game, Wayne Fereday conceded a corner and the resulting set-piece saw Steve Bruce find the back of the net with a diving header. But Rangers didn't let United settle and were soon putting the visitors under pressure. Colin Clarke had an excellent chance but his shot was saved and by this stage, Gray was giving the visitors lots of problems down the right wing. And he played a big part in the equaliser. One of his great strengths was the massive throw-ins he was able to launch into the opposition penalty areas. From such a throw-in, Andy Gray found the head of Colin Clarke and his flick-on was tucked home by Andy Sinton on the edge of the six-yard box. Had he been a Queens Park Rangers player for a longer period, Gray would have gained a reputation for having what was perhaps the longest throw-in of anyone who wore the blue and white hooped shirt. A claim that can usually be attributed to either Jack Robinson or Jay Emmanuel-Thomas-both of whom turned out for the club, many years later.

Just a couple of minutes later, Manchester United were back in the lead when Clayton Blackmore caught the Rangers defence cold. A Brian McClair volley from outside the area gave them the chance to double their lead, but to the great relief of the home support, his shot went wide. In terms of results, this was the worst United team for years, finishing the season eleventh, which would be two places below QPR. But on the evidence of the first 45 minutes, you wouldn't have known it from their performance. But throughout the game, Rangers continued to threaten the United goal and Gray had the look of a man who was capable of something special. That special moment came about from a David Seaman goal kick.

His punt upfield was headed by Clarke towards Sinton and his pass left Mark Stein with just Steve Bruce to beat in order to get a shot on goal. As the ball bounced up from a heavy Stein touch, Bruce handled the ball in an attempt to block the danger. Upon viewing of the footage once again, you can see that the handball took place right on the very edge of the penalty area, which usually means that there is the possibility that the referee could either award a free-kick or point to the penalty spot. As it happened, he gave neither and simply waved play on. Now there was the chance that Rangers supporters would walk away at the end of the game feeling cheated. Or at least they might have done were it not for Andy Gray. With the crowd still fuming about that Steve Bruce handball, the culprit's clearance went only as far as Gray who was facing the Paddock as he collected the ball. From 30 yards out, he turned and sprinted into the penalty area brushing aside an attempt by one United defender to stop him and then unleashed a shot that gave Jim Leighton no chance of stopping as it flew into the top left corner of the net. QPR had equalised in a match that was fast becoming a classic and once the celebrations abated, some fans were quick to say it was the most powerful shot they ever saw from a Rangers player. There was even a theory that had Leighton got his hands to the ball, it was hit with such force, it would have taken him into the back of the net, too.

Manchester United tried to regain the lead again, and came closest, when a McClair header went wide. QPR thought they had won the game when an attack which started when Andy Gray blocked a United clearance, gave Stein the chance to set up one of his teammates. His cross pinballed around the penalty area for a few seconds before Clarke tucked home from a couple of yards out. Celebrations would be short lived as the linesman ruled the goal offside. As the match was drawing to a close, it looked like it would be honours even, when Ralph Milne attempt to pass to a United teammate. Andy Gray intercepted the ball and from a few yards inside his own half, had just one thing on his mind. On a night when he tormented not one, but two full-backs who failed miserably to stop him causing havoc, Gray seemed to find extra reserves of energy as the game went on. His run in the 89th minute took him past both Blackmore and Mal Donaghy like they didn't exist and finished with an exquisite shot from 25 yards out. To beat Manchester United was memorable enough. But to do so with two stunning goals, of which the second came in the final minute, looks like a tick in every box of the 'wish list', a fan might have drawn up before the game started. This was incidentally, the first season in which videos featuring all of the league matches and goals went on sale. If Rangers fans needed any motivation to go out and buy a copy, then Andy Gray had certainly played his part. The thought of more performances like this one and goals of a similar quality, was a mouth-watering one.

This win over United was the anti-penultimate game of the season. By the time that the next campaign got underway, he was no longer a Queens Park Rangers player, having joined Crystal Palace. As is often the case, he was on the Eagles team for the opening game of the season at Loftus Road in August 1989. Many fans were left wondering how he could go from a five-star performance in a stunning with over Manchester United, to being offloaded for only slightly more money that was paid for him a few months earlier. He has always claimed that it was a surprise that he was allowed to leave the club. Though looking back at his career, with the exception of Crystal Palace, Gray never seemed to settle at any of the clubs he was at, for very long. He is one of many players to have played for the England national team on just a single occasion, with an appearance in a Euro' 92 qualifying game away to Poland. Graham Taylor's team got the 1-1 draw that sealed their place in the tournament in Sweden the following summer. But Andy Gray's performance was poor and rightly or wrongly, often finds his name being mentioned whenever discussion turns to England's worst ever international player.

Returning to the point made at the beginning of this chapter, it is a fascinating comparison between himself and Dennis Bailey who both enjoyed their finest hours as QPR players, in match winning efforts against Manchester United. On the one hand you have Bailey remains so well liked not just for that hat trick, but also coming across as perhaps the nicest guy ever to wear a Rangers shirt, as he remained as humble, honest and down to earth after that hat trick, as he was before the greatest day of his football career. In comparison, there has never been much in the way of affection for the former Palace and Villa player. There are a couple of reasons for this. Gray played just eleven matches for Queens Park Rangers with the aforementioned two goals. Fans inevitably never got to know the man or see him build up a series of performances that would establish him as an influential figure at the club. Instead he remains something of an enigma whose star shone even brighter than the Loftus Road floodlights that night back in 1989, before departing in surprising circumstances. His reputation with the QPR support was not done any favours when he played for Tottenham Hotspur in a bad-tempered 2-1 defeat at Loftus Road in 1992. When he scored the equaliser for Spurs in the second half, he was responsible for some of the most over-the-top celebrations ever seen from a visiting player. What little admiration some Rangers fans had for Andy Gray, disappeared with his reappearance in West London.

Yet whatever faults he had, on that memorable evening Gray played the game of his life as Queens Park Rangers beat United. It may well be a very long time before we see another QPR player emulate him with a matchwinner against them at Loftus Road. To do so with a wonderful individual performance accompanied by two strikes that would be worthy of inclusion in any Goal of the Season competition, would hopefully be a feat enjoyed and appreciated more than it was in the 1988/89 campaign.

22 *Parker Scores Sixth*
Queens Park Rangers 6 Luton Town 1
1990/91

The Hatters had been a thorn in QPR's side for years. They were the visitors for the first ever match on the Loftus Road AstroTurf in August 1981. They won that match, along with their next two visits to W12. Eventually, Rangers beat them on the plastic pitch in January 1987 in an FA Cup Fourth Round replay, and later that year, also recorded that elusive first win over them in a league game on that surface. But wins and draws in West London for Luton, both comfortably outnumbered their defeats here.

Yet under different circumstances, there might have been something resembling a mutual admiration between the two sides. Both got promoted to the First Division in the early 1980's, and it was something of a golden era for the two teams, in terms of the number of years in top flight, very respectable league placings and cup finals reached. Given the size of Luton Town and QPR, both clubs well and truly 'punched above their weight', for a number of

117

years. They would like Queens Park Rangers, go down the road of getting their own Astroturf pitch for their Kenilworth Road ground. This would at least take away a bit of the controversy that surrounded the presence of our own unpopular surface. And when under controversial chairman David Evans they introduced the much-hated membership scheme which attempted to ban all away fans (with mixed results, it must be said), the Hatters became one of the most despised teams in the country. So much so, even many years later when financial hardships and a massive points deduction caused them to drop out of the Football League in 2009, there were many fans around the country who had no sympathy for them, as a result of the choices they made a couple of decades earlier.

Although they could not be classed as 'local rivals', there has for many years and an assortment of different reasons, been plenty of animosity between supporters of the two teams. QPR's own particular and unusual rivalry with Luton Town probably began in September 1970. Rangers hosted the Hatters and a 1-0 defeat against them was masterminded by a couple of very familiar faces. They were managed by legendary manager Alec Stock and Luton's goal scorer that day was none other than former midfield stalwart Mike Keen. The 2-0 win at home to Luton in April 1973 on the way to promotion to the First Division when Terry Mancini scored with a header and Don Givens finished off a brilliant run from Gerry Francis, was a feisty affair. No fewer than four goals were disallowed-three of which came from the Hatters. The visitors also had Gordon Hindson sent off. Although most of the media who were present, were of the opinion that the referee made the right decisions for all of the disallowed goals and the sending off. Not that is this sent the visiting fans home, feeling any happier.

When QPR visited Kenilworth Road in August 1974, it came off the back of Chelsea being the previous team Luton played host to. Chelsea's hooligan element ran amok, smashing up the town as well as causing trouble during the game. As a result, visiting Rangers supporters were met with a heavy-handed police escort throughout the afternoon, complete with the obligatory snarling Alsatian dogs that accompanied them to and from the ground. The match itself, was notable for a controversial incident, when Queens Park Rangers were awarded a penalty. As Stan Bowles spot kick found the back of the net to cancel out John Ryan's effort for the home side, another football came flying out of the terrace behind the goal and to the amazement of most people in the ground, referee Les Hayes ordered a retake. The Rangers players led by skipper Terry Venables were furious, but Hayes was unmoved. Thankfully Bowles scored with the retake. In the lead-up to his second attempt from the spot the maverick number ten indicated where he would place the retake. Upon finding the net, then bowed to the home fans. Later on, he made a couple of gestures towards John Faulkner after he was booked for fouling Bowles. As a result, Stan Bowles incurred the displeasure of Luton Town manager Harry Haslam, as well as the home fans. The man known throughout the game as 'Happy' did not live up to that moniker, claiming that Stan Bowles should have been sent off for inciting the crowd. On the Monday after the game, Gordon Jago drove up to Luton, to smooth things over, after there was talk of legal action against the Rangers player.

If there was still a strong rivalry between both clubs by the time the 1990/91 season had begun, it almost seemed like Don Howe had gotten dragged in the mire, if you read his notes in the programme, for the visit of the Bedfordshire outfit. For many decades, the manager's column in the Queens Park Rangers matchday magazine, has been an exercise in diplomacy, as the man in charge would usually welcome the manager, players and the supporters of whoever happens to be visiting Loftus Road, on the given afternoon. This would often be accompanied by the obligatory complimentary remarks, even if the away team were in an appalling run on form. Yet on this occasion, Howe came out with the following comments suggesting that Rangers were on the verge of thrashing someone.

"I have a strong feeling that once we start scoring, we could get a hatful. I have watched our players in training and know that they have the ability, and someone in the First Division will be on the receiving end".

It should be noted that Don Howe was a highly respected figure in the game as well as being a consummate organiser. He was the last person you would expect to come out with brash statements like this. Yet by the end of the day, Howe was not only proved right, he was probably never more accurate with his timing throughout a lifetime in football, than he was on that autumn afternoon back in the early 90's. On the pitch, the win would be inspired by Roy Wegerle. It would be a very satisfying afternoon for him, given that he became Rangers' first million-pound signing when he arrived from Kenilworth Road, nine months earlier. His departure was met with comments from one Luton director, claiming that he wouldn't be that much of a loss because he was not a prolific goal scorer. Wegerle would respond in the best possible manner, by producing one of the best all-round performances of the decade, from a Queens Park Rangers player.

The first goal came early in the game when Paul Parker picked up a Luton Town clearance, and passed to Ray Wilkins. The veteran midfielder found Roy Wegerle whose run took him towards the corner flag. But with a couple of defenders around him, it looked like the best that the

Rangers striker could hope for, was to deflect the ball off of one of them to get a throw-in, in order to keep possession. Instead, he not only managed to evade the presence of the pair by skilfully running clear of them, he also dispossessed another opponent, before his charge towards goal. Completing an excellent individual passage of play, Roy Wegerle wrong-footed one further Hatters player, before a low shot from 16 yards out, found the bottom left-hand corner of the net. There were no more goals in the first half, and with Luton not looking particularly overawed, not to mention the fact that they had an outstanding record at Loftus Road over the previous decade, their fans were probably still confident of a comeback.

Just three minutes into the second half, QPR went 2-0 ahead. Wegerle linked up well with David Bardsley and the right-back sprinted along the wing and his superb cross found Andy Sinton at the far post to head home. Sinton turned creator just seven minutes later, when his right-footed cross, found the head of Ray Wilkins, whose glancing header was well directed into the bottom right corner of the net. Both Andy Sinton and Wilkins can boast outstanding goals for Rangers during their playing careers with us, but when they both scored with headers in the same match, even the pessimists among our number, were probably convinced that this would be our day. Welsh midfielder Ceri Hughes managed to get a goal back when the Queens Park Rangers defence failed to clear a Luton Town free-kick. But rather than herald a comeback, it simply inspired Howe's team to turn the screw with some even more memorable goals.

A 60-yard ball up the pitch from Parker, was good enough to pick out Roy Wegerle, who outmuscled one of the Luton players. He then sprinted into the penalty area, and as two defenders were closing in on him, he found the same corner of the net as the Ray Wilkins header, just a few minutes earlier. There were still 27 minutes remaining and it was beginning to look like the only remaining issue was just how many goals Rangers would score that afternoon. It only took another two minutes for the next goal to arrive, and it was the same combination linking up. Another ball forward from Paul Parker found Wegerle on the same left flank. Some fans might have expected him to try and beat another couple of defenders to complete his hat trick. Instead, the new hero in the number ten shirt had a different trick up his sleeve. He used the time he had on the ball to collect and then turn another defender, before delivering a cross of his own to the far post which picked out Mark Falco. The big striker attempted a shot that most players would have found a difficult opportunity to execute. But in the case of Falco, he thrived on opportunities like this and a spectacular volley on the turn with his left-foot, found the opposite corner of the net. By this stage, the quality of the goals seemed to be getting better and better, as the afternoon went on. Yet somehow, the five aforementioned goals would all be eclipsed by someone whose name did not usually appear on the scoresheet.

Paul Parker is a name that regularly features in the greatest All Time XI of supporters. Mention that his signing for £200,000 from Fulham was one of the finest transfers QPR ever made, and you will not start too many arguments in West London. He was lightning fast, brilliant in the air, a superb tackler and reader of the game. And as seen in this Luton game, even his distribution was better than some people might have given him credit for. But his one weakness was a lack of goals. In three previous seasons, each of which he was outstanding in, he had failed to score a single goal for Queens Park Rangers. But with the lead at 5-1 and perhaps having been inspired by what his teammates did, Parker sprinted into the Luton half of the pitch. He found Andy Sinton and a one-two between the pair of them saw the England international defender free in the penalty area, and to the delight of every single home fan, slotted the ball past the advancing figure of Alec Chamberlain, for the sixth QPR goal of the afternoon. So popular was he with supporters, the lack a goal in his first three years as a Queens Park Rangers player, was never a source of criticism. But at the same time, we were all desperate to see him finally get his name on the scoresheet in a blue and white hooped shirt. A fine goal yes, but not the best of the afternoon. Yet it was without question, the most popular of this rout.

Towards the end of the game, Don Howe bought young striker Les Ferdinand off the bench. With just a couple of minutes remaining, he was fouled in the penalty area. The defender got nowhere near the ball, and the award of a penalty, was surely a formality. Only, the referee never pointed to the spot. In the context of the match, it made no difference. But it did inevitably deny Roy Wegerle of the opportunity to bag himself a hat trick. He was the designated penalty taker at the time, and was enjoying a good run from the spot. One cannot help but wonder whether the match official felt some sympathy with the away side.

With Paul Parker's goal being the end of the scoring, it was a day to remember. Ironically, Luton Town had actually had more efforts on goal than the home side. But that was something of a misleading statistic. Some of their chances came early in the game. Tony Roberts had a couple of problems with one or two early shots, leading the chants of 'dodgy keeper' from the away fans. Although that line of chanting soon dried up, when goals started going in at the other end of the pitch. Also, whereas Rangers were clinical, many of the Luton efforts on our goal, were missing the target, altogether. The thrashing of the Hatters had the unusual distinction of being the third time in just six years that QPR had scored five goals in the second half of a match at Loftus Road. The others being the 5-5 draw with Newcastle in 1984, and the 5-2 victory over Leicester City in the FA Cup in 1987. Ironically, against Luton Town, it was the only one of these three examples of this five-goal blitz that did not take place on the Astroturf.

From being something of a bogie team to Rangers, in just 90 minutes, that school of thought was blown out of the water. It was a memorable win for numerous reasons. And on the very day the manager predicts that such an occurrence would happen. When you have Roy Wegerle looking like the latest skilful player worthy of wearing the number ten shirt, Mark Falco getting a brilliant volley, along with both Andy Sinton and Ray Wilkins scoring with headers, it felt like the type of day when anything was possible from Queens Park Rangers. But the icing on the cake was our outstanding defender finally scoring a goal for the club. The Sunday newspaper headlines that read "PARKER SCORES SIXTH", were among the most unusual and welcome, that QPR supporters ever saw.

23 *Most Vital Draw*
Derby County 1 Queens Park Rangers 1
1990/91

If you asked a group of QPR supporters the question "Which former manager was responsible for the worst losing run, in the last fifty years"? you would probably hear the same names being suggested. Most likely those of Ray Harford, Mark Hughes or Steve McLaren, for example. As it happens, none of them were to blame for this somewhat unwanted record. The man in question, was actually the much-respected figure of Don Howe. The 90/91 season had started off well enough, with three wins, three draws and three defeats, from the opening nine league matches of the season. All three wins were memorable for an assortment of reasons.

The first home win of the campaign was a 1-0 victory over Chelsea. A match in which Roy Wegerle converting the first of eight penalties he scored for Queens Park Rangers during their First Division campaign. This before Chelsea were awarded a spot-kick of their own. Kerry Dixon took one of the worst penalties Loftus Road ever saw, which sailed well wide of the goal. The win over Luton Town has already been discussed in the previous chapter. The third of those victories came as a result of beating Leeds United 3-2, having being a couple of goals behind at one stage. This was also the game when Wegerle scored with a solo goal that saw him beat five men, before his shot from outside the penalty area, beat John Lukic. It won the ITV Goal of the Season and remains a strong contender for being the greatest QPR goal of all time. All good and well up to this point. Then the wheels came off big time.

A nightmare losing run over a two-month period, saw Rangers lose eight consecutive matches in the league, along with exits in both the League Cup and the ZDS Cup. The latter incidentally, saw influential defender Paul Parker depart with a long-term injury. Alan McDonald also found himself in the injured list at around the same time. And if that wasn't bad enough, reserve team central defender Brian Law would also find himself fighting for space on the physio's treatment table. By now, Danny Maddix was the only fit experienced central defender Howe had available to him. Though Maddix was in very good form, he couldn't look after the centre of the defence all on his own, and the need for support alongside him, was urgent. Following a 3-1 defeat at home to Arsenal, the Queens Park Rangers manager bought in the very first loan signing in the history of the club, in the form of Gus Caesar from the aforementioned champions-elect. Caesar was already a much-maligned figure at Highbury, because of a nightmare performance in the 1988 League Cup Final, when his mistake gifted Luton Town one of their goals, in a shock 3-2 victory for the Hatters

After what amounted to two and a half years in the wilderness, the Arsenal defender was given the chance resurrect his career with the guarantee of some first team football. It did not take long before both he and the Rangers supporters must have wished that he had remained in the wilderness. In a loan spell that lasted just five matches, he made errors in four of those games that lead to opposition goals, along with conceding a penalty in the home match against Sunderland. Gus Caesar had become as much a figure of ridicule during his brief spell at Loftus Road, as he was at Highbury. It felt like he simply carried on from where he left off, following his nightmare back at Wembley in the spring of 1988. There was no getting away from the fact that Don Howe had blundered by bringing him to QPR in the first place. But despite the presence of Gus Caesar and that horrible losing run, there was still considerable support for the manager. Most fans understood that it was a tough act to replace players the calibre of Parker and McDonald, at such short notice. And the general consensus was that Howe and the team were good enough to get themselves out of the mess they were now in.

Two days before Christmas, Rangers visited Derby County's old Baseball Ground. Off the back of a losing run that had now gone into double figures, something positive was desperately needed. Thankfully, the Rangers manager was by now joined by a trusted lieutenant alongside him, with whom he enjoyed a successful working relationship with at Wimbledon, previously. Bobby Gould had been in charge of the Dons while Don Howe was his assistant, but were now in opposite roles. With a reputation for being able to spot talented players, Gould was able to single out a couple of defenders who would bolster the defence. They came in the form of Andy Tillson who joined from Grimsby Town, for a fee of £400,000. Tillson had started out his career as just a part-time footballer, who also trained to be a landscape gardener. He would get his break with non-league Kettering Town when he was signed by then manager, and former Queens Park Rangers central defender David Needham.

Alongside him was Darren Peacock, who was previously with Hereford United. Like Andy Tillson, Peacock stood at six foot two inches tall. Though with his trademark long hair, he looked like he would have been more at home in the line-up of a heavy metal band, than a top-flight football team. In an interview in a match programme a few weeks later, Darren Peacock admitted that the move was a complete surprise and two days before his Rangers debut, he had no idea that Howe was even interested in signing him.

Having the two new defenders come into a team that was fast becoming accustomed to losing, was not the perfect way to start their new careers with QPR. Don Howe later admitted that he would have preferred it had the pair had the chance to play a few reserve matches, before blooding them in the first team. Circumstances however, did not allow for that luxury. Though as it happened, it would not be necessary and they both looked comfortable as First Division footballers, from the moment that they turned out for the club.

A stylish defender, Tillson immediately appeared as confident on the ball as any Rangers centre-half since Glenn Roeder. At the time, Howe favoured a central defence with three men which allowed one of them freedom to roam forward when in possession. Andy Tillson looked like a natural in that role. Meanwhile, Darren Peacock's job on his debut was to mark the experienced striker Mick Harford. A man with a fearsome reputation throughout a playing career that lasted almost 20 years. During his first match in a Queens Park Rangers shirt, Peacock completely marked Harford out of the game.

QPR took the lead with a goal that would in the modern era, have had referees running straight towards the VAR cameras. A free-kick some 35 yards out saw Ray Wilkins cleverly play the ball to the left, where Simon Barker found himself in plenty of space. Barker's cross into the box looked like it would be comfortably covered by the highly rated defender, Mark Wright. But his attempted clearance was very poor and fell nicely into the path of Roy Wegerle. From 15 yards out, Wegerle's volley was far too good for Derby's ageing keeper Peter Shilton, who was rooted to his goal line. The strike from the R's forward smashed the underside of the crossbar before bouncing down back out of the goal and into Shilton's hands. Peter Shilton quickly looked towards the referee hoping that the match official would signal that the ball did not cross the line. As it happened, Roy Wegerle's shot was not even debatable and footage of the game reveals that it was comfortably two foot over the goal line. His goal at the Baseball Ground against the Rams was his fourteenth of the season.

Don Howe's men now found themselves in the novel position of actually leading during a game. The only time that had actually happened during that nightmare run of defeats was against high-flying Arsenal. In comparison to the jittery defending, going behind in matches, worrying about the lack of communication between the defence and the new Czech goalkeeper Jan Stejskal, all of a sudden, the confidence appeared to return to the side. Then there were a couple of late setbacks to deal with. Off the back of an excellent debut that impressed the travelling fans, Darren Peacock picked up a knee injury late on in the game. At first it was a worry. As Peacock later explained, it was the same leg that he broke a couple years earlier. And as a result, five months in plaster meant that in the long-term, one leg would be slightly shorter than the other. Thankfully, there was no such serious damage on this occasion. But supporters would have to wait a couple of weeks before they got the chance to see him in action at Loftus Road. And it meant the return of the much-maligned Gus Caesar for a couple more games. Equally disappointing, was a last gasp equaliser when a Derby County attack was not cleared and Dean Saunders scored from inside the six-yard box.

Although Rangers conceding a late goal that meant two points dropped, the long run of consecutive defeats was over. Losing had become a habit and QPR needed to bring that run to an end. Sure enough, that single point proved to be the springboard to better things. Three days later, Queens Park Rangers got another draw against Liverpool. Wegerle's goal at the Baseball Ground turned out to be the start of strong run of good results. Don Howe's side lost only two games in a sixteen-match run that started in the East Midlands just before Christmas. Though curiously, Bobby Gould departed after just two months at the club, to take up the job as manager of West Bromwich Albion. But he was a valuable asset to have at the club during his brief stay. As a result of the arrival of the two new defenders and that excellent run in the league that followed, Rangers steered well clear of any potential relegation battle and a mid-table finish was secured. Howe's reputation had also recovered, following that run of defeats towards the end of 1990. The same however, could not be said for Gus Caesar. The latter part of his career saw him drop down the divisions, followed by a spell in Scotland with Airdrie, before Caesar saw out his playing days in Hong Kong. To this day, he is still regarded as one of the worst players who ever put on a QPR shirt, off the back of that doomed loan spell.

In the context of the 1990/91 season, that draw at Derby County, must go down as one of the most important in the history of the club. When a team loses that many games, it is inevitable that even the better players in the team start to doubt themselves. Just that single point against the fellow strugglers, gave everyone some closure, from that horrible losing run. As a result, the team never looked back. Throughout that difficult period, the Rangers support continued to back Don Howe. Chairman Richard Thompson who could have easily have hit the panic button, also held his nerve and importantly, backed the judgement of Howe and Gould with new signings that strengthened the defence. Thankfully, we never needed to wonder would another manager have been able to save the club, had Don Howe being sacked?

24 *Another Giant Slayed*
Queens Park Rangers 4 Leeds United 1
1991/92

Ask QPR supporters to talk about the famous 4-1 win in the 91/92 season, and many of them would happily regale you with numerous stories of the day. Such as Dennis Bailey's hat trick at Old Trafford on New Year's Day, the brilliant team performance, going two goals up within minutes of the kick-off, and Alex Ferguson's high-flying team getting well and truly destroyed. And if that wasn't enough, there was the small matter of ITV screening the match live, so millions of people up and down the country got to watch Manchester United being given a footballing lesson. Making it an even more satisfying afternoon, serving as both pundit and co-commentator to Brian Moore, was former United striker Dennis Law. After spouting the United viewpoint for most of the game, he finally ate humble pie, and awarded his namesake the Man of The Match award for his three goals. Definitely one for the QPR annals, of which there is no doubt. Yet going back to the original question, other fans would have responded by asking 'which one'?

Leeds United were involved in a keenly contested battle all season with their Manchester rivals, for what would be the last of the old First Division championships, when they arrived at Loftus Road in March 1992. But Rangers came into this match, off the back of a stunning 4-0 win over Manchester City, who had themselves been among the top six sides all season. On that occasion, two goals from Les Ferdinand, a penalty from Clive Wilson and another from Simon Barker, sealed a brilliant win. It is doubtful that any supporter left that match thinking that QPR could take their game to the next level, just four days later.

In front of a loud and lively crowd, both teams attempted to make a statement of intent, as soon as possible. It would be Leeds who would do so. After they sprayed a few passes around the Rangers half of the pitch, Jon Newsome got a cross in from the right-hand side, and Gary Speed managed to outjump Alan McDonald to head beyond Jan Stejskal. Rather than be intimated, this was an era when Queens Park Rangers tended to save their best performances for the strongest of opponents. and they quickly put pressure on Leeds with Andy Impey forcing a good save out of John Lukic. From the resulting corner, their defence was unable to clear, and Ferdinand from just six yards out, scored with what by his standards, a rare left-footed goal. With plenty of time still to play in the first half, this already had the feel of a great game. Both sides had their chances before the half-time whistle, but there would be no more goals for a while, at least.

During the second period, Andy Sinton came close with a shot that just deflected wide from well outside the area. Even McDonald was getting in on the act, when he brilliantly controlled the ball, before turning to beat one defender, and his curling shot from inside the penalty area, only just went wide. Leeds United had a few attacks of their own, and another Newsome cross was almost finished by Rod Wallace. Ironically, Wallace's failure to connect with that cross, was the platform for Rangers to take the lead. And that came about thanks to one of the best team goals ever scored under the Loftus Road floodlights. David Bardsley calmly saw off the challenge of David Batty and this gave Impey the chance to race forward, as the home crowd roared him on. He passed to Ray Wilkins who in turn, picked out Sinton. The R's winger found his path blocked, so passed the ball back to his experienced teammate. What followed was a moment of inspiration. Wilkins was the only player on the pitch who spotted the run of Bradley Allen into the penalty area, and the young QPR striker was too quick for Lukic. Defenders Chris Fairclough and Chris Whyte tried to get to the goal line to block his shot, but from a narrow angle, Allen found the back of the net to give Rangers the lead. After accepting the congratulations of his teammates, Bradley Allen then went towards the Loft and pointed to someone in the crowd and applauded the said individual. It remains a mystery as to whether it was a friend he invited to the game, a member of the famous clan, or someone who might have been giving him stick, whom he went to acknowledge.

Following Allen's goal, the confidence began to flow through the Queens Park Rangers side and they seemed to know that Leeds were there for the taking. Ray Wilkins cut out a United pass and this gave Les Ferdinand the chance to launch yet another attack. Both he and Bradley Allen had shots blocked, but that man Wilkins saw the right pass once again, and he found Andy Sinton, whose low left-footed drive found the bottom right hand corner of the net. That was two Rangers goals in two minutes, and Sinton had now scored in both of the memorable 4-1 wins over the United's. A short while later, Ray Wilkins and Allen almost set up Andy Sinton again, but this time, his shot from about the same angle from which he scored, was saved by the giant Lukic.

With Rangers defending so well, the Leeds opportunities dried up, and it started to seem like Wilkins had shared his gift for brilliant passing, to his teammates. Bradley Allen set up Andy Sinton who almost scored his second of the evening, but was denied by John Lukic. Shortly after that, Darren Peacock superbly picked out Sinton for yet another goalscoring chance. With just the keeper to beat, Whyte tripped him from behind, and the referee immediately blew up. In the Manchester City game just days earlier, Andy Sinton was the victim of another professional foul-this time from goalkeeper Tony Coton. Surprisingly, Coton only received a yellow card. Another view of the highlights from the win over Leeds, reveals that as soon as he was brought down, Sinton appears to mouth the words 'Not again'. This time there would be no such leniency from the referee, and Chris Whyte was shown the red card. The Leeds players protested the sending off and tried to delay the taking of the penalty, but to no avail. Clive Wilson sent John Lukic the wrong way as his spot kick found the left corner of the net. Wilkins almost curled in a shot in to make it five on the evening, before a point-blank save from Stejskal brought a wonderful night at Loftus Road, to a close.

What an incredible four days it had been for supporters, players and indeed, manager Gerry Francis. Two wins, both in such an outstanding manner, and both with four goals coming against two of the strongest teams in the country. Yet hard as it is to believe, here we were in the month of March, and these were just QPR's third and fourth home league wins of the season. If an explanation was required as to how that was possible off the back of two stunning victories, it was a mixture of conceding last minute equalisers, failure to convert chances in matches where Rangers were dominant, and the occasional inspirational performance from a visiting keeper.

Yet for the all the brilliance that was undoubtedly on display in that win over Leeds United, time has not been kind to this victory. It rarely gets discussed on the QPR Facebook forums, in the same way as the one over Manchester United earlier in the same season, still does. In his otherwise superb book on great Rangers matches, Mike Donovan omitted this game. Likewise, a DVD featuring the best Queens Park Rangers games of the 1990's, did not include the win over Leeds United. Truth be told, this great win, has lived in the shadow of the earlier 4-1 thrashing. Which is most unfair.

Both wins were outstanding, albeit in very different ways. Rangers went ahead in the game at Old Trafford and once they got the second, Manchester United never really looked like they would salvage anything from the game. In comparison, Francis' side had to come from behind against Leeds, and the game was level at half-time. A brilliant performance in the second half saw QPR tear Leeds United apart, in a season when no-one else did. And of course, there is the small matter that it was Leeds and not Manchester United who won the title in the 1991/92 season. Any supporter who sat and watched both of these incredible wins one more time, would be in no doubt that they deserved to be mentioned in the same breath. Although it would be wrong to try and say that one was better than the other. They were both amazing victories in their own unique way. Finishing that season in eleventh place, obviously Rangers did not maintain that level of performance too often. But thinking back to both of those 4-1 victories will leave no fan in any doubt that it was an incredible period to be supporting Queens Park Rangers.

25 *The Summit of English Football*
Coventry City 0 Queens Park Rangers 1
1992/93

It is amazing to think that just nine days earlier, there was anger and bitterness. In particular, QPR manager Gerry Francis was seething. And with good reason, it must be said. This was the first season in which top flight English football was played under the banner of the Premier League. It was also the first year in which SKY television would screen league matches live, on both Sunday afternoons and Monday nights. This being the first-time games would be played at such unusual times, the scheduling was not so kind to some teams. Most notably, Queens Park Rangers. For the opening match of the season, the R's had to play on Monday night away to Manchester City, quickly followed on Wednesday at home to Southampton, Sheffield United at Loftus Road again on Saturday afternoon, and Coventry City away, the following Tuesday. A punishing four matches in nine days, whereas most of the other teams in the newly formed Premier League, would get eleven.

There was a cruel irony with regards to Rangers being picked for the first Monday night game. During the previous four years, ITV had exclusive coverage of First Division games, while BBC did likewise with the FA Cup. In those four years, our only appearances on live terrestrial television were in the 6th Round of the 1990 FA Cup at home to Liverpool, in a highly entertaining 2-2 draw. Along with that amazing 4-1 win at Manchester United, in January 1992. The truth is that the only chance QPR ever had of getting picked for a live television game, was to face one of the big teams. United, Liverpool, Arsenal, Tottenham Hotspur and Everton, didn't so much dominant the schedule for live games, as they monopolised it. The running joke among football fans all over the country during that period was that BBC and ITV might as well have called their respective shows *'The Big Five, Live'!* Yet the moment that there was an appearance that would play havoc with the individual plans of most sides, the great and the good of English football were nowhere to be seen. Francis let it be known in no uncertain terms that he was furious about having to start the season at a disadvantage to everyone else. The response from the Premiership and SKY TV was to state that someone had to play that night, and as we would soon see, television was dictating when teams play their football matches, and not the other way round. But in one last defiant snub to the new paymasters of the game, Gerry Francis refused, along with his players, to conduct any media work with SKY in the lead up to the match at Maine Road.

On a night where fans were greeted with skydivers, cheerleaders, and the slogan 'A Whole New Ball Game', this occasion felt more like a circus, than a football match. Manchester City took the lead in the first half, thanks to David White. But on 47 minutes, Andy Sinton equalised with a sensational left-footed shot from 30 yards. Just two days later, Rangers came from a goal down at half-time, to beat Southampton 3-1. An eventful second half saw Les Ferdinand score twice from close range, and David Bardsley scored from well outside the area, with one of the best free-kicks Loftus Road, ever saw. There was even time for Southampton's Micky Adams to get sent off after he thought it was a good idea to have a dust-up with QPR's big striker Garry Thompson. At the conclusion of the melee that involved most of the players on the pitch, Adams saw red, but Thompson wasn't even booked. Concluding a remarkable period of less than five days, Queens Park Rangers beat Sheffield United 3-2, with goals from Ferdinand, Simon Barker and Dennis Bailey. Ferdinand's goal when he scored after just collecting the ball yards inside the United half and preceded to beat three players before scoring with a 25-yard piledriver, did much to bring him to the attention of those who weren't QPR supporters. It was incidentally, another great addition to the list of brilliant strikes at a time that the new season had only just got underway.

With seven points from the opening three matches, a trip to top-of-the-table Coventry City was next. If Rangers could win at Highfield Road and other results go the way Francis and the team, then they could be in first place themselves, by the end of the evening. The first real opportunity of the night went to Ray Wilkins, but his 25-yard volley just missed the target. Coventry had a couple of chances of their own, when Robert Rosario and Micky Gynn-who stood at six foot three inches and five foot four inches tall respectively-both came close. Still in the first half, Bardsley nearly scored his second superb free kick in a week, but Steve Ogrizovic pulled off the save. As Queens Park Rangers took control of the game, Clive Wilson picked out Andy Impey and his one-two with Ray Wilkins, almost forced a goalscoring opportunity for the young winger. Just before half-time, Alan McDonald found Les Ferdinand with a long pass up the pitch. Ferdinand cleverly chested the ball down and while it looked like there was a half chance for the taking, he unselfishly picked out Impey and from fifteen yards out, smashed the ball into the bottom left-hand corner of the net. It was incidentally, Andy Impey's first league goal.

For the start of the second half, Coventry City bought on substitute John Williams. Nicknamed 'The Flying Postman' owing to his former profession and lightning turn of pace, the striker had made a name for himself at the 1992 League Cup Final. But not in the manner that you might think. In a competition to find the fastest player in English football, each club was allowed to enter one member of their team, in order to find out who was the quickest player in the game. Representing Swansea City at the time, Williams won the prize of £10,000 in the final for finishing first, beating our own Tony Witter incidentally, who was among the favourites to claim the cash prize, having easily won his London heat.

But it was our own quick forward who was more dangerous, and Les Ferdinand almost doubled the lead when he headed wide. Unfortunately, the said goalscoring opportunity saw him have a clash of heads with one of the City defenders, and Ferdinand would later go to hospital with concussion. Someone giving the Rangers defence plenty of problems was winger Peter Ndlovu. The Zimbabwean got a number of crosses into the box and the threat of Rosario kept Jan Stejskal on his toes. Impey and substitute Gary Penrice both had opportunities of their own, before Coventry City were forced to play the last few minutes of the game with just ten men. On a night when Les Ferdinand was not the only player to leave the pitch badly hurt, Micky Gynn was stretched off after the home side had used all of their substitutes.

This did not deter the hosts and they continued to take the game to QPR. Robert Rosario failed to convert a great chance with ten minutes to go and Stejskal was forced to make a great save from a rasping drive from Ndlovu. With the two injuries in the second half, it was no surprise that there was plenty of added time. The Rangers fans had an agonising six extra minutes to sit through, before the referee blew the final whistle. At the start of the match, the home fans chanted "We are top of the League" in the direction of the away supporters. They in response, sang "We'll be top at 10 O'clock". And sure enough, they were. For the last time in the history of the club.

From a position of feeling like Queens Park Rangers had been given the thin end of the wedge from the rest of the newly found Premier League, Gerry Francis and the team, were now looking down at all 91 other teams in English football. Whilst we will never know, you cannot help but wonder if Francis had taken a leaf out of Alex Ferguson's book, when he found out the scheduling for the start of the 92/93 season. It was as if he and the team took what was a negative, and turned it into a positive. On many occasions, Ferguson would adopt a 'siege mentality' if he thought that his own team were ever getting a raw deal. And not talking to the media, was another position that the Scotsman was prone to adopting, when he wasn't happy with them.

Alas, it proved to be a short stay at the top of the Premier League. Three days later, QPR visited Stamford Bridge and despite having a number of good goalscoring chances, Les Ferdinand and Dennis Bailey both had off days. Rangers played as well as they had in any of the four matches that took them to the top of the league, but were caught by a late Chelsea goal that came against the run of play. Despite their best efforts, perhaps the punishing schedule of five matches in just twelve days, was catching up with the team.

With two further matches the following week-both of which finished in goalless draws against Arsenal and Ipswich Town, meant that it was now seven games in just nineteen days. No wonder Gerry Francis felt hard done by, when he saw that every else was at least getting an extra two days, to handle such a busy period of football.

Yet despite all of the problems Queens Park Rangers would have had playing so many matches in such a short space of time, they did for a brief period, top the league. Even if it was for less than 72 hours. It was only the third season that QPR managed this impressive feat, under the guise of either the original First Division or Premier League. The other two occasions were in the 1975/76 season, when Rangers were within minutes of actually winning the title, itself. And at the start of the 87/88 season, the opening of the campaign, saw Jim Smith's side top the league for the first few weeks.

Decades later, the achievements of those teams cannot be understated. The club's miserable experience of Premiership football in the 2010's where Queens Park Rangers had three seasons of non-stop struggle, makes you realise just how difficult it will be to emulate what the three previous R's sides had managed. Each year, the strongest teams in the Premier League usually go to the top of the table immediately. Even if QPR could make a return to the top flight at some point in the future, the likelihood of a fourth appearance at the top of the table, is a very slim one. The game has changed too much for that to happen. By definition, it makes all supporters appreciate what Gerry Francis and his team managed back in August 1992. Especially when circumstances regarding the somewhat ridiculous scheduling of matches, were not exactly in their favour. Given half the chance, Rangers supporters would have been happy if the season came to its conclusion, at the end of that game at Highfield Road.

26 *Spot-Kick Legend*
Grimsby Town 2 Queens Park Rangers 1
1992/93

Think of all of the great and influential penalty takers QPR
have had over the years, and some outstanding names
come to mind. Among them were Jim Langley, Mike
Keen, Terry Venables, Gerry Francis, Terry Fenwick, Alan
McDonald, Roy Wegerle, Clive Wilson and Heidar
Helgusson. One of those names will probably come as a
surprise to many people. But when called upon, McDonald
did indeed earn his place among his peers, as a penalty
hero for Rangers. Even if it was in surprising
circumstances, and came in a cup tie that he and his
teammates were very fortunate to win.

Back in 1992, the Second Round of the League Cup was
played over two legs. As a Premiership side, Queens Park
Rangers entered the competition at that stage and were
drawn to face Grimsby Town. The first leg was held at
Loftus Road and under normal circumstances, Gerry
Francis and supporters alike, would have wanted a

comfortable victory against the team that were a division below ourselves, to ensure the tie was beyond the visitors, by the time the second leg took place. Grimsby however, had other ideas. At the time, the Mariners had become an established side in the second tier of English football and would indeed finish the 1992/93 season in a very respectable ninth place in the league.

Things started well enough in the first half, when a move started by Andy Sinton saw him find his teammate Clive Wilson and his cross was met by the incoming Les Ferdinand, who couldn't miss from just four yards out. But that was the only goal of the first half which would undoubtedly have given Grimsby Town hope. In the second period, they equalised when Tommy Watson started and finished a move that took in a few passes that was too slick for a stagnate Rangers defence. Thankfully, an in form Ferdinand had the final say of the evening when some fine passing from the midfield duo of Ray Wilkins and Simon Barker, saw the latter flick a pass over the heads of a couple of Grimsby defenders and the Rangers' striker got his second of the evening, with a powerful shot at the near post. QPR won 2-1 on the night, and Les Ferdinand's burgeoning reputation grew yet further as a result. But the visitors were far from out of this cup tie.

In the second leg, both teams would be missing a key player. In the case of Rangers, Ferdinand was injured which would have been a relief to the opposition who might have had a point if they claimed he was the difference between the two sides in the first meeting. Stylish central defender Andy Tillson was also unable to play, as a result of the fact that he was on loan from QPR in the first place. The Blundell Park pitch was in excellent condition on the night, so that didn't look like it would be a 'great leveller' with the visit of Gerry Francis' side. The howling wind throughout the game, however, may well have been. Andy Impey had the best of the chances early on for Rangers with a shot from outside the area, but the Mariners were enjoying plenty of possession and put Darren Peacock and Jan Stejskal under plenty of possession, having a couple of fine goalscoring opportunities of their own. They were gaining in confidence as the game went on, emphasised by the fact one of the Grimsby players had the temerity to nutmeg Ray Wilkins of all people. Queens Park Rangers may have thrashed Tottenham Hotspur 4-1 just three days earlier, but that cut no ice with the hosts.

With the match goalless at half-time, Gerry Francis would have wanted to see a better display as the second period got underway. As the rain started to come down quite heavily, QPR managed to exert some pressure, and Clive Wilson just failed to finish a chance that he helped create. But just when it look like Rangers might take control of the game and as they enjoyed the best of the deteriorating conditions, an attack from the home side took them into the penalty area and in an attempt to get in a tackle in, Andy Sinton only managed to poke the ball beyond Stejskal, and into the back of the net.

Rangers had to battle to get their way back in the match. Sinton very nearly equalised when his shot was well saved by Rhys Wilmot. But from the resulting corner, Wilkins swung the ball in, and Alan McDonald's flick-on was stabbed home from close range by Dennis Bailey. As things stood, that Bailey goal would be enough to take QPR through to the next round. The Mariners would require one more goal just to take the game into extra-time, and a second, to cause a cup upset. They hadn't previously looked overawed in either match thus far, and they didn't start playing that way, now. Within a couple of minutes, Grimsby's Gary Croft almost curled a low shot past Jan Stejskal, after the Rangers defence failed to clear the danger. Shortly after that, a low cross was just missed by two of the home forwards, when the slightest touch from either would have taken the ball into the net. With ten minutes remaining, a cross from the left, was powerfully headed home by Neil Woods to make it 2-1 to the Mariners, and it must be said that it was thoroughly deserved. Rangers best chance to equalise came when substitute and veteran striker Garry Thompson was through on goal, but his appalling shot had neither power or accuracy and that chance came to nothing. Shortly after that, McDonald made his second telling contribution of the evening by brilliantly clearing a shot off the line, after a terrible mix-up between Stejskal and Clive Wilson. Extra time would be needed.

Supporters who came all the way from London to follow QPR would have hoped that even around this point, qualities like class, experience and fitness would have started working in our favour. But again, Grimsby just would not give up or play like they were a team from a division below Rangers. Chances for an R's winner were few and far between in extra time. Perhaps the best of them came just a couple of minutes from the end, when Holloway's shot went through a crowd of players and over the bar. Queens Park Rangers were nearly beaten in the dying moments of play, when a shot from close range was somehow smothered by our giant Czech keeper. Seconds later, the referee blew the final whistle and penalties would be required to find a winner.

Ironically, Grimsby Town had gotten to this stage of the competition thanks to a penalty shootout, following two 1-1 draws with Barnsley in the first round of the competition. If that gave the hosts a slight advantage, QPR got one of their own, when all of the penalties were to be taken in front on the travelling fans. The Mariners would go first, and Tommy Watson hit his perfectly, into the top right-hand corner of the net. First up for Rangers, was probably the calmest man on the pitch, in the form of Ray Wilkins. He matched Watson, by finding the other top corner of the net, himself. Next up was Neil Woods, who may well have been the best player on the pitch all night, but his low shot was well saved by Stejskal who dived to his left. Andy Sinton calmly put Rangers into the lead, and in the process, made amends for his earlier own goal. Sinton incidentally, had an interesting history when he came to penalties for Rangers. Both of which came in the 92/93 season. This was one of them and earlier in the season, he took one in the 90th minute of a home match against Middlesbrough. He converted it to make the final score 3-3. All of which suggests that Andy Sinton would probably have made a great penalty taker in his own right, had he been given the role on a regular basis. Jim Dobbin scored the next one for Town, and then it was the turn of Clive Wilson.

As it happened, he was the club's regular penalty taker at the time, and only missed out on taking the aforementioned penalty against Middlesbrough because he wasn't on the pitch at that time. He was a most reliable spot-kick taker over four years, but on this occasion, put it too close to the keeper who saved to his left. A disappointment, but in fairness to Wilson, he never missed another one as a Queens Park Rangers player. Both sides converted their two remaining penalties. On each occasion, Ian Holloway and David Bardsley sent the keeper the wrong way. Now, there would be sudden death. And with Rangers going second, a miss spot-kick from one of our own, would mean elimination-unless it followed hot on the heels of one from Grimsby. By this stage, there is a danger that you are now turning to some very reluctant volunteers who probably never expected to be in this situation.

First of the sudden death penalties was taken by the Mariners' Gary Childs. An emphatic strike into the top left-hand corner, was as good as any of the first ten that were taken, and many of those were pretty good. Now it was the turn of Dennis Bailey. A player who had his share of injuries and disappointing performances since that magical day at Old Trafford, at the start of the year. But at the same time, were it not for his goal, Rangers wouldn't even be in the position of having the chance of going through to the next round. Wilmot went the right way for Bailey's penalty, but it was powerfully struck, and found the right corner of the net. Resembling that famous match against Newcastle United from 1984, the scores were now 5-5, and Tony Rees stepped up for Grimsby. His penalty was placed well towards the corner, but lacked a bit of power, and Jan Stejskal was able to grab the ball with both hands. The next penalty taker could send QPR into the next round.

As a disconsolate Rees walked away, up stepped Alan McDonald. The Northern Irish defender was probably our best player on the night, and must have thought he had seen everything in a long career as a Queens Park Rangers player. But this would have been a 'first' for him. Off a long run-up, McDonald attempted to find the bottom left-hand corner of the net. Rhys Wilmot went the right way, and even got a hand to the ball, but he was unable to stop it and Rangers had at last, seen off this most enterprising and determined of opponents. Alan McDonald was immediately swamped by teammates, but so too was Stejskal. Our first overseas goalkeeper had a very good record when it came to penalties. Obviously, this evening is a good example of that fact. But he also saved one in the 1990/91 season against Sunderland, in a memorable 3-2 home win. And one of QPR's most memorable top flight away wins came at Newcastle United in the 93/94

148

campaign, when Jan Stejskal pulled off a brilliant save in the final seconds of the game, in an amazing 2-1 victory. It was harsh on the Mariners who probably deserved to win, but McDonald and his teammates would remain in the competition.

For Queens Park Rangers, it would be the last penalty shootout win for a very long time. They would lose the next three, among them, a humiliating FA Cup defeat to Vauxhall Motors which represented an all-time low in the modern history of the club. But wins over Swindon Town in the 16/17 season and Bristol City in 19/20, has at least given supporters fonder memories of sudden death shootouts. The club's record overall reads won five and lost four. Not a German-like return in terms of those won. But equally, not England-like, in terms of heart-breaking moments, either. A respectable enough history when it comes to these most dramatic of finales.

When looking at all thirteen penalties that were taken at the end of the Grimsby Town v QPR cup tie, the one from Alan McDonald was far from being one of the best. But it was still a pressure moment that required a hero. By definition, McDonald was the seventh Rangers player to take a penalty that night, meaning that there were at least four more players who fancied taking one, less than him. After so many years as a Queens Park Rangers stalwart, no-one would ever doubt that he would shirk his responsibilities. Even allowing for the fact that he would probably have never imagined finding himself in a situation like this. Ultimately, Alan McDonald can justifiably take his name among the list of great penalty heroes to have worn the Rangers shirt. Even if he is the unlikeliest player to appear in such illustrious company.

27 *Same Again, Please*
Queens Park Rangers 3 Swindon Town 0
1992/93

Between 1983 and 1996, fourteen different FA Cup Third Round draws, saw Rangers get drawn at home on just two occasions. Aside from runs to the Sixth Round in 1990 and 1995, the club's record was pretty dismal during this time. But at least fans could console themselves with the fact that much of that was down to the misfortune of getting drawn away from home, so often. Which is in stark contrast to the last couple of decades where as many disappointing cup exits have come at Loftus Road, as in away matches. Ultimately in 1993, it was something of a novelty when QPR did get a Third-Round home tie. Discounting a couple of replays, it was six years since it last happened at this stage of the competition, courtesy of that memorable 5-2 home win over Leicester City.

Swindon Town who were going along very nicely in the league below Rangers, would be the visitors. In charge of the Robins was Glenn Hoddle, who by now, player-manager. In the space of just a couple of years, Hoddle had started to build up a reputation for playing good football at the County Ground, and all without the aid of a big budget. For good measure, they were in the hunt for promotion to the top flight, for the first time in their history. When you take that into consideration, being drawn at home to Swindon Town in the cup, was a potential 'banana skin', and not the type of opponents to be taken likely.

The Queens Park Rangers line-up for the visit of Swindon Town was Tony Roberts; David Bardsley, Clive Wilson, Darren Peacock, Alan McDonald; Simon Barker, Ray Wilkins, Ian Holloway, Andy Sinton; Les Ferdinand, Gary Penrice. As anyone who is old enough to remember the 92/93 season will recall, that was a very strong side. Back then, it would have been unthinkable for Gerry Francis or any other manager of the time, to make wholesale changes for an FA Cup tie like this. Contrast that with the modern era when sometimes all eleven players will be replaced from the previous league game. In the Swindon Town line-up was David Kerslake, who as a QPR youngster, once held the record for the most appearances for the England youth team, with no fewer than 29 of them. Alongside Kerslake was Glenn Hoddle who was playing in the somewhat unfamiliar role of sweeper. Whilst the two teams playing their strongest sides for this Third Round tie might have felt like a throwback to another era, because this match was being played on a Monday night for the benefit of SKY TV, the Fourth Round draw was already made and both sides already knew that a home tie against Manchester City or Reading, was up for grabs.

An entertaining first ten minutes saw both sides play some attacking football with Les Ferdinand constantly worrying the Swindon defence, particularly David Mitchell who was played as an emergency centre half, after captain Colin

Calderwood missed out through injury. But the first goalscoring chance of the night came when Holloway was careless with the ball and striker Steve Whyte just had Roberts to beat but struck his shot over the bar, in the 15th minute. Two minutes later, Craig Maskell had a golden opportunity when he took the ball round Tony Roberts and with just David Bardsley on the goal line to beat, also shot wide. The visitors could count themselves very unlucky not to be ahead. As well as having the two best chances of the game, they were also passing the ball around in a manner that their player-manager would have approved of. Then out of nothing, there was a complete reversal of fortune.

In the space of just five magical minutes, Queens Park Rangers scored three times thanks to a brace from Ferdinand and a third from Penrice. The latter coming from a fine shot on the turn. After an absorbing period of pressure from the Robins, Rangers managed a purple patch of their own in which even Alan McDonald almost managed to score his first goal in four years. Thereafter, there was a feeling from both sides that the tie was already settled. Swindon to their credit, still played an attractive style of football and did have their chances to get a goal back. Including one where Hoddle almost scored with a free-kick from 30 yards out. Whilst the margin remained at three goals, Rangers seemed happy to sit on their comfortable lead, without the need to go chasing after more goals. One of the most fascinating elements of the night was the contrast between the two veterans.

The combined age of the pair was 71 years and five months, with Wilkins older than Hoddle by slightly more than a year. Although Hoddle was no longer playing in the midfield role for which he was famous, it was interesting seeing the range of passing of the pair. Both were outstanding exponents when it came to distribution and they also seemed to make the best use of the time, as well as the space that they had on the ball. Which was in stark contrast to what was happening with the national set-up. England were in the middle of a World Cup qualifying competition that would end with disappointment, when Graham Taylor's side miserably failed to make the tournament in the USA, in 1994. The England manager resigned within days his final qualification match. Taylor had tried various midfielders including Geoff Thomas, David Batty and the much-maligned Carlton Palmer, but none of them had the ability to hold the ball, keep possession and find teammates with the highest quality of passing that came so natural to both of these veterans. How Graham Taylor must have wished that he had a player with the vision of a Ray Wilkins or Glenn Hoddle available to him, only ten years younger.

Running out 3-0 winners meant that QPR were through to the Fourth Round of the FA Cup. A comfortable victory, even though the score line somewhat flattered Rangers. But there was something very unusual about the first and second goals that night. So much so, you were unlikely to see a repeat of it in any match, let alone another one involving Queens Park Rangers. For the first goal, an Andy Sinton corner was only partially cleared as far as Darren Peacock. The big defender passed to Ian Holloway and his cross into the area was met by a powerful header by Les Ferdinand to give Rangers the lead. For the second, a Sinton corner was not fully cleared and Peacock picked up possession. He passed the ball to Holloway and his cross into the penalty area was met by an unstoppable header from Ferdinand. Yes, Francis' side had managed the rare feat of scoring two goals that were almost identical to one another. Even watching the highlights one more time, you could be forgiven for thinking that you were simply seeing the same goal twice.

As an occurrence, it just doesn't happen. It is the equivalent of throwing a dice and having it continually land on the number six. For example, with QPR taking the lead the way they just did for that first goal, the likelihood of the same four players having the opportunity to link up again is very small in its own right. And even if it did come about, the law of averages would have meant that there was less chance of Peacock, Holloway and Ferdinand all successfully managing to execute the same passage of play. And even if they did, there was still the Swindon defence to contend with. Having been caught out in that manner just a couple of minutes earlier, the natural instincts of the Robins stoppers would be to prevent a repeat of what just happened. Instead, every single element of that move went the way of Rangers, as they doubled the score line.

With that comfortable, if slightly unusual win ensuring progression in the competition, they then faced Manchester City. That game attracted national media attention when Les Ferdinand managed to return from injury for this game thanks to the aid of an oxygen tank. With hindsight, the R's striker was rushed back too quick, and had by his high standards, a poor match when he missed a couple of key goalscoring opportunities as City won 2-1. That victory over Swindon Town was the only one in the FA Cup for Gerry Francis in his first spell as Queens Park Rangers manager. It remains a pity that the team that Francis was in charge of between 1991 & 1994, couldn't manage anything resembling a proper cup run and in turn, the chance of some silverware. The highs that were reached on many occasions in the league, were never replicated in the knockout competitions. Yet three decades later and in the hundreds of matches that have taken place since, no group of QPR players have ever managed to replicate what Ferdinand and friends managed back on that cold Monday night at Loftus Road in January 1993. And given how slim the odds are on seeing a repeat of what happened against Swindon Town, that feat may well remain one of those once-in-a-lifetime oddities.

28 *Les Bids Loft Farewell*
Queens Park Rangers 2 Everton 1
1993/94

Just four months after the Hillsborough disaster which claimed the lives of 96 Liverpool fans in April 1989, the Taylor Report was released. Its aim was to establish the causes of the tragedy and make recommendations regarding the provision of safety at sporting events, thereafter. Many of those recommendations were indeed implemented as a result of the report, but none were as far-reaching as the decision that all major football stadiums should become all-seater. Terracing at every football ground in the country was the norm, so there would be drastic changes at all of them. Ultimately, it was end for all of the famous standing areas of so many football grounds around the country, and our own beloved Loft was no exception.

The standing area behind the School End, had already converted to being all-seater, in the summer of 1993. Before the 93/94 season was out, the Loft would follow

156

suit. It had been a strange season with a mixture of highs and lows. On the plus side, QPR had built up a very impressive away record with a number of excellent wins on the road. Les Ferdinand was for a while, the first choice England striker. At 37 years of age, Ray Wilkins was still in outstanding form. And despite not being a regular in the side and often the subject of ridicule by a minority of fans, Devon White had a knack of scoring important goals whenever called upon. But there were negatives as well. The relationship between owner Richard Thompson and manager Gerry Francis, was deteriorating fast. Fans were in constant fear of another one of our key players being sold, which was the cause of Francis' anger with the departure of Daren Peacock to Newcastle United. Results against some of the weaker teams in the Premiership, were surprisingly poor. And a 2-1 defeat away to Stockport County was one of the biggest shocks of the FA Cup 3rd Round.

Everton would be the visitors to Loftus Road for the final match in which home supporters could watch from the Loft, whilst it was still officially a standing area. Rangers had not come into this game in outstanding form, after a series of disappointing results. But if the Super hoops had worries of their own, it was nothing compared to the ones Everton had. They were struggling in the league, and not necessarily safe from the drop. And their record against Queens Park Rangers was not impressive. Of their six previous visits to West London, they had lost four and drawn two, in the league. And QPR's previous two visits to Goodison Park, saw us win 5-3 and 3-0. And just for good measure, each of the three previous meetings between the sides had seen a different Queens Park Rangers player score a hat trick.

In the first half, it did not look like Rangers would extend that great run against Everton. It was 0-0 at half-time and the most memorable incident in the opening period of the game, was not one Les Ferdinand would probably want to remember. An attempted shot from outside the penalty area went so far over the crossbar, it actually cleared the upper tier and the roof of the away end, going out of the ground in the process. It was beginning to take the look of an afternoon in which the famous terrace would depart with a whimper, rather than a bang. Sure enough, in the 64th minute of the game, Swedish winger Anders Limpar's defence-cutting through ball found Tony Cottee and his shot beat Tony Roberts. If Everton thought that they were going to end their dismal record against Rangers, they did not have much time to dwell on that idea.

Just two minutes later, QPR soared forward in great numbers and a Clive Wilson cross was only cleared as far as David Bardsley. The right-back's shot looked like it could be heading for the top left-hand corner of the net until it struck Gary Ablett and fell into the path of Ian Holloway. He then crossed into the area, and although Ferdinand could not get his head to the ball, Devon White did. White's header hit the back of Les Ferdinand, and in the ensuring scramble, the giant forward put the ball into the back of the net. But just which part of his anatomy did he score with? Well, the answer to that question is his right hand. He had the good fortune to have Ferdinand being an obstruction between the offending hand and the referee Martin Bodenham along with most of the Everton side. Bodenham incidentally, had the unique distinction of being the only man ever to referee Premiership football and be an umpire of First-Class cricket, in Britain. Devon White was very lucky to get away with this moment of, well, skulduggery. Yet how ironic was it that the striker who was affectionately known as 'Bruno' because of his physical similarity to the popular boxer Frank Bruno, should score his last ever goal for Queens Park Rangers, by punching the ball into the net?

So, Rangers were back in the game, but the fact remained it would have been a pity if the last ever goal in front of the home fans standing in the Loft, was a cheeky effort that went in off of somebody's hand just inches the right side of the goal line. Thankfully, that would not be the case. Everton tried to put Tony Roberts under pressure from a back pass, but his calm ball forward found Bardsley. Seeing Les Ferdinand ahead of him, an inch-perfect punt up the field found his teammate. Ferdinand still had to deal with the attention of a couple of defenders, but beat one of them for pace, and superbly rode an attempted tackle from another. And with that, he struck a low right-footed shot into the bottom corner of the net which gave Rangers the lead. With no further goals, victory was secured on this historic day. And there was no better way to do so than with QPR's most prolific and influential goal scorer of his generation, finding the back of the net with the type of goal that he scored with on so many occasions. If it wasn't a fairy tale end for the Loft in its dying days as a standing area, then it was pretty damn close.

For Everton, that game, and in particular, White's goal, very nearly had serious implications. Their manager Mike Walker was furious with the decision and was in no doubt it was a handball. The defeat left them in a serious battle to avoid relegation. They would only survive when they overturned a two-goal deficit to beat Wimbledon 3-2 on the final day of the 1993/94 season. With Queens Park Rangers still having three more home Premiership matches of their own, there would be something of an eerie end to this campaign. Aside from little pockets of supporters in the corners, the Loft was already being ripped apart in anticipation of the seating that would replace it, come the following August.

As it happened, QPR were unable to win any of that trio of games. One of those was a highly credible 1-1 draw with Arsenal, despite the fact that Ferdinand, Trevor Sinclair and Alan McDonald were all absent through injury. And showing that bad luck can just as easily follow the good variety, Rangers had two penalty appeals against the Gunners turned down. Despite being the whipping boys of the Premiership all year long, Swindon Town somehow managed to come to Loftus Road with relegation already secured, and won 3-1. The last game saw Queens Park Rangers comfortably dominate West Ham United, but fail to score in a goalless draw, despite a barrage of opportunities. To look at the footage of those three matches, does not make for great viewing, and not just because none of them ended in victory. The sight of the famous old terrace being turned into a pile of rubble, was a sorry one. The Loft departed with very little fanfare on the part of the club, which was a shame given that so many supporters would have had great memories of it. But a little while earlier, one fan captured the spirit of standing in the Loft at Queens Park Rangers, and he wasn't even a real person.

In the early 1990's, the BBC screened two series of the Anglo-Australian comedy/drama series Boys from The Bush. It starred Geordie actor Tim Healy as Reg Toomer, a Rangers mad private detective who moved to Melbourne, Australia, almost two decades earlier. Reg never really took to life down under, and takes every opportunity he gets to talk about London and his beloved QPR. In the second series of the show, Reg gets the chance to return to London for the first time. Even though that happens to be during the British summertime, he doesn't turn down the chance to visit Loftus Road. In perhaps the most iconic scene of the entire series, he walks into an empty stadium and from the Loft starts a one-man chant of "Come on You R's"! before setting foot on the hallowed Loftus Road turf. He then imagines he is playing upfront for Rangers, screaming for his boyhood hero Rodney Marsh to cross the ball for him, and with that, heads home a goal in front of an adoring Loft. What followed was Reg Toomer running much of the length of the pitch to celebrate screaming Rodney's name. The camera view of his celebrations came from the top of the away end and offers great views of the Paddock, as well as the Loft. It was a view of Loftus Road that would disappear within two years. Even if you didn't watch games from those parts of the ground, it would still have been sad to see them consigned as become part of our history. Thankfully, one supporter caught what it meant to support Rangers from the terraces. Even if he happened to be of the fictional variety.

29 *Macca's Bizarre Return*
Queens Park Rangers 1 Swindon Town 2
1997/98

When a former player returns to Loftus Road with his new side, sometimes they will get a great reception, and on other occasions, less so. Generally speaking, much will depend on how they performed with us and the circumstances behind their departure. When Alan McDonald returned with his then current side Swindon Town in March 1998, there was no doubt whatsoever that he would be guaranteed a rousing welcome from the QPR support. McDonald made his debut for the club in 1983, and over the following 14 years, would make almost 500 appearances for the club. Adjectives like effort, determination, leadership and loyalty can often be bandied about when talking about footballers who have played for Rangers, but Alan McDonald earned them all. A favourite son of Northern Ireland as well as Queens Park Rangers, he represented his country on no fewer than 52 occasions, and remains to this day, the club's most capped international footballer.

So, following the pleasantries that came with the appearance of our former captain and long-serving stalwart, the game kicked off and Rangers had a great start to the game. A ball forward from defender Steve Yates to Kevin Gallen, found the QPR striker down the left, and his powerful run gave him the opportunity to cut inside and deliver a low right-footed cross. Mike Sheron was tackled by McDonald and as a result the ball fell kindly for Nigel Quashie, whose low shot found the bottom corner of the net, after just eight minutes of the game. The lead lasted for exactly a further eight minutes as the pace and power of Swindon forward George Ndah was too much for Karl Ready, and the Rangers defender brought him down in the penalty area. From the resulting spot-kick, veteran winger Mark Walters equalised for the Robins.

Just 21 minutes in, came the moment that looked like it would swing the game the way of Ray Harford's side. A punt upfield from Rangers saw one of the visiting defenders head the ball back to his keeper. Not looking where he was, future R's stopper Fraser Digby came forward to grab possession. So much so, QPR forwards Gallen and Sheron protested that he had handled outside his penalty. After much discussion between the referee and linesman, Digby was shown a red card-much to the anger of his teammates. Upon viewing this incident again, it was a tad harsh on the keeper who would join Rangers late in 2001. It was debatable whether he was actually outside his area as he collected the ball, and at least part of his body appeared to be inside the penalty area.

But regardless of the rights or wrongs of what just happened, Swindon were now down to ten men. During the 1997/98 season, teams could pick three substitutes and it was entirely at the discretion of the manager whether one of those was a goalkeeper. Under normal circumstances, the chances of requiring a second goalkeeper were slim in comparison to the need for a third outfield substitute. Only today, this match did not fall into the category of 'normal circumstances'. The Robins did not have a recognised keeper to replace Fraser Digby. If everyone thought that was unusual, it was nothing compared to what was about to happen. Alan McDonald took the keeper's jersey and promptly took his place between the sticks.

Rather than leave Swindon demoralised, the turn of events seemed to inspire the visitors following the red card. First of all, Scott Leitch hit the post with a brilliant left-footed shot from almost 35 yards out. Then on the stroke of half-time, Iffy Onuora scored with a header on what was his debut. The home side going behind off the back of Digby being dismissed, was not what either set of supporters would have expected after 45 minutes. But without a recognised goalkeeper, an extra man on the pitch and a highly experienced manager in Ray Harford overseeing things, surely it was only a matter of time before the stand-in keeper would be beaten. And if the equaliser went in early enough in the second period, there was a strong likelihood that a second goal would quickly follow.

Although Rangers dominated possession in the second period, the comeback failed to materialise. There was next to nothing in the way of genuine goalscoring opportunities and about the best chance came to Kevin Gallen, but his shot went over the bar. McDonald started to look more and more confident as the game went on. Because of his long association with QPR, the last thing the majority of home supporters would have wanted for him to endure a humiliating afternoon with a series of blunders. But at the same time, it was a complete mystery as to why he was not once tested with any shots from outside the area. After all, his lack of experience would probably have meant this represented the best hopes of an equaliser.

On a day that Rangers looked like they couldn't have scored if the match went on for a further two hours, the final whistle was met with one of the most hostile responses to a home defeat in living memory. Even though there have been many by a worse score line, rarely had a loss at Loftus Road come in such embarrassing circumstances. The nature of this pitiful capitulation did not escape the notice of either Ray Harford or owner Chris Wright, and this led to a rash move that would come back to haunt the club before long. Within days of the 2-1 loss to Swindon Town, Vinnie Jones was signed for a fee of £500,000. He would play just nine times for the club- none of which was in a winning cause. And the following season, by which time he was player coach, stormed out of the club after he did not succeed Harford as QPR manager. For many months thereafter, Rangers were still paying his wages while he was busy promoting his new career as an actor. An even more humiliating episode in the club's history, than the Swindon defeat.

Looking back, it is both a mystery and a disgrace that Alan McDonald was not allowed to see out his career in West London, with a coaching role of his own. Surely his many years of service had earned him that right. Aged 33, he still had something to offer the club that he served so well, especially off the back of his performances in the 1996/97 season. Strong personalities with QPR's best interests at heart should never be taken for granted. You only have to look at how Steve Morrow found himself hopelessly out of his depth as Rangers captain, immediately after McDonald departed Loftus Road. It is interesting to try and imagine would the team have fared any better against Swindon Town on that fateful day back in 1998. had Alan McDonald been in the Queens Park Rangers team that afternoon and they faced an identical scenario? One thing is for certain, he would never have accepted such a tame capitulation, in the manner that his former teammates did.

30 *Pollock Saves Rangers*
Manchester City 2 Queens Park Rangers 2
1997/98

For a while, the fortunes of Queens Park Rangers and Manchester City could not be separated. Both finished in the top half of the table, in the very first Premiership season of 1992/93. The two sides would suffer relegation in 1996 and at the time, most pundits seemed to believe that both Rangers and City would come straight back up the following year. Once again, the two sides matched each other by failing to mount a promotion challenge. In the 1997/98 season, both teams seemed intent on matching each other yet again, by having a poor season and taking residence in the bottom half of the table. With the penultimate fixture of the campaign seeing QPR go to Maine Road, the likelihood was that their paths would finally go in different directions. A win would go a long way towards keeping Manchester City in the division. Whilst a victory or draw, would do likewise for Ray Harford's team. The biggest worry coming into this match was that Rangers were struggling to win games and badly needed a hero to step up and come good in this vital relegation battle. Thankfully such an individual existed. Only, he wasn't wearing a Queens Park Rangers shirt.

Rangers got off to the worst possible start when Nigel Quashie conceded a free-kick just 16 seconds into the match. From the resulting set-piece, City favourite' Georgi Kinkladze gave the home side the lead with a strike from 30 yards out. It couldn't have been a worse start. But if Kindladze's moment of brilliance gave the home side cause for optimism, it seemed like his teammates did everything they could to get QPR back into the game. Manchester City keeper Martyn Margetson picked up a back pass from a teammate. The referee awarded Rangers an indirect free-kick from inside the penalty area. Before Margetson and his colleagues had time to contemplate arranging a defensive wall, Kevin Gallen and Mike Sheron caught the hosts napping, and the former passed the ball to the latter, who tapped home before some of the City players had a chance to even return to their own penalty area. On any other day, this blunder would have been remembered for a very long time. But as a result of what happened minutes later, that Sheron goal became a mere footnote to the events of the afternoon.

Another Rangers attack saw Sheron pass to the experienced David Bardsley. The popular right-back was renowned for his brilliant crosses, and many of the best headed goals in the history of Queens Park Rangers, came as a result of an assist from his right foot. Perhaps a sign of how far the R's had slipped from the days when he and his teammates were a force in the Premiership, Bardsley's pass across the pitch was tame and posed next to no threat. Yet for some reason, Manchester City's Jamie Pollock came charging towards Bardsley's ball that went across the pitch. He then proceeded to scoop the ball over both Gallen and one of his own teammates. Then from 12 yards out, headed the ball over the despairing dive of Martyn Margetson which finished up in the back of the net. It is said that if someone does something that is particularly embarrassing, they wished that the ground would open up and swallow them. This would have been the exact moment that Pollock would have hoped that the Maine Road pitch was directly above a sinkhole that was about to give way. Had he been up the other end of the pitch, it would have been lauded as a moment of individual brilliance, instead of the moment of madness it actually was.

The rest of the match was not short of further drama. City's Kevin Horlock hit the crossbar with a rasping shot. Also, in the first half, Kevin Gallen was brought down for what was the most obvious penalty you would see all season, but the referee failed to award anything. Later in the second half, loanee Neil Ruddock failed to clear the ball properly after he was put under pressure by a couple of Manchester City attackers. From the resulting opportunity, a cross was met by Shaun Goater who put the striker Lee Bradbury in with the easiest of chances, after he had missed a number of opportunities, earlier in the game. It would be a nervy conclusion to the match for Ray Harford's side. And their task was not made any easier when Nigel Quashie was sent off for striking Paul Dickov. From the footage of the match, you can see there was a bit of needle between the pair, but it was irresponsible for the young midfielder to behave like that in such an important fixture. Had it come earlier in the match, it might have come at a high cost in terms of the result and our future in the division. Eventually, the final whistle was blown, and barring a couple of completely freaky results the following weekend, Rangers were safe.

A miserable afternoon for Jamie Pollock was made worse by the fact that his own goal was directly responsible for

QPR staying up and sending Manchester City down. The following weekend, City won 5-2 at Stoke City, and Rangers lost 1-0 at home to Bury for their final matches of the campaign. But by then, those results made no difference to the league standing of the two teams. He would not be allowed to forget that costly error. Shortly afterwards, he made news when an internet poll was sabotaged by Queens Park Rangers supporters and Pollock was voted the most significant individual of the previous 2,000 years. He comfortably saw off Jesus Christ into second place, incidentally. That goal was included in the BBC sports shows, 'A Question of Sport' and 'They Think It's All Over'. Every DVD specialising in own goals and howlers, featured this moment, as did any list of Top Ten Own Goals. And on his birthday, he was inundated with greetings cards. Most of which originated from London. In March 2002 before he even turned 28, Pollock retired from the sport. It felt like that moment in the relegation battle against Rangers, defined his entire career.

Closer to home, although his own goal was a source of humour, it only served to gloss over a multitude of sins. QPR won none of their last ten league matches of the 1997/98 season, and only two of the 23 games played in the second half of the season. Even all three of the teams that got relegated won more matches than Rangers in this campaign. Much of the football under Ray Harford was memorable only for the fact that it was completely forgettable. And even as supporters breathed a collective sigh of relief at staying up, everyone would have been aware that just about the only chance of this team improving the following season would be if there were 'Jamie Pollock' moments from the opposition, on a more regular basis.

Speaking of the man of the moment, the paths of Queens Park Rangers and Pollock did cross on one more occasion.

Albeit, in an indirect manner. Manchester City were promoted at the first time of asking, and in November 1999, came to Loftus Road. Jamie Pollock was one of the substitutes and when his name was mentioned over the loudspeaker in the stadium, an enormous roar went round the ground. As it happened, he was not one of the substitutes that would come on. Though one could imagine that he would have got cheered every time he touched the ball. He could well have become the first opposing player at an English football ground to make obscene gestures towards the home supporters, and still have been cheered and applauded by them. Fascinating as it might have been, we never did see just what the reaction to his appearance on the pitch would have been like. Though given what happened to Jamie Pollock in the aftermath of that 2-2 draw at Maine Road, any QPR supporter with an ounce of compassion would freely admit that he had probably already suffered enough.

31 *End of Away Day Misery*
Wolverhampton Wanderers 1 Queens Park Rangers 2
1998/99

On September 20th 1997, Stewart Houston's R's side won 3-2 at Crewe Alexandra, thanks to goals from John Spencer, Danny Maddix and Trevor Sinclair. Fans who travelled up to Cheshire to follow QPR probably had no idea that it would be the last time they would see an away win for a while. It must be noted that just weeks later, Houston and his assistant Bruce Rioch were sacked after a series of poor results. After John Hollins took over as caretaker for a few matches, Ray Harford was appointed as the new manager of Queens Park Rangers. Fans who met Harford found him open, friendly, knowledgeable and happy to give up his time to meet the supporters. At one forum staged not long after he took charge, most people were impressed with how Ray Harford seemed to have identified all of the problems with the side that he had inherited.

Changing the fortunes of QPR, proved to be much harder for the experienced former Blackburn Rovers and West Bromwich Albion manager. Very few positives came about during the Harford era. Among the worst aspects of his time in charge, was the inability to win a single game away from home. Of course, the home record wasn't exactly a source of non-stop enjoyment either. Ray Harford had only overseen four home league wins in ten months, by the time his side visited Oxford United, in September 1998. A year had now elapsed since the previous away win at Gresty Road. This match seemed to be the perfect opportunity to finally end the club's miserable away record. Oxford were struggling in the league and had just lost 7-0 away to Sunderland. But rather than being a great chance to end the winless run away from home, what followed was a nightmare. Rangers went a goal behind in the first half, following some sloppy defending. By this time, Rangers supporters would have feared the worse. Not only did Rangers fail to win away under Ray Harford, they never once recorded a victory under his management after going behind in a game. All of which suggested that this side was lacking a number of qualities. Confidence, self-belief, effort, pride, team spirit, fitness. You can take your pick.

In the second half, Oxford United doubled their lead with perhaps the most ridiculous goal Queens Park Rangers have ever conceded. Goalkeeper Lee Harper unnecessarily came tearing out of his penalty area, in an attempt to clear the ball. He only succeeded in hitting it off the backside of the advancing Oxford forward. The ball then bounced around the QPR half of the pitch and following another couple of failed efforts by the Rangers defence to clear it, Matt Murphy tried a speculative shot from some 45 yards. Rather than being an effort of rare power or a clever chip that eluded everyone, it was an innocuous effort that bounced off the ground four separate times and only found the back of the net because Harper took an age to get back to his goal line. Rarely in the history of Queens Park Rangers did the team look like they were less interested in playing for the manager, than on this afternoon. The Oxford United forwards swept forward and scored twice more, as the Rangers defence offered little resistance.

Even a stunning 25-yard left-footed volley from Tony Scully in the dying moments of the game, meant next to nothing for those who had to watch this shambolic performance the home side ran out 4-1 winners. Harford resigned in the aftermath of the Manor Ground fiasco. Soon after, his now former assistant Vinnie Jones stormed out of the club, after not succeeding the man who signed him for QPR. For many years, Jones felt hard done by because he never got the job. But the fact that he was still a volatile figure on and off the pitch as he was sent off in a reserve match weeks earlier and already had bust-ups with members of the first-team squad. He had no prior coaching or managerial experience, nor did a single member of the Rangers side come out in support of his appointment. And Vinny Jones own role alongside the erstwhile Ray Harford in taking the club to the foot of the table, all suggested that appointing him as the new manager would have been an act of complete and utter lunacy.

Instead, Rangers turned to Iain Dowie. The former Northern Ireland international was a very different personality to Jones. Whilst the latter had become something of a toxic presence at the club, Dowie was quietly doing a good job with the reserves, winning more matches than the first team, it must be said. On that basis, he was put in temporary charge, for the visit to Wolverhampton Wanderers. After the events of three days earlier, this had the look of a damage-limitation exercise.

174

QPR had lost all of their five previous league matches away from Loftus Road, so a trip to Molineux was hardly a mouth-watering prospect.

To use a phrase that was often favoured by a well-known former QPR manager, sometimes what was needed was "the rub of the green", in order to get out of exactly the rut Rangers were in at this point in time. And that was exactly what happened for the first goal of the evening. Initially, Mike Sheron did well to see off one Wolves player as he tried to start an attack. His attempt at a one-two with teammate Kevin Gallen failed to come off, but when one of the defenders tried to clear his lines, he only succeeded in hitting the ball off of Gallen and all of a sudden, Sheron was able to beat what was left of the Wanderers defence to tap home from six yards out. And so, we had yet another entry in the long list of bizarre goals, Queens Park Rangers have been gifted over the years.

The second goal did not take long to arrive. Once again Mike Sheron and Kevin Gallen linked up well on the left side of the Wolves half. Gallen then ran to the bye-line and his cross evaded no fewer than four defenders, as Sheron was on hand to tuck home his second of the evening. At the time, the man who scored both of QPR's goals was the club's record signing. For many years, he was regarded as a £2.7 million flop, and his name would often get mentioned when internet discussions among fans turned to find out who was our 'worst ever centre-forward'. Truth be told, he was nothing of the sort. Unfortunately, his problems were in fact two-fold. Firstly, he failed to justify the huge price tag that he arrived at Loftus Road with. And secondly, he was starting to play some of his best football for Rangers, at the time he was offloaded to Barnsley, for little over half what was paid for him, just 18 months earlier.

From coming into this game with an embarrassing record away from home, Queens Park Rangers now found themselves two goals up in a matter of minutes. It was one of those matches where you were not sure which of the two teams would have been more shocked at the turn of events. But just how would QPR cope with being a couple of goals up away from home, especially given this was a scenario the previous management never had the luxury of worrying about? As it turned out, pretty well. Wolverhampton Wanderers did pull a goal back late into the game, but Iain Dowie's side held on for the win on the road. A small matter of one year, and nine days since it happened previously.

And so, this rather embarrassing statistic was no more. It was a night to be happy for many of those involved. First of all, there was the travelling support who had to contend with one miserable trip after another, so this night would have been all the sweeter. Iain Dowie also deserved some credit, not just for overseeing this long-awaited win, but also giving back a little bit of hope, in the process. And although he could never be regarded as a success at Loftus Road, this was at least one of the better days that Mike Sheron would enjoy in a Rangers shirt. Had he joined QPR for a more modest fee, or had the luxury of a longer stay in West London, perhaps his legacy would look somewhat different.

This result must also have felt like one final kick in the teeth for Ray Harford. He arrived in West London with a fine reputation, and was able to impress those fans that he came into contact with. But in less than 12 months, his stock fell alarmingly. Whether it was the results, transfers, the brand of football being played, or the aforementioned away results, there wasn't any aspect of his tenure that can be viewed in a positive light. The win at Wolverhampton Wanderers less than 48 hours after he resigned, felt like we were getting immediate closure on a period few fans look back on with any warmth or enthusiasm.

32 *Kiwomya's Mystery Goal*
Queens Park Rangers 3 Ipswich Town 1
1999/00

For many years, there was a common perception among supporters that every single time that a former player faced Queens Park Rangers, he would score against us. There was a time when there was a certain amount of truth to that school of thought. Clive Allen did so on numerous occasions. Even those considerably less prolific than Allen, seemed to get in on the act. Nigel Quashie moved to Nottingham Forest in the summer of 1998. He failed to score a single goal in his first season and a half with his new club, yet finally found the back of the net in January 2000, upon his return to Loftus Road. Likewise, Ian Baraclough scored just once in 125 appearances for QPR, so naturally enough, did likewise on his return to West London, with Notts. County. Incidents like these only fuelled the belief that we were almost cursed, when it came to former players biting the hand that used to feed them.

Of course, there was no such curse and as the years have gone by, it is an occurrence that has happened less frequently. But if you were to turn that scenario on its head, there have been many examples of Queens Park Rangers players scoring against their former clubs. In the 1988/89 season, Mark Falco managed this feat in each league match against Tottenham Hotspur. And in one of the most famous cup ties under the Loftus Road floodlights, Kenny Sansom scored with an absolute cracker, against Arsenal, in the FA Cup in 1990. But no goal against a former team was ever as bizarre as the one that was scored against Ipswich Town on a bright sunny day in April 2000.

The 1999/00 season was to be a year of respite and surprisingly good results under the auspices of Gerry Francis, following two years of relegation struggles. This was thanks to the canny management of Francis, an unbeaten home record than somehow lasted until the turn of the New Year, and the surprising number of goals that came from Stuart Wardley. A player that was signed as a utility defender or midfielder, and went on to score an astonishing 14 goals that season, after being signed for a miniscule £15,000, from Saffron Walden Town. He would never enjoy that level of goalscoring form, for the remainder of his career.

With Rangers having already secured a place in the top half of the league, Ipswich Town arrived in West London, having already been thrashed 4-1 in the reverse fixture. This thanks to goals from Gavin Peacock and Wardley, along with a brace from Swedish striker Rob Steiner, for a truly memorable away-day victory. The first half of the match at Loftus Road was pretty unremarkable, with little in the way of significant action. But the second half burst into life when a shot from Richard Langley was only palmed away by goalkeeper Richard Wright and Peacock tucked home from close range. It took just 20 seconds of the second period to take the lead. Minutes later, the lead was doubled when a short pass from Chris Kiwomya found Sammy Koejoe, and his low powerful shot from 15 yards out, found the back of the net. Koejoe is now largely a forgotten figure, but was something of a novelty when he joined QPR in 1999. Although he was born in the Suriname capital of Paramaribo, he learned his football in the Netherlands, and can be regarded as the first Dutch player to turn out for Rangers. He took his goal in fine style, and the way he sprinted into the box and struck his shot powerfully and low into the corner, was uncannily like what we saw from Les Ferdinand, on so many occasions. Unfortunately, it was one of only three goals that he managed in 32 appearances, in a spell that lasted just over two years. Nor was his form particularly outstanding, whilst he was with QPR. Perhaps had he managed to resemble Ferdinand on a few more occasions, things might have been different.

Ipswich got back into the game when Langley fouled future R's manager Jim Magilton to concede a penalty. Magilton took it himself, to make it 2-1. With no further goals as the game went into injury time, it looked like the points were sealed. Then in one final twist, Wardley did well to keep the ball in, passing to Kevin Gallen in the process. Gallen managed to cross the ball to Chris Kiwomya. Close to the penalty spot, the Rangers striker was in a great position, but it looked like any attempt to get a shot on goal, was about to be blocked by one of the Ipswich defenders. But the attempt at the aforementioned block was a poor one, and all of a sudden, Kiwomya had time and space for a shooting chance, which he took and it beat Wright. But as he turned away to celebrate, something was wrong. If he had just scored, why wasn't the ball in the net?

How could Kiwomya be so jubilant to get one over on his old side, when the ball had bobbled past the goal and finished up somewhere between one of the photographers on the touchline, and the advertising board for HMV, which was nearer the corner flag than the Ipswich goal? We also had the sight of fans behind the goal celebrating, whilst others in different parts of the ground were not sure what had happened. And even some of his teammates were a bit slow to join in the celebrations, considering that the victory had just been confirmed. A couple of the Ipswich Town players were complaining to the referee, about what just took place. However, on closer inspection, it was indeed a goal. Footage of the match reveals that the ball had gone into the goal, but had come back out again.

"He's burst the net" exclaimed a jubilant Tony Incenzo on the official video of the 1999/00 season. If the subject ever came up among Rangers supporters, most of them would love to see something as outrageous as a Queens Park Rangers player bursting the back of the net with a shot of immense power. But Kiwomya's shot, whilst well taken, could hardly fall into that category. Unlike say, Andy Gray's rocket in that superb win over Manchester United in the 88/89 season. Or a certain Gareth Ainsworth goal that will feature in a future chapter. Instead it was the result of some faulty stitching, that meant the third goal happened as a result of going into the net, and straight back out. It could have happened with any of the three QPR goals that afternoon.

And so, Rangers recorded a fine double over Ipswich Town, with seven goals scored, and just two conceded. Which was no mean feat considering that the Tractor Boys would win automatic promotion at the end of the season. And in the finest tradition of the classic cartoon series Scooby Doo, they would have won the title, if it wasn't for those pesky West Londoners. For now, Chris Kiwomya can claim to be the only player ever caught on film, bursting the net in the process of scoring a goal for Queens Park Rangers. Most supporters would love to see it happen for real one day at Loftus Road. Preferably with a shot more powerful that the one that sealed this win in 2000. And if such an occurrence is accompanied by the entire net collapsing under the weight of such a powerful shot, at least this time teammates and supporters will be in no doubt as to what just happened.

33 *New Faces*
Queens Park Rangers 1 Stoke City 0
2001/02

During the Flavio Briatore era, and then the years of Queens Park Rangers yo-yoing between the Premiership and Championship, it had become routine to see a whole batch of new faces turn up in the playing squad, when a new campaign would get underway. This meant that QPR rarely had anything resembling a settled side, for many years. And looking back at the previous two decades, more often than not it was a policy that failed to benefit our football club. Yet none of those numerous examples of upheaval in the late noughties and early tens, came close in comparison with what happened around a decade earlier.

The 2000/01 season represented one of the lowest points in the history of Queens Park Rangers. The club crashed down to the third tier for the first time in 34 years. Owner Chris Wright threw in the towel, having presided over a couple of poor managerial appointments in Stewart Houston and Ray Harford, not to mention numerous other bad decisions. Even Gerry Francis who initially helped keep Rangers in the division and followed that up with a mid-table finish in 2000, was overseeing a team in freefall, and resigned before the campaign came to its pitiful conclusion. With the club in administration, there would be a cull, the likes of which supporters have never seen, before or since.

An unprecedented 20 professionals left the club. They fell into a number of different groups. First there were the prized sellable assets. Admittedly, they were few and far between. But one of the players who did actually come out that season with any credit was young striker Peter Crouch. He clearly had a great future, and Portsmouth snapped him up, with Rangers getting somewhere in the region of £2 million, once you take sell-on fees, into consideration. Versatile and lightning fast wide player Jermaine Darlington was not without his merits, and he joined Wimbledon for £300,000. A fee that felt like a 'kick in the teeth' given that Rangers payed almost twice as much for the hugely disruptive figure of Vinnie Jones, who made the opposite journey, just a couple of years earlier.

Crouch and Darlington were the only ones QPR could command money for. Other long-serving figures also headed for the exit. Among them, Karl Ready, Danny Maddix and Paul Murray. Numerous signings were made in the years preceding the 2001 relegation, and their days in West London were numbered too. Among them were Steve Morrow, Lee Harper, Tony Scully, George Kulcsar, Ian Barraclough, Ludek Miklosko, Keith Rowland, Chris Kiwomya, Tim Breacker and Michel Ngonge. The rest of those who left departed, were made up of former youth team players who would not make the grade. The slashing of the Queens Park Rangers playing squad was a painful exercise, but also a necessary one, given all of the financial problems that existed. Only now, manager Ian Holloway had a new problem to deal with.

What was leftover in the dressing room, would hardly fill up a team sheet, let alone have a squad in place that would be big enough to handle a 46-match league programme. A lot of new faces needed to be recruited and that would have to be done with little in the way of funds to spend. It goes without saying that transfer fees were out of the question, so any new signings would be made up of free transfers. But Rangers did have one thing in their favour, and that was Ian Holloway himself. A thoroughly committed midfielder throughout his career, which included his spell at Loftus Road between 1991-1996, he became QPR manager following a five-year spell in charge of Bristol Rovers. The third tier of English football would have been a complete mystery to many a Queens Park Rangers supporter. But it was a level that Holloway very familiar with.

QPR were drawn at home to Stoke City for the first match of the 2001/02 season and many of the Rangers players would have been as much a mystery to our own fans, as they were to Stoke's traveling support. For the record, the starting line-up against the Potters was as follows. Chris Day; Terrell Forbes, Aziz Ben Askar, Steve Palmer(captain), Marcus Bignot; Alex Bonnot, Mark Perry, Paul Bruce, Karl Connolly; Stuart Wardley, Andy Thomson. Of those eleven mentioned, only Perry, Bruce, Wardley, Connolly and Thomson had previously turned out for Queens Park Rangers, and an astonishing six players were making their debut. No wonder most of those of a blue and white hooped persuasion had no idea just how this season was going to pan out. Thankfully, everything would be fine.

Around halfway through the first period, Stuart Wardley fed Andy Thomson a pass into the Stoke penalty area, and calmly finished to give QPR the lead. It was to be the first of 21 league goals he got in the 2001/02 campaign. Disappointingly, he remains to this day, the only Rangers forward to get twenty league goals in a season, in the 21st century. Further chances came the way of Ian Holloway's side, with Thomson again, Marcus Bignot and Steve Palmer all having chances to increase the lead. But in the end, just the one goal separated the two sides. Later in the second half, striker Leroy Griffiths came off the bench meaning that he became the seventh Queens Park Rangers player to make his league debut for the club, that afternoon.

A most creditable start to the season, especially as Stoke City were one of the division's favourites for promotion. Sure enough, they went up through the Play-Offs, the following May. QPR were unable to make their own bid for an immediate return to the second tier, finishing the season in eighth place. But if ever there was a season in which consolidation and rebuilding was needed, then this was it. There was no guarantee that Holloway's newly assembled outfit compiled at the minimum of expense were going to be a success. Had his recruitment policies been as poor as some of his predecessors as Rangers manager, the years of struggling that began back in 1995, might have continued. Big clubs like Manchester City, Leeds United and Sunderland, have in the last 25 years, had to come down to this level. Portsmouth and Coventry City who could boast numerous seasons in the top-flight, would fall down to a division Queens Park Rangers have never had to occupy. And even Luton Town and Notts County whom QPR faced in top flight as recently as the 1991/92 campaign, have both suffered the ignominy of dropping out of the Football League, altogether.

Instead, a new and very different looking Queens Park Rangers side from the one that played in the 2000/01 relegation year, was been assembled. It was able to hold its own, and although a few of the personnel would come and go, Ian Holloway was able to strengthen the side slowly, with the arrival of each new signing over the next couple of years. By way of a nod to Flavio Briatore some years later, it was almost as if Holloway had his own 'Three Year Plan' in order to get QPR promoted. Albeit, without a single wealthy benefactor in sight. It was not a straight forward return to the Championship. Not least because the club's financial problems that hung-over Loftus Road like a giant rain cloud that wouldn't disappear for years on end. But in May 2004, a combination three years of hard work, numerous canny signings and the best team spirit in a generation, made it happen with a memorable 3-1 win at Sheffield Wednesday. And to think, it all began when no less than seven players made their debuts for Queens Park Rangers back in August 2001.

34 *The Curse of Nine*
Queens Park Rangers 4 Wycombe Wanderers 3
2001/02

In what turned out to be the first of two very bad-tempered affairs against the Chairboys in the space of well under a year, Wycombe came to Loftus Road towards the end of December 2001, just three days after QPR and Brighton & Hove Albion had played out a goalless draw at the same venue. There would be no lack of goals on this occasion, although the fact that the opponents that day managed to bring some respectability to the score line, only went to prove that not for the first, or last time, Rangers have an uncanny ability to fail to take advantage of a generous numerical advantage, when it comes their way. We will look at that in greater detail in due course.

It all started off in the right spirit, and with the first goal going the way the home fans would have wanted. Kevin Gallen held onto the ball well by the Wanderers touchline, before Karl Connolly provided support for him. Connolly's shot was saved but only went as far as Andy

Thomson, who tapped in from just a couple of yards out. It was the Scottish striker's 18th league goal of the season. Three minutes later, a Wycombe cross into the box saw Terrell Forbes and Andy Rammell go for the ball. Forbes somewhat bundled the striker to the ground and a penalty was awarded. A couple of QPR players had half-hearted protests to the referee, but he was never going to change his mind. Steve Brown made in 1-1, with the resulting spot-kick.

Still in the first-half, a through ball into the area found Gallen and just as he had the opportunity to take the ball clear of the Wycombe Wanderers defence, he was caught by a late tackle from Jason Cousins. The sort of mis-timed challenge that would usually happen at least a couple of times on any given weekend, in English football. Referee Phil Prosser blew his whistle and pointed to the spot for the second penalty of the afternoon. Despite the fact that the footage showed that it was definitely a clear-cut penalty, most of the Wycombe players were incensed with the decision. None more so than midfielder Keith Ryan. He ran over to Kevin Gallen and started manhandling him while the QPR striker was still on the ground. Once that happened, it was inevitable that a melee quickly followed. Thankfully, despite that happening, the Rangers players managed to keep their composure, considerably better than their opponents did. Among them, was Jermaine McSporran, who somehow had even more to say for himself than Ryan. Once the protests stopped, both of those Wycombe players were shown the red card. Emulating that Derby match featured earlier on, two opposing players were sent off, as a result of a single incident. And even more unusually, neither of them was Cousins who committed the foul in the first place. Before Rangers had the chance to take the spot-kick, McSporran returned to the pitch to start remonstrating with the referee once more.

Eventually, the game continued and Thomson stepped up to take the penalty. Unfortunately, his effort was weak, and keeper Martin Taylor went to right way to comfortably make the save. Upon viewing the match highlights once again, the reaction of the Wycombe players was well over the top. You cannot help but wonder if the long hold-up initially started as a ploy to put off Andy Thomson before he took the penalty, but got out of hand. If that was the case, it had worked owing to the fact that it was saved. But all of the protests about the penalty award in the first place, had come at a heavy price. With over half the match to go, Rangers now had a two-man advantage.

It was level at half-time but just minutes into the second period, Doudou and Terrell Forbes linked up well on the right, and Kevin Gallen scored from close range. The third QPR goal of the day was by far the best, and one of the R's goals of the season. Karl Connolly started the move in the middle of the pitch, before passing to Thomson on his left. The cross was partially cleared and this was met with a stunning volley from Connolly on the edge of the area, that found the top right-hand corner of the net. It looked like Ian Holloway's men were starting to take a stranglehold on the game, thanks in no small part to the extra men they had on the pitch. But a free-kick in the 64th minute from Dannie Bulman, somehow went through the Rangers defensive wall and past the keeper Fraser Digby, to bring the score back to 3-2. During another attack, Doudou produced a wonderful defence splitting pass to put Gavin Peacock in with a chance. The veteran midfielder slotted home to double their lead. Then late on, QPR defender Aziz Ben Askar was judged to have fouled Andy Rammell, and he converted what was the third spot-kick of the afternoon.

With that, the match was over and Queens Park Rangers

had slightly the better of this seven goal stormer. The mere mention of a game finishing 4-3, will usually mean that the match was an absolute cracker, and if the R's are on the right end of that score line, then even better. Yet for over half of the match, we got to enjoy a two-man advantage that should have ensured that the game would have come to its conclusion without thinking that the Chairboys might have got an unlikely equaliser. But unfortunately, Rangers have an appalling record when it comes to putting matches to bed, when they have the rare luxury of a two-man advantage. This game and the one from Chapter Ten are two such examples. Let us look at a few more.

In the 1992/93 season, QPR faced an Everton team that had goalkeeper Neville Southall and Paul Rideout sent off before half time. Rangers went into the break 1-0 ahead, and would go three goals up at one stage, before the visitors pulled back two goals in quick succession. At one stage, they even pushed for an equaliser, before Andy Sinton wrapped up the points, with the fourth Queens Park Rangers goal of the afternoon, which also gave him his hat trick. The next time it happened, we did not even have the benefit of actually getting something from the match. Gerry Francis' side were already trailing 2-1 at home to Manchester City in a 94/95 Premiership game, when keeper Andy Dibble and Richard Edghill were both sent off in the space of seven minutes, leaving QPR the best part of 15 minutes to salvage an equaliser. Sadly, they failed and supporters had to leave the ground to the City fans chanting of "Nine men, we only needed nine men.....", to the tune of the famous song Blue Moon.

Another lower profile example came in the 2002/03 season. During a particularly poor run of form, Rangers visited Luton Town who had striker Steve Howard dismissed very early on and captain Kevin Nicholls did likewise, not long after the second period began. The response from the visitors was a poor one. During a forgettable loan period that lasted just three matches, Callum Willock missed a number of chances. One match that most definitely couldn't be described as 'low profile' was the 1-0 win over Chelsea, in the 11/12 season. Long before he became a hate-figure at Loftus Road in his own right, Jose Boswinga was sent off for a challenge on Shaun Wright-Phillips, when the latter was through on goal. And Didier Drogba also get a straight red card for a lunge on Adel Taarabt. Both of which happened before half-time. Victories over Chelsea are always sweet, but Queens Park Rangers were made to work hard for the remainder of the game, as the nine visitors that were left on the pitch, continually pressed for an equaliser.

The one exception to the rule when it comes to making heavy work when it is eleven versus nine, was the 6-0 win over Crystal Palace in May 1999. A strange match all round, owing to the fact that it came off the back of five successive defeats, hundreds of black and white balloons were still on the pitch after kick-off, and Palace's Andy Linighan playing for QPR that afternoon, because his parent club were in such financial dire straits, they were just glad to get him off the wage bill. The sight of much-maligned players like George Kulcsar and Tony Scully scoring with inch perfect 25-yard shots and volleys from a tight angle, along with the fact that the Palace defenders were so immobile they might as well have been wearing concrete football boots, only served to make the day feel even more surreal. On top of all that, Chinese international Fan Zhiyi was sent off for needlessly pushing the referee and defender David Woozley also got his marching orders, when he pulled Scully back, and prevented him from scoring. Even if we were to say that Rangers were aided in their efforts to avoid relegation thanks to playing against nine men, it was the only completely successful example, in seven different attempts. Playing with two extra men is not a scenario that you would expect to have to deal with on a regular basis. But most of the occasions it did happen over the years, Queens Park Rangers responded poorly to the gift that came their way.

The next time Wycombe and QPR met, was during the following season at Adams Park. If there was bad feeling in the 4-3 match in December 2001, that paled into comparison with what took place in August 2002. Four players were sent off in that game which Wanderers won 4-1, including Marc Bircham and Marcus Bean. A record in a competitive match involving Queens Park Rangers. In Bean's case, he became the third player in just over a year, to be dismissed on his Rangers debut, following Justin Cochrane and Danny Shittu. Although Paul Furlong scored for Rangers, he had another goal disallowed, as did Karl Connolly,. With the disallowed goals, sending offs and the result, referee Rob Styles became a hate figure among Queens Park Rangers supporters. After that, if a primary school in Shepherd's Bush caught fire and Styles ran inside and successfully rescued every single child, he would probably still have been despised among Loftus Road regulars. Helping make history in that bad-tempered afternoon in Buckinghamshire, Andy Rammell and Danny Senda were also dismissed for the home side. That was of little benefit to Rangers when the Chairboys went down to nine men. But then that has been a familiar story over the years.

35 *Langley Makes Bittersweet History*
Oldham Athletic 1 Queens Park Rangers 1
2002/03

Play-Off matches became part of the landscape of domestic football, in the 1986/87 season. Although it took on a very different look to what fans know today. When it was introduced, the team which finished nineteenth out of the twenty-two teams in the old First Division, would take their place in a semi-final that would also involve the three sides that finished third, fourth and fifth, in the Second Division. The participants were Charlton Athletic from the top flight, ironically avoiding relegation thanks to a 2-1 win over Queens Park Rangers on the final day of the regular league season. They were joined by Ipswich Town, Oldham Athletic and Leeds United, who were all vying for their place at the top table of English football. Charlton and Leeds won their respective semi-finals, and would meet over two legs to decide who would play in the top flight, in the following season. Two 1-0 wins meant that the teams would need a third match to separate them. Played at the neutral venue of St Andrews, Birmingham,

Leeds United took the lead, only for the unlikely figure of Charlton Athletic centre-half Peter Shirtliff to score twice, which kept the Addicks in top flight. A year later, Chelsea faced Middlesbrough for the same prize. Chelsea were beaten 2-0 at Ayresome Park, before winning 1-0 at Stamford Bridge. The game was as much remembered for the rioting from the home fans, which spilled out onto the pitch and the streets outside the ground, at the final whistle. But with regards to on field matters, Chelsea became the only team ever to be relegated from the top flight, as a result of the Play-Offs.

All of which was very amusing to QPR supporters, but these end of season dramas, were an alien concept to our own club for many years. Rangers would remain in the top flight for almost another decade, after their introduction in the 86/87 campaign. Following relegation in 1996, a year later Stewart Houston's side fell a few points short of a late bid to sneak into the Play-Offs. Thereafter, Queens Park Rangers only ever looked like they would leave the second tier of English football, via the wrong end of the table. Which of course, is what happened at the end of an excruciating 2000/01 season. A year of consolidation followed in 2001/02, as the club tried to rebuild. Despite a horrible run around November 2002, QPR managed to sustain a genuine Play-Off challenge throughout the second half of the following season, spending a couple of months occupying the sixth place. A late surge saw Ian Holloway's side jump to fourth place, as the league came to its conclusion. The R's curious relationship with the Play-Offs was about to begin.

Rangers were drawn to face Oldham Athletic, and a familiar figure was managing our opponents. It was none other than Iain Dowie, who was player-coach at Loftus Road for a few years, before being part of the huge exodus from the club in the summer of 2001. These sorts of matches are rarely easy and QPR did not have a good record against the Latics. As a result, the media liked to make a big thing about Dowie getting one over on his former club, whenever Oldham beat Queens Park Rangers. The last thing supporters would have wanted was to have those comments rammed down our throats once again, only this time, probably tenfold given what was riding on the outcome. The first leg would be at Boundary Park.

On 29 minutes, the home side made the breakthrough. 39-year-old midfielder David Eyres scored with a free-kick that took a deflection that was just about big enough to catch out goalkeeper Chris Day. An ageing hero and a fortuitous goal were both elements that made it feel like it was not going to be QPR's day. Eyres was actually older than Dowie who was his manager. But early in the second half, loanee Tommy Williams saw off the close attention of one of the Birmingham City defenders to deliver a high cross to the far post. With immaculate timing, Richard Langley arrived in the penalty area and his drive was too good for the Latics keeper David Miskelly.

As history has shown, Play-Off matches involving Queens Park Rangers do not tend to be high scoring affairs because all 22 players on the pitch, know what is at stake for these games. As a result, Langley's goal was so vital. Unfortunately, the midfielder had a rush of blood to the head, by picking up two yellow cards in the space of less than 60 seconds. The first of which was for an alleged dive, and the latter for a backward head-butt on the veteran David Eyres. With ten minutes remaining, Rangers had to survive an onslaught from Oldham, but survived until the final whistle. All things considered, a very satisfactory result, but a bittersweet afternoon for Richard Langley. Despite that goal, Ian Holloway was furious with him, as he would now be suspended for the second leg at

Loftus Road.

What happened next is indelibly etched into the memory of every single Queens Park Rangers supporter, old enough to remember the 2002/03 season. That of course was one of the most famous wins under the Loftus Road floodlights, followed by the late heartbreak at Cardiff's Millennium Stadium. Although Langley suffered the misfortune of leaving the game early, not helped by his own actions it must be said, he did still score the goal that meant Rangers had a slightly better than even chance in the second leg of the tie against Oldham Athletic. Yet as history has shown, among QPR players who have scored goals in Play-Off matches, his own effort has long been forgotten. Meanwhile, everyone else has scored in those games has written themselves into Queen Park Rangers folklore. Let's look at those individuals.

Just ten days later, Rangers beat Oldham Athletic 1-0, thanks to a late goal from Paul Furlong. A few months earlier, the veteran striker was targeted with chants of "Chelsea reject" from the crowd, as he took the brunt of fans anger, off the back of a shock FA Cup dismissal to Vauxhall Motors, which was followed up just three days later by a 4-0 home defeat to Cardiff City. Over the course of the 02/03 campaign, Furlong found his goalscoring touch, and his winner in the Play-Off second leg was complete redemption in the eyes of even his fiercest critics. If the term 'zero to hero' hadn't existed, Paul Furlong would have invented it.

Moving forward eleven years, QPR hosted Wigan Athletic in the second leg of a Play-Off semi-final, following a goalless draw in Lancashire. After future R's defender James Perch gave the visitors the lead, Charlie Austin took over the proceedings. Austin was not in need of a redemption of his own, as he had already enjoyed a great first season at Loftus Road. But the equaliser in normal time, followed by the extra time winner, sealed an evening that was regarded as one of the most memorable since Paul Furlong's goal against Oldham, in 2003. As for Bobby Zamora? His own career and that moment in 2014, will be looked at in greater detail, in one of the upcoming chapters. In stark comparison, Richard Langley's goal at Boundary Park has been long forgotten, whereas Furlong, Austin and Zamora are all still lauded for their own personal Play-Off moments. Many fans, even those who went up to Lancashire back in May 2003, would struggle to remember who even scored that equaliser in the first leg. Which is something of a mystery, when you think about it.

Had Langley scored an 89th minute consolation at Oldham in a 5-1 defeat that meant Rangers were all but out of the tie, it would have been understandable why no one gives it a second thought. But the reality was very different. Without that goal, Paul Furlong could have replicated his strike at Loftus Road, and Queens Park Rangers might still have failed to reach the final. Also, had the Latics won 1-0, they might have come to West London with a slightly different game plan. But the fact was they didn't and the game was there for the taking, for Ian Holloway's team. Even the keenest of supporters would be hard pushed to find an explanation as to why Richard Langley's goal has never got the credit it deserves. Perhaps the most obvious reason is that every other Play-Off goal was scored in front of a large QPR following-either at Loftus Road or Wembley.

A look at the club's record in the 21st century, reveals a complete lack of anything resembling a genuine run in either the FA or League Cup competitions. A long and embarrassing run of results, fans rarely talk about even among our own number. In contrast to those knock out games, Rangers have enjoyed considerable success in the

Play-Offs. Their record to date reads won three matches, drawn two, lost just the one. And that was against Cardiff City who were playing on their own doorstep, so to speak. With two semi-final wins, and victory in the 2014 Final, Rangers can boast a 75% success record in terms of their progression in these matches. In many ways, the Play-Offs have superseded the cups, when it comes to moments of drama, excitement, and euphoria. Regardless of the fact that he picked up a red card on the same day, that all started on the day that Richard Langley did his part to help Queens Park Rangers reach the 2003 Play-Off Final.

36 *The Astonishing Ainsworth*
Rushden & Diamonds 3 Queens Park Rangers 3
2003/04

Whenever any professional footballer worthy of the name joins a new club, he will inevitably want to make a good impression with the team he is now part of. Gareth Ainsworth would have been no exception, when he came to Loftus Road on a free transfer in the summer of 2003. The winger was hugely experienced, and his list of former clubs included Preston North End, Cambridge United, Port Vale, Wimbledon and Cardiff City. But at the age of 30, he was still young enough to offer something substantial to Queens Park Rangers. He would make his debut in the club's opening match of the 2003/04 season at home to Blackpool.

Despite their famous tangerine shirts not actually clashing with our own blue and white hoops, the Seasiders in their infinite wisdom, decided to wear an all-black strip. It must rank as one of the all-time great kit blunders ever seen at Loftus Road, as temperatures soared into the high eighties, that afternoon. A mere three minutes into the game, Ainsworth opened his account when he poked home a Gino Padula corner. Cue the famous air guitar celebration that would be seen on numerous occasions. It was the start of a great afternoon as Richard Langley made it 2-0 before the first-half ended. In the second 45 minutes, Kevin Gallen got a third and Ainsworth got his second of the afternoon, when his run into the Blackpool penalty area saw him beat the keeper with a shot from a tight angle. A towering header from captain Steve Palmer completed the scoring, on what was an excellent afternoon for Queens Park Rangers, and outstanding debut for Gareth Ainsworth. But if he thought that his first appearance for the R's was memorable, it would pale into insignificance as a result of the game that took place just 16 days later.

Being in the third tier of English football, meant that fans who followed QPR away from home, would get the chance to visit some new and unfamiliar grounds. It is doubtful that any stadium would have been more unfamiliar than Nene Park. This was the home of Rushden & Diamonds. A team that unusually, was formed by the merger of Rushden Town and Irthlingborough Diamonds in 1992. It was the brainchild of Dr Martens owner Max Griggs. In just nine years, Rushden & Diamonds got in the Football League and two years later, got promoted to what was then the Second Division. All things considered, it was something of a meteoric and fairy tale rise for this once little-known outfit.

Just minutes into the game, a quick breakaway from the home side saw them breakaway down the right side of the pitch. Rangers keeper Chris Day misjudged the cross and Rushden took the lead. But QPR did not let their opponents enjoy the lead for long. In one attack, Ian Holloway's side stormed forward in great numbers. With Tommy Williams in possession wide on the left, his cross-field ball found Ainsworth on the opposite side of the pitch, and it seemed like the perfect chance to either run to the by-line and put in a cross, or perhaps cut inside and try to get a left-footed shot on goal. Instead from some 30 yards out, he struck a perfectly executed volley that found the opposite corner of the net. Just about everyone realised that they had just witnessed something very special. Even the Rushden supporters applauded to a man. Only one person wasn't impressed. Moments after the ball hit the back of the net, defender Barry Hunter berated his keeper for not stopping Gareth Ainsworth's shot. On that season's DVD, Holloway singled out Hunter, finding his reaction to this goal, absolutely hilarious. The winger's afternoon was far from over.

Minutes later, Ainsworth robbed one of the Rushden midfielders of the ball and ran forward. From well over 35 yards out, there was another shooting opportunity, albeit one that would have favoured the keeper because he was so far out. But perhaps off the back of what happened earlier in the game, he had the confidence to take another shot at goal. Remarkably, another long-range effort was perfectly hit, as he found the same corner of the net. In the space of just a few minutes, Gareth Ainsworth had made the Goal of the Season contest a non-event, such was the high quality of both strikes. And all by the time he played just his fourth league match for Queens Park Rangers. Early in the second half, Paul Furlong poked home a long ball forward, and with the score at 3-1 with just ten minutes remaining, an away win seemed like a mere formality. But there would be one final and cruel twist. Future QPR coach Paul Hall pulled a goal back before in the final minute, Onandi Lowe scored when his close-range shot hit the post and went in.

A remarkable afternoon which both teams could boast something to remember. The two goals from Gareth

Ainsworth from a Rangers viewpoint, and an unlikely comeback for the home side. On the one hand it would have been disappointing for the visiting fans not to have left with all three points. Yet such was the quality of the first two QPR goals, it pretty much made the result an irrelevance. Had Rangers comfortably won that afternoon with a couple of goals of the 'bread and butter' variety, few fans would even remember it. But instead, no-one has ever forgotten Ainsworth's astonishing efforts that afternoon. Any nomination for the best ever Queens Park Rangers goal would have to include his first goal of the afternoon. And if you drew up a list of the twenty best R's goals of all time, the other would have little trouble finding its way on to that illustrious list, either. It is without question, the finest 'brace' scored by Rangers player. And just for the record, Ian Holloway's side still won automatic promotion come the end of the season.

Ainsworth would go on to enjoy a long and happy seven-year association with Queens Park Rangers, making 141 appearances and scoring a very respectable 36 goals. Yet in terms of quality, none of the other 34 goals came close to those scored on that memorable afternoon in August 2003. But as Gareth Ainsworth said at the time, it was "the best goal I ever scored, followed by the second-best goal I ever scored". The years that followed were not so kind to Rushden & Diamonds. They were relegated at the same time QPR got promoted. A year later, they dropped out of the Football League. The sale of Rushden to a Supporters' Trust failed to work out, and by 2011, the club effectively went out of business. Queens Park Rangers made only that one visit to Nene Park, but few people who attend that game will ever forget the events of that afternoon. Least of all, Ainsworth, himself.

Queens Park Rangers 1 Swindon Town 0
2003/04

The term 'Fortress Loftus Road' has a wonderful ring to it. Close your eyes and you could almost conjure up images of a packed ground with fans almost on top of the players. Noisy home support backing the R's, making our home such a difficult place for opposing teams to visit and get anything resembling a positive result. That all sounds very nice, though the reality is usually something very different. But every once in a while, that term does ring true. Ironically, one of the few times that happened, was under the ill-fated leadership of Mark Hughes. During an otherwise appalling period under the Welshman, QPR put together a great run of home wins which kept the club in the Premiership in the 2011/12 season. A run of consecutive games Hughes may well have got carried away with, when he made brash claims about no further relegation battles as long as he was in charge at Queens Park Rangers. But for a longer and more significant run in which Loftus Road was a place where away teams dreaded visiting, let us go back a further eight years.

Between 2001 and 2004, Rangers had three successive seasons in what was then, the Second Division. It was a noticeable feature that during that time, Ian Holloway strengthened the squad, with each transfer he made. Among them were new skipper Steve Palmer, Kevin Gallen (returning for a second spell), Marc Bircham, Paul Furlong, Gareth Ainsworth and Martin Rowlands. With the arrival of each of them, QPR were able to rebuild and grow stronger, following a largely miserable period between 1995-2001. This was reflected especially when it came to results at home. In the 2001/02 season, Holloway's side lost just two home league matches. The following season, it was four home defeats. Admittedly, there were a few bad days at the office. Rangers managed to lose three consecutive home league matches during the 02/03 season-all off the back of the humiliating FA Cup defeat to Vauxhall Motors. And coming to Loftus Road held no fear for either Tranmere Rovers or Northampton Town, who both enjoyed successive wins in West London. But on the whole, it was becoming a tougher place for visiting teams to get anything.

A few years earlier, Queens Park Rangers had gotten used to the likes of Arsenal, Liverpool, Chelsea and Manchester United turning up for home matches. This inevitably meant capacity crowds and no shortage of away supporters finding their way into the home sections of the ground. One of the few good things about falling into the third tier of English football was that all of a sudden, Rangers were now one of the 'big teams'. From packed away ends just six years earlier, the number of visiting supporters would now on some occasions, struggle to nudge three figures. For all of the previous financial hardships and new-found lowly status, it was also a period when the home support made their presence felt, in a way that has rarely happened before or since in the modern era of the club.

By the time the 2003/04 season got underway, that was starting to benefit QPR on a regular basis. From the moment Holloway's side thrashed Blackpool 5-0, they never looked back when it came to results at Loftus Road. They won the first three league matches at home, scoring nine times, with none in reply. When Wycombe Wanderers held Rangers to a goalless draw in the following home game, it was the only time all season when we would not score in a match hosted in West London throughout the entire campaign. By the time everyone was celebrating the New Year on 1 January 2004, Queens Park Rangers had only conceded three goals at home in the league. Even champions-elect Plymouth Argyle were well beaten 3-0. All of a sudden, the term 'Fortress Loftus Road' did not feel out of place. On the rare occasions that Rangers enjoy run of positive results like this, it is usually accompanied by a certain level of pressure that comes with keeping it going. But as it happened, Rangers were saving their poorer results and performances for away matches, where they were nowhere near as dominant. If anything, the long unbeaten run at Loftus Road seemed to inspire them to just keep up this remarkable sequence of results throughout the campaign.

By 1 May, as QPR were about to host their final Loftus Road fixture of the season, they had at this point remained unbeaten. Not surprisingly, this meant that they were very much in with a chance of promotion. If they could win their last two matches, they were guaranteed automatic promotion. If not, it was a second successive year in the Play-Offs. After the disappointment against Cardiff City some 12 months earlier, fans much preferred the idea of the not going through that, for a second successive year. The last home league game of the 03/04 campaign, saw Swindon Town come to Loftus Road. The Robins incidentally, were managed by Andy King who 23 years earlier, became the first Queens Park Rangers player to score on the Astroturf pitch. In an ideal world, Rangers would have faced a team who were in around 17th or 18th place. By definition, a side who were not in danger of getting relegated but at the same time, had nothing left to play for. The Robins were however, not what you would call a 'gimme'. They had Play-Off aspirations of their own. But having already clocked up 22 matches without losing at home, this side were by now, used to making Loftus Road such a tough place for visiting team to get.

Before the game started in front of 18,396 fans, Ian Holloway came out onto the pitch with a microphone to give a rousing speech. As a personality, there were always some supporters who could not warm to him, and they certainly made their voices heard during Holloway's second spell in charge. But whatever you might have thought of him as a person, you could never doubt his passion and enthusiasm. And a scenario like the one Queens Park Rangers were in at the end of the 2003/04 campaign, was definitely bringing out the best in him. His team made the perfect start after ten minutes.

A throw-in from Steve Palmer found Kevin Gallen and for one moment, looked like he would have been trapped by the corner flag, as he had two Swindon players surrounding him. But Gallen cleverly saw off the attention of both opponents and got in an excellent cross, which was met by the head of Paul Furlong. His nod down went nicely into the path of Martin Rowlands, and he couldn't miss from just six yards out. In a season in which Rangers scored a number of spectacular goals in an overall tally of 80 in the league, this was far from being one of the best. Certainly, Rowlands alone, had scored some better ones. But this was one of the most important. And it was interesting to note that all four players involved were bought to the club (or back to West London in the case of Kevin Gallen) during Ian Holloway's time as manager.

Following that goal, Rangers enjoyed the best of the remaining chances in the game. Also, in the first half, Gallen turned superbly in the Swindon penalty area, but his shot was well saved to prevent QPR from doubling their lead. In the second period, Rowlands very nearly headed in his second goal of the afternoon. But the Robins somehow managed to execute a goalmouth scramble to keep the score at 1-0. Following the final whistle and with three sides of the ground still comparatively full, Holloway took the microphone once more, to whip up excitement among supporters for the following weekend's deciding game at Hillsborough. When Bristol City beat Barnsley just 24 hours later, it was confirmation of just how important this win over Swindon Town was. It meant that Queens Park Rangers could still decide their own fate.

To see just how dominant Rangers were at Loftus Road during the 2003/04 season, let's take a look at the statistical breakdown of the 23 home league fixtures. QPR won sixteen of them and drew seven, which of course meant that they lost none. 47 league goals were scored, whilst only twelve were conceded. With figures like that, the term 'Fortress Loftus Road' certainly carried some credence. The achievements of the 03/04 side meant that they emulated two of the most celebrated sides in the history of Queens Park Rangers. With Kevin Gallen(17 league goals), Paul Furlong(16), Martin Rowlands(10) and Tony Thorpe(10) all getting into double figures, it was the first time a Rangers side had managed this feat since the 1966/67 season. In case you were wondering, on the previous occasion, the quartet was Rodney Marsh(30), Les Allen(16), Mark Lazarus(16) and Roger Morgan(11). Ian Holloway's men also emulated the 1975/76 team, by going the entire season at home, unbeaten. You know a QPR team have done something pretty special when it matches the achievements of both of those great teams.

By comparison, the away form that year, was somewhat indifferent. Only six wins were picked up on the road. Not an embarrassing total, but not a particularly high number, for a team that won automatic promotion, with 83 points. At the time, that was just two points shy of the club record, set by the 82/83 side, under Terry Venables. Therefore, it is interesting that the one match fans remember most from that campaign is the 3-1 win at Sheffield Wednesday on the final day of the season. Understandable, given what that victory meant. But looking at the 2003/04 season as a whole, although promotion was sealed in South Yorkshire, that feat was undoubtedly managed thanks to results at Loftus Road, over a very enjoyable nine-month period.

38 *The Hand of Bean*
Gillingham 0 Queens Park Rangers 1
2004/05

In the pre-VAR days, handballs were a curious thing where footballers were concerned. Some individuals were never allowed to forget their moments of shame. For example, Thierry Henry will never win any popularity contests in Ireland, as a result of his handball on the way to setting up William Gallas to score in a World Cup qualifier that sent France to the 2010 tournament, and meant that the Irish would miss out. And decades on, Diego Maradona has still never been forgiven by many from these shores, for that 'Hand of God' incident, at the 1986 tournament. Closer to home, fans do not tend to dwell on those moments involving Queens Park Rangers players. But there have been a few of them.

Devon White's handball against Everton during the same match in which Les Ferdinand scored the last goal in front of the Loft, has already been discussed. In a 2-0 win over Coventry City in 1993 when Andy Pearce gifted Rangers perhaps the most ridiculous own goal, pre-Jamie Pollock, defender Darren Peacock was guilty of controlling the ball with his hand on his way to scoring from close range. In an otherwise undistinguished first loan spell at QPR, Paul Furlong charged down a back pass in a home match against Crewe Alexandra in August 2000, which resulted in the goalkeeper's attempted clearance hitting the striker's fist before bobbling into the net. And more recently, Nahki Wells final goal during his second spell in West London, saw the ball hit both his arm and hand on the way to his winning effort against Leeds United in January 2020. But when it comes to notorious handballs from Rangers players, Marcus Bean stands head and shoulders, and perhaps we should say hands, above all others.

QPR visited Gillingham's Priestfield Stadium in August 2004. Following promotion, the previous May, this was Rangers fifth Championship match of the season, and they had failed to win any of the previous four. Although Ian Holloway would have been desperate for the first 'three pointer' of the campaign, it is doubtful he would ever have imagined that it would come in such a controversial manner. Rangers had much of the early play, and Lee Cook came close when his shot hit the outside of the post, following his run into the penalty area from the left flank. Then on the half hour, an attack that took unusually took in crosses from both wings, firstly from Kevin Gallen on the left and then Martin Rowlands on the right, saw the latter drive a low ball into the six-yard box. With that, the Queens Park Rangers midfielder Marcus Bean attempted a back flick that was not quite executed well enough, and he fell over in the process. Yet somehow, Gills keeper Steve Banks wasn't able to get hold of the ball, and this gave Bean the chance to bundle the ball home. Despite being on the ground at that very moment, he still gave QPR the lead.

The Gillingham players were not happy and in particular, Andy Hessenthaler was absolutely livid. Gillingham's player-manager made a point of chasing referee Mike Thorpe halfway up to pitch, protesting that the ball had gone in off of Bean's hand. Did he have a point? Absolutely. With the game being televised, we had the luxury of seeing this goal from another couple of camera angles. One of which proved that Marcus Bean didn't just handle the ball as he scored, he punched it into the back of the net. Almost as noteworthy, was the reaction of the youngster. When Diego Maradona scored with his hand in the 1986 World Cup quarter final, he immediately looked around at the linesman to see if he got away with the indiscretion, which he did. Bean was having none of that. He immediately ran up the pitch before stopping to raise his arms in the air, and except the congratulations of his teammates. If he felt any guilt about the goal, he certainly did not show it. Indeed, perhaps the lack of any doubt on his own part, may well have helped make up the mind of the match officials, regardless of the protests and the scrappy nature in which the attack was finished.

In the second half, the home side dominated the proceedings, and had a string of chances but were unable to convert any of them. In the aftermath of the game, naturally the Gills felt a little bit hard done by, even though they wasted their own opportunities to get back into the game. And fans who travelled to Kent to cheer on Queens Park Rangers, would probably have pointed out that the visitors were not awarded a penalty in the same match, leading some of those in attendance to claim this was a wonderful example of 'winning ugly'.

Hammersmith-born Marcus Bean joined QPR at a very young age, before making his debut in the 2002/03 season. He would spend the next four seasons at Loftus Road making 67 appearances and scoring twice. Yet he never seemed to be regarded as an automatic starter over a sustained period during that time. Which was a shame given that upon his departure, it would take many more years before the youth system would produce players that would regularly play for the first team. Bean managed some 440 league appearances for seven different clubs in a 17-year career. Which suggests that his talents were appreciated more, elsewhere.

Rightly or wrongly, that handball is one of the things supporters will remember most about Marcus Bean's time as a Queens Park Rangers player. As with the other examples mentioned at the start, these moments that evaded the attention of the referee and his linesmen, are all controversial and let's be honest, would have left our own supporters fuming had the roles being reversed. Though for the record, every one of them was instrumental in QPR winning each of the five matches they happened in. But it is with good reason that the goals from Peacock, White, Furlong, Wells and Bean aren't remembered with too much fondness. After all, they were simply moments of good fortune that Rangers were very lucky to get away with.

39 *The Petrified Forest*
Queens Park Rangers 2 Nottingham Forest 1
2004/05

There was an unusual sub-genre of matches in which QPR did not enjoy a great deal of success up to May 2005. When facing a team that were fighting to stay in the same league as Rangers, you could hardly say that there was a thoroughly ruthless streak on show from the men in blue and white hoops. At the end of the 1986/87 season, Charlton Athletic went a long way towards maintaining their top-flight status, thanks to a 2-1 home win over Jim Smith's Queens Park Rangers side. With nothing to play for at the end of the 96/97 campaign, the R's visited Bradford City who needed a victory to ensure that they would remain in the second tier of English football. The Bantams easily won 3-0 and the only thing that the travelling fans from London will probably recall that afternoon was the pitch invasion from the home fans as they ran towards the away end and applauded the Rangers support. The memorable 2-2 draw at Maine Road in 1998, did at least go the way of Ray Harford's beleaguered QPR side. It pretty much guaranteed their status in the same division for the following year. But both of the goals that came our way, were as a result of Manchester City errors. And as history has proved, those howlers along with that result simply glossed over the fact that Rangers had plenty of their own problems that would soon need to be dealt with. City sent themselves down, rather than Queens Park Rangers dealing the final blow.

When Rangers hosted Nottingham Forest for the final home match of the 2004/05 season, we had another opportunity to deal a fatal blow to a wounded opponent. Only unlike the aforementioned games, this one would be on home turf. It was also the chance for a little bit of payback-and not because of our abysmal record over the years at the City Ground, either. In January 2005, an FA Cup Third Round tie saw Forest belie their lowly league status and easily beat QPR 3-0. One of the goals came from 40 yards out when Kris Commons chipped the ball over keeper Chris Day. Not for the first or last time, there is nothing like an FA Cup tie against Queens Park Rangers to bring out the best in an opposing team. But that was then, and today there was a very different scenario which did not require a calculator. Beat Nottingham Forest, and they would go down to the third level of English football.

Rangers made an excellent start to the game, and Wes Morgan had to clear a ball off the line from Paul Furlong in the early stages of the match. Lee Cook nearly scored with a shot from 25 yards. But on this occasion, his shot went just wide of the right-hand post. With Forest surviving the early exchanges, they might have thought that luck would be on their side on this sunny May afternoon in West London, and take their relegation battle to the final day of the season. But before the first half came to a conclusion, midfielder Darryl Powell pressed the self-destruct button.

On 31 minutes, Powell was sent off for a second bookable offence, when he went for an aerial challenge with his arm raised high, which immediately left Martin Rowlands lying on the floor in a heap. This after he was earlier booked for a foul on Paul Furlong. After almost 400 league appearances, and a further 21 for the Jamaican national team, his final match as a professional would see him getting sent off in a game in which his team would get relegated. A minute before half-time, an in swinging free-kick from Cook was headed into his own net, by John Curtis. This was by the way, the same John Curtis who would join Rangers two years later, playing just four matches before having his contract terminated. To this day, Curtis still regarded as one of the poorest QPR players of the 21st century. Following Powell's dismissal and that moment of misery for John Curtis, the travelling support must have known that it was not going to be their day, off the back of those incidents.

On the hour, a QPR corner was cleared off the line, before finding its way to the left side of the penalty area. Some neat interchanging of passes between Tony Thorpe, Kevin Gallen and Marc Bircham, eventually saw the latter have a shot from a very tight angle. Despite the level of difficulty, Bircham expertly curled the ball into the top corner of the net. It looked like the game was over for Forest. Upon going 2-0 ahead, some of the Rangers fans taunted the visitors with the chant *'Going down, going down, going down...'.* The visiting supporters decided that if there was one area in which they could come out on top, it would be in terms of the noise from the stands. In 2005, veteran English singer Tony Christie enjoyed a new lease of life, when his song (Is This the Way To) Amarillo, reached number one in the UK Singles Chart. To the same tune, Nottingham Forest fans started singing *'la la la la la la la la la, la la la la la la la la, la la la la la la la la'*, *Forest score a goal for me'!* This chant went on and on. And when they weren't not singing that, they were in full voice belting out *'We're going to win the LDV'*. Gallows humour at its finest.

On 77 minutes, Ukrainian-born German player Eugen Bopp obliged the away fans, with a smart finish from just inside the Queens Park Rangers penalty area. A few minutes later, Gareth Taylor, who previously had a rather forgettable loan spell at Loftus Road in 2000, headed over the bar for Nottingham Forest. With that, their chance was gone, Ian Holloway's side had done just enough. QPR had put the final nails in the coffin for Gary Megson's side.

Inevitably, a team gets relegated as a result of not being good enough over a 46-match programme, and not what happens in a single afternoon. But it was nonetheless, odd to see Queens Park Rangers condemn Forest to the drop. Despite some mocking from R's fans that afternoon, Nottingham Forest were not necessarily one of those teams whose demise would have been celebrated, in London W12. Had for example Norwich City been on the wrong end of this loss, QPR supporters, especially those with long memories, would have seen it as payback for that infamous defeat at Carrow Road in 1976. Likewise, had Brentford or Fulham suffered a similar fate, there would have been little sympathy from Loftus Road regulars. Instead, it was something of an oddity, rather than a day of celebration, when Nottingham Forest slipped down to the third tier, for the first time in their history.

Four years earlier, Queens Park Rangers had gone through the same experience, when getting relegated to that level. Still reasonably fresh in the memory, our own supporters would have known exactly how they were feeling. They would have felt the same way we did, at the end of the 2000/01 season. Although there was also a bit of unwanted history for Forest. It was the first time that a team that had won a European club title, dropped to the third level of their own domestic league. And it was Rangers who were responsible for sealing their fate. A far cry from being double European Cup winners. For all our own failings in the past, QPR supporters could at least console themselves with the fact that Nottingham Forest had much further to fall, than we ever did in the early part of the century.

40 *One Size, Two Goals, No Hat trick*
Queens Park Rangers 2 Barnsley 1
2008/09

A few of the chapters here have looked at club records set by various Queens Park Rangers players and teams, over the years. There are though, some landmarks that have yet to be achieved. For example, no QPR defender can lay claim to scoring a hat trick. Though one such individual did come within a whisker of managing this very rare feat. Yet the fact that he even had the opportunity to do so, looked like it was the result of a team behaving like they were going to lay waste to the majority of sides that they would face in the Championship. But before we come to that, let us take a look at the years that preceded the start of the 2008/09 season.

Financially speaking, it was a pretty miserable time in the history of QPR. Obviously, there was the period when most of the squad headed for the exit, following administration and relegation, in 2001. Fans had to wave buckets outside the ground before home games, in order to help the club to keep going. And with the club treading water rather than completely leaving their money problems behind, there was the ever-present danger that Queens Park Rangers could return to administration. Only this time, because of a change of rules a few years prior, that would now mean points being deducted. But in the 2007/08 season, all that changed.

Motor racing magnates Flavio Briatore and Bernie Ecclestone, along with one of Britain's richest men Lakshmi Mittal, joined the board of directors at Loftus Road. All of a sudden, from years of penny-pinching, the club was now being financed by some high-profile billionaires. Sure enough, there would be major changes among the playing personnel, as well as in the dugout. QPR got their first overseas manager, in the form of Luigi De Canio. What the Italian may have lacked with his limited grasp of English, he more than made up for with his charm, humour, and an improvement in the team's fortune. Both results and the quality of football improved drastically following a poor start to the league campaign, helped in no small part to the new faces that arrived on his watch. Much to the disappointment of so many fans, De Canio left Rangers by 'mutual consent' in May 2008, to return to his homeland.

But with the new owners in place, and Iain Dowie succeeding the popular Italian, hopes were high for the new season. The opening day fixture saw Barnsley visit Loftus Road. If confidence was sky high among the home support, it may well have been mirrored by the players. Perhaps as we would soon see, there might have been too much confidence among the first team squad. Just five minutes into the match, Ian Hume put the visitors ahead. A disappointing start, but not a complete disaster. There was still plenty of time to come back into the game, and inevitably, even the best Queens Park Rangers sides will have to deal with a few tests of character like the one they now found themselves in. As it happened, they responded in fine style, and it was all thanks to the man with one of English football's more imaginative nicknames.

Fitz Hall was one of many new signings made during the 2008 January Transfer Window, when he joined from Wigan Athletic. At six foot four inches tall, Hall who was known to fans all over the country as 'one-size' was an imposing central defender, who was by now with his seventh different league club. From an Emmanuel Ledesma free kick, Fitz Hall nodded home after the keeper was unable to gather the ball. A goal from one of the central defenders who went forward for a set-piece, is the type that you would expect a few times a season, so there was nothing that unusual about QPR's equaliser. The same could not be said about Rangers second goal, just two minutes later. Another corner saw Barnsley only clear the ball as far as Hall and with an acrobatic volley, he found the corner of the net from 15 yards out, that flew across a crowded penalty area. One of the club's best goals of the season and not the sort of thing that you see that often from a Queens Park Rangers centre back.

In the second half, Barnsley's Darren Moore brought Dexter Blackstock down and referee Neil Swarbrick pointed to the penalty spot. From going a goal behind after just five minutes, the R's now had the chance to pretty much seal the victory. To the great surprise of almost everyone inside the ground, Fitz Hall stepped forward to take the penalty himself. This wasn't according to any pre-match plan. As a result, the stakes just got a whole lot higher. Find the back of the net, and he would have made a wonderful bit of history, that would still be talked about to this day. Fail, and he and his teammates would be made to look pretty foolish.

The resulting penalty saw Fitz Hall go for placement rather than power and Tykes keeper Lee Steele had little problem saving it. With Barnsley's Marciano van Homoet's red card being the only significant moment thereafter, Queens Park Rangers won their opening match of the 2008/09 season. Courtesy of an unlikely matchwinner, who sealed all three points with a spectacular goal. Yet, he blotted his copybook somewhat, with that poorly taken penalty. There is a reason that the likes of Alan McDonald, Danny Shittu and Richard Dunne did not take corners, and it wasn't just because we were hoping that they would be on the other end of those set-pieces. That reason is because there is inevitably someone else in the team better suited to that particular role. It always felt like the same philosophy applied to that penalty kick. Though surprisingly, manager Iain Dowie had a different point of view.

On the official 2008/09 DVD, Iain Dowie claimed Fitz Hall was the designated penalty taker all along, despite most people thinking that it was Blackstock. After all, the striker scored with one towards the end of the 2007/08 season, in a 3-3 draw at Wolverhampton Wanderers. Successful penalty takers who willingly give up that role are about as rare a breed as, well, defenders who score hat tricks. Dowie also said that he would be happy for Hall to take the next one-which was an even bigger surprise than the theory that the giant defender was on spot kick duties, in the first place. Given that 'One Size' never did take any further penalties during his time as a Queens Park Rangers player, we can be pretty certain that Dowie was having us on, all along. And that being the case, let us look at the thinking behind that incident.

The match was still in the balance and by failing to convert the spot kick, Rangers still only led by a single goal. There was a chance that Barnsley could come back into the game, off the back of that saved penalty. And had that happened, it would have been red faces all round. That is not to say that under a couple of different scenarios, giving Fitz Hall the responsibility might have been a good idea. If Iain Dowie's team were giving Barnsley a hiding, and had for example, been 5-1 ahead, then no-one would have begrudged the central defender the opportunity to take home the match ball. After all, had he missed from that point in the game, it would have made no significance difference to the outcome. Likewise, if it was the 46th league match of the season, and nothing was at stake, then supporters could at least have seen the logic behind the chance to see a bit of history.

But the fact is that it was the first and not the last league match of a pivotal campaign, that was supposed to herald a bright new future for Queens Park Rangers. Instead, it was something of a strange season, with a few anomalies along the way. Dowie was sacked after just 15 games in charge. Yet he can by a strange twist of fate, claim to have the highest winning ratio of any manager in the history of QPR (with 53.3%) with eight wins during that time. Clearly Flavio Briatore was no fan of such statistics. Without the aid of penalties, Hall was unable to add to his goal tally for the season, yet those two goals still made him the joint third highest league scorer in the 2008/09 campaign, with only Dexter Blackstock and Heidar Helgusson scoring more than him. Although Rangers finished the campaign in a respectable eleventh place, with just 42 league strikes, it was one of the few occasions that they managed less than a goal-per-game, over the course of a league season. All of which was a far cry from when Rangers played host to Barnsley, on the opening day of the campaign.

To be fair to Hall, it was a great shame that he never scored with that penalty. It would have been a most impressive feat that would have ensured his place in the history of Queens Park Rangers. And it would have made this chapter of the book, look very different. But it does beg the question 'Should he have been allowed to take it in the first place'? Well, let us imagine we found ourselves with a similar scenario in the next home game in Shepherd's Bush. QPR find themselves 2-1 ahead and one of the central defenders has a brace to his name when a penalty award gives him and his teammates the chance to double their lead. Now let us ask ourselves once more who should take it; the designated taker or the defender who has already scored twice? I would have no hesitation in saying our regular spot kick expert. The well-being of the team should always come ahead of the individual. This was one of those scenarios that was so rare that it is doubtful we will ever see a repeat of it. But if we did, let's hope that a common sense approach would be taken to the situation. It certainly wasn't back in August 2008.

41 *Nineteen and Counting*
Queens Park Rangers 2 Cardiff City 1
2010/11

When Neil Warnock was appointed manager of Queens Park Rangers in February 2010, some supporters were somewhat sceptical. There were two reasons for this. Firstly, Warnock was the fourth different manager QPR had during that season. All of the chopping and changing that Flavio Briatore was responsible for, had become tiresome for the fans. Then there was Warnock himself. The much-travelled manager had previously overseen a number of promotions in a long career. But his personality was not to everyone's liking. His reputation for arguing with match officials, was as well founded, as his record at getting teams up to the top flight. He would have to win some supporters over. With Rangers in freefall when he joined, Neil Warnock comfortably managed to steer the team clear of a relegation battle towards the end of the 2009/10 season. He also seemed to enjoy a better relationship with Briatore than some of his predecessors, which meant that the club might finally have some much-needed stability. Both of which ensured that Queens Park Rangers were in a more settled position than it had been for the previous couple of years. Warnock used the time he had before the start of the new season most wisely, in terms of the playing personnel that was bought in.

The Yorkshireman had worked previously with Irish international goalkeeper Paddy Kenny, and in no time at all, he was racking up clean sheets for fun, totalling an astonishing 25 over the course of the Championship winning season. Shaun Derry and Clint Hill also arrived during the pre-season. Both had passed their 30th birthdays, and it is fair to say that neither of them caught the imagination of the QPR support at the time. But they immediately became key figures in the team, and both enjoy a level of popularity that remains strong to this day. Attacker Jamie Mackie was another signing that exceeded most expectations. He scored on his debut and would get eight goals in his first seven matches. Unfortunately, a serious injury would curtail his season. And even more important in ensuring this side would win the Championship, was Adel Taarabt.

The exciting Moroccan had previously had loan spells in the 2008/09 and 09/10 seasons, and had dazzled with a serious of memorable performances and goals. Neil Warnock decided not only would he bring Taarabt in on a permanent basis, he would also make him captain of the team. An almost unheard move for a player who was just 21 years old. It may well have been rare for a Queens Park Rangers manager to show so much faith in a single individual. But equally rare was the way in which Adel Taarabt would repay Warnock with interest. Nineteen league goals and the same number of assists, was an unprecedented return from these two key areas, from any QPR player in the last few decades.

When the season got underway, a series of draws and mostly wins, ensured a lengthy unbeaten start. Neil Warnock almost seemed like a different character, too. In post-match interviews, he was beaming and claiming he joked with the assistant referees and the fourth officials, that he was enjoying his time as manager more than ever and finding the football more entertaining than any period in his long managerial career. Was this really the same man who was notorious in the game for a long list of arguments with match officials, and who was once responsible for a dressing room rant, in which the language was even more blue than the one that finished the football career of former Leyton Orient manager John Sitton? It certainly seemed that way.

As Rangers went from strength to strength, even Warnock's 'shorts' became a talking point. He wore them at the start of the season, which began in glorious sunshine, and decided to keep wearing them as long as the team were unbeaten. But if the shorts were a suitable choice of attire in August, they became less so, as QPR remained unbeaten as autumn was drawing to a close. Neil Warnock admitted that his wife thought he was 'bonkers' but also that he hoped that "the lads will keep me shivering all winter". Many supporters will have their own regular matchday routine, especially if it is deemed as being lucky. Whether that is taking the same route to the game, drinking in a particular pub, or like Warnock, wearing a certain item of clothing (although shorts in cold weather, would rarely fall into this category). Whatever you might have thought of the Yorkshireman, you could never accuse him of a lack of enthusiasm or failing to get into the spirit of what was happening in this most exceptional of seasons.

By the time Cardiff City visited Loftus Road on 27th November, Rangers were still unbeaten as they were about to play their 19th league game of the season. This would be one of the most anticipated fixtures of the season, as Cardiff were in second place behind QPR at the time, and a win would take them to the top of the table. The away side took the lead when a slip from defender Kaspars Gorkss, gave City the chance of a quick attack. They took advantage of this unexpected gift and seconds later, Craig Bellamy scored from close range. The big Latvian responded in the best possible manner when just five minutes later, he headed home a left-footed cross from Tommie Smith. Both sides had found the back of the net within the first 20 minutes of the game and many people would have thought that it would be a high-scoring affair.

As it happened, there was only one more goal and what a goal it was. Cardiff City seemed to clear a Rangers corner well enough, but a ball upfield was headed on to Adel Taarabt, and he would produce a bit of magic. He flicked the ball past one defender, before driving his way into the penalty area. He then executed a couple of stepovers to take the ball past another Cardiff player, which gave him a shooting chance which was despatched into the top left-hand corner of the net. An example of how Taarabt's goals and assists weren't just plentiful during the 2010/11 season, they were also very important. Although it was an outstanding goal, it didn't even come close to being his best of the campaign. Truth be told, goals of the highest quality were almost becoming routine for our talented young captain. That was the end of the scoring although in stark contrast to what you would normally expect, City manager Dave Jones was fuming that the referee Kevin Friend did not award that his team a late penalty when he claimed that future R's forward Jay Bothroyd was brought down by Matthew Connolly. Neil Warnock meanwhile, said that he thought Friend had done an excellent job refereeing the game and had got that penalty decision right. This was certainly a season that threw up more surprises than usual.

Eventually, all good things come to an end and in the very next match at home to Watford, Rangers long unbeaten run came to a rather limp conclusion as the Hornets easily won 3-1 at Loftus Road. Typically, it was a loss that was covered live by the SKY TV cameras. It was of course disappointing that the run was over, but let's put that into some perspective. That home defeat was our 20th league match of the season. We were almost into December and thoughts had turned to Christmas, before QPR were even beaten. And it was all overseen by a manager many fans had their doubts about, just months earlier. Another benefit of this remarkable unbeaten run was that Queens Park Rangers had built the foundation that would ensure the Championship would be won in the following spring. Although Warnock was probably as disappointed at anyone that the nineteen match unbeaten run came to an end, he could at least console himself with the fact that he would not be as cold standing on the touchline at future matches as the shorts could go back in the wardrobe, until the next warm spell of weather.

42 *The International Brigade*
Queens Park Rangers 1 Southampton 3
2012/13

Some club records come about as a result of a long-run of unbeaten matches, or a particular achievement on the part of a certain Rangers player. Whilst others happen somewhat by accident and in the most unexpected of circumstances. When QPR played host to the Saints during the 2012/13 season, the record in question definitely fell into the latter of the two categories.

Both sides came into this match needing a positive result. In the case of Queens Park Rangers, a win was by now desperately required. This was their 12th Premiership fixture of the season, and Mark Hughes side had yet to record a single victory in the league up to this point. All of which was a far cry from the Welshman's claim that *"the club would never face another relegation battle while he was in charge"* in the immediate aftermath of avoiding the drop at Manchester City's Etihad Stadium, in May 2012. Hughes did not lack self-confidence as a manager but as one bad result followed another, each important decision he made was not standing up to scrutiny. The signings in the summer of 2012 were largely past their best, injured, or most unforgivably, looked like they didn't care about what was happening on the pitch. The disciplinary record was appalling as soon as Mark Hughes arrived at Loftus Road, and never got any better. For the home game against Southampton, attention would turn to his team selection. The starting eleven that afternoon was as follows:

Julio Cesar; Jose Boswinga, Anton Ferdinand, Ryan Nelson, Armand Traore; Samba Diakite, Alejandro Faurlin, Esteban Gennero, Adel Taarabt, Junior Hoilett; Djibril Cisse.

QPR supporters were well used to seeing other Premiership teams play with line-ups consisting entirely (or pretty much near to) of foreigners. But it was still a surprise to see that happen when it came to those who wore the blue and white hoops. Among this side that started this key game, only Ferdinand was either English or British. With Rangers hosting fellow strugglers in the form of Southampton, fans hoped that this side, regardless of the fact that it was populated by a record number of foreign players, would finally get that much needed win. Instead what followed was a horror show. Ricky Lambert scored for the visitors after 23 minutes, before Jason Puncheon added a second just before half-time. Despite the fact that the team were second best all afternoon, Junior Hoilett pulled a goal back early in the second half. But a miserable afternoon for the home fans was complete when the sole Englishman in the starting XI-Anton Ferdinand-turned the ball into his own net for the Saints third goal of the afternoon.

A look at the subs bench told its own interesting tale, about what a mess the club was in that afternoon. Among those on standby were Rob Green. The England keeper was bought in by Hughes, yet quickly jettisoned when Cesar arrived just weeks later. Two of the biggest cheers of the afternoon were for the appearance of Shaun Derry and Jamie Mackie from the bench. Both players were instrumental in the Championship win in 2011 and helping the club avoid relegation a year later. Yet, their battling qualities were overlooked in favour of players who encapsulated the type of qualities that were fast turning the club into a national laughing stock. Manchester United loanee Fabio replaced Jose Boswinga, who was one of the worst performers on the day. At the time it seemed like a bad afternoon for the Portuguese full-back, whereas the truth was we were nowhere near scrapping the bottom of the barrel with that man. And if Mark Hughes was looking for inspiration elsewhere from his substitute bench, it is doubtful he saw any when he turned his head towards Keiron Dyer and Shaun Wright-Phillips warming the dugout. Days later, Hughes was sacked as manager of Queens Park Rangers.

His final game in charge was a strange one, not least for the fact that it went down as the match in which QPR selected the most foreign players in the history of the club. Of the starting XI, Mark Hughes signed seven of them, so must take most of the responsibility for the way his side failed in such a spectacular manner. You will have already seen the line-up on that fateful afternoon against Southampton, but if you looked at the clubs that they were signed from, that also makes for very surprising reading. The teams that this multi-national eleven came from included Inter Milan, Real Madrid, Chelsea, Lazio, Manchester United and Arsenal. At the time, it looked like most of the names that you would have found in a Champions League quarter finals draw. A former manager who enjoyed his fair share of success in the English game, once cannily observed "It is a bad idea to sign a player who is taking a stepdown to join you, as he will think that he will be doing you a favour". The manager in question would have not have been impressed to see so many players coming from some of the biggest sides in Europe, all in such a short space of time. And the results were all the proof needed to see that they never gelled as a unit.

Then there is the debate about whether that many overseas players should be in an English top flight team in the first place. There are two sides to this particular argument. If every team in the Premiership replicated what Hughes did in his final match as QPR manager, there would not be enough English footballers in 20 starting line-ups to fill up a World Cup squad. Which is a poor advertisement for the England team as a whole. But equally, a large percentage of our own fans would freely admit that they would favour the well-being of Queens Park Rangers over the national team, any day of the week. And besides, no Rangers player has represented England since Les Ferdinand did so in September 1994, during a friendly international against the United States of America. So, it's not like the fortunes of club and country have been intertwined any time recently. You could also argue that if such a multi-national line-up was improving the fortunes of the club, there would at least have been a valid reason for this starting line-up.

But rather than improve the team, the new players were leading Rangers into freefall. The Hughes signings brought little in the way of flair, even less in terms of valuable points. With the benefit of hindsight, some of the new players were responsible for much of the bad feeling with others who were already at the club, who saw lots of new teammates arrive on big wages, but doing little to justify those salaries. The reputation of Mark Hughes has never recovered around West London as a result of what happened in the 2012/13 season. Not just for the results, signings and poor league position he was responsible for, but also for the way he remained completely unapologetic about the mess he left behind. One thing we can all agree on is that during that fateful campaign, Hughes took the club in a direction that they had never been on previously. And given the monumental mess that was made, a direction we will do well never go down, ever again.

43 *Another Hitchcock Cameo Appearance*
Queens Park Rangers 1 Ipswich Town 0
2013/14

Anyone with a keen interest in classic old films will probably be aware of the fact that the person who made the most appearances in the films of legendary director Alfred Hitchcock, was Hitchcock himself. The man known as 'the Master of Suspense' memorably made almost 40 cameo appearances in his own pictures. Whilst Hitchcock cameos were famous in Hollywood, they didn't have any relevance to Queens Park Rangers. Or at least that was the case until 2013.

Rangers hosted Mick McCarthy's Ipswich side for what was the third league game of the 13/14 season. Harry Redknapp's team did create a number of chances, and could probably have felt a little bit hard done by not to be leading, as both Charlie Austin and Clint Hill struck the visitor's crossbar. But as the game went on and with the visitors seemingly happy to play for the point, it was beginning to feel like a goalless draw. With just seven minutes remaining, 20-year-old striker Tom Hitchcock came off the subs bench to make his debut for the club. His father Kevin incidentally, was a former Chelsea goalkeeper and by now, a coach at Loftus Road, himself. Hitchcock senior had been part of Mark Hughes coaching staff at Blackburn Rovers and Tom was also on the books at Ewood Park, although he failed to make an appearance for the first team, whilst he was still a teenager.

We can pretty much imagine that when the young striker came on late in that Ipswich game, he would have dreamed of scoring the winning goal and immediately become a hero to the QPR support. The odds of that happening on most occasions, are pretty slim. The lack of time on the pitch, his inexperience, and the fact that the visiting defence had already managed to hold Austin and friends at bay for over 80 minutes, were elements that would on most days, have gone against the new man. But on that afternoon back in 2013, the dream debut did actually happen for Hitchcock-and in the final minute, too. In a last-gasp attack, Shaun Wright-Phillips got a cross in from the left which found Charlie Austin. The big striker's pass across the penalty area was met by Tom Hitchcock who scored from just inside the six-yard box. In a matter of minutes, Hitchcock had gone from unknown, to Rangers matchwinner.

Under normal circumstances, the player in question could look forward to further appearances and supporters would have been keen to see how his career progressed. Only, neither of those things happened. He was promptly loaned out to Crewe Alexandra and then Shrewsbury Town, where he scored a total of eight goals in 17 appearances, including a hat trick for the Shrews against Gillingham. Meanwhile, Harry Redknapp set about making up for the shortfall of available strikers by raiding the loan market.

First up, was former Uruguayan international Javier Chevanton. The 33-year-old had enjoyed a long career with a succession of European clubs, Including Leece, Monaco and Seville. But his time in West London, consisted of a mere two appearances. Then prior to the closure of the January 2014 Transfer Window, no fewer than four forwards arrived at the club, in very quick succession. They were Kevin Doyle (Wolverhampton Wanderers), Will Keane (Manchester United), Modibo Maiga (West Ham United) and Dellatorre (Deportivo Brasil). Redknapp did not want for quantity when it came to forwards to choose from. As for the quality of those who turned up in W12? Well, that was another matter.

Queens Park Rangers were ever-present in the Play-Off places all season, though the arrival of the new frontmen did not really have any significant effect on the amount of times that the ball found its way into the opposing net. The good work in the latter part of the season was mainly down to the water-tight defence, the ever-reliable goal threat of Charlie Austin, and latterly, a fit-again Bobby Zamora was starting to make significant contributions with almost every appearance he was making. By the end of the 2013/14 campaign, none of the four loanees forwards were signed on a permanent basis. Nor was there any great desire on the part of the supporters for any of them to extend their time with QPR. Kevin Doyle started both the Play Off Semi Final and Final games against Wigan Athletic and Derby County. But the overall view was that he was a good signing about three years too late. Among the quintet, he was by far the best of the bunch. And in total, Harry Redknapp's five loan strikers played a combined number of 29 games between them, and collectively managed a mere three goals, in the 2013/14 season

During the home Play-Off Semi Final tie against Wigan

Athletic, an announcement came over the loudspeaker that Tom Hitchcock won the award for Queens Park Rangers Young Player of the Season. A few weeks later, he was released by the club. Given that Hitchcock would in time find himself dropping down to non-league football, Redknapp would probably have pointed to this as his justification for giving the young striker a free transfer. But when you look at the lack of goals and disappointing performances from the five loan strikers signed by the veteran manager, it would probably be wise for Harry Redknapp not to dwell on some on his selections from this period. So, history shows Hitchcock's QPR career lasted less than ten minutes, yet he can claim a last-minute winner in that sole outing. And it happened in a season that culminated in promotion. Maybe, just maybe, Tom Hitchcock had the perfect name for a footballer who made a memorable cameo appearance for Queens Park Rangers.

44 *Record Shutout*
Queens Park Rangers 2 Barnsley 0
2013/14

The Ipswich Town match in which Tom Hitchcock scored the winner which was featured in the previous chapter, was the start of a run that saw a club record, few fans were aware of. In the previous game, Rangers drew 1-1 at Huddersfield Town, with the Terriers striker James Vaughan scoring for the home side. Little did we know that he would be the last opposing player to trouble our goal for a very long while. Rangers followed up that draw with the aforementioned 1-0 win over Ipswich. After that came back-to-back 1-0 wins away to Bolton Wanderers and Leeds United. We then saw our fourth successive 1-0 win, with a home win over Birmingham City. By now, supporters were beginning to notice that the team were not only building up a nice winning run (QPR won as many matches in the league in the month of August 2013, as they had in the entire 2012/13 Premiership programme), there was also a most satisfying run on clean sheets. It got many thinking what is the highest number of consecutive League matches Queens Park Rangers played without conceding a goal?

As it happens, two great keepers from the past shared this somewhat obscure record. Legendary post-war goalie Reg Allen managed seven successive shutouts in the 1946/47 league season. And almost forgotten among the achievements of the 1966/67 side, Peter Springett also kept seven successive clean sheets as Rangers stormed towards the league title. To overhaul what both Allen and Springett had managed, would take a monumental effort of the part of the 13/14 team. But because fans only really began to take note of the record after that win over Birmingham City, we were already halfway there. Next up, Brighton & Hove Albion were the visitors. This match finished goalless and on any other day, would have been regarded as a tame and forgettable affair. But on this occasion Harry Redknapp's team were now up to five clean sheets. It was about now that many fans were beginning to talk about this side making history. Next up was a trip to Yeovil Town. Yet another 1-0 win was racked up, and it was in this match that Rob Green pulled off a couple of great saves, that were instrumental in making sure that history would be made. It also equalled Phil Parkes best run of clean sheets, with that sixth successive shutout. The fixture list was kind to Queens Park Rangers, as two home matches would follow. Goals from Joey Barton and Charlie Austin gave QPR a 2-0 win over Middlesbrough. Their seventh league win of the season, but surprisingly, their first by more than a single goal. Green was now on level terms with Reg Allen and Peter Springett. The only question remained was whether he and his teammates could own the record outright?

Barnsley came to Loftus Road on a sunny October afternoon and as it happened, they were just the type of opposition we would have wanted for an afternoon like this. Bottom of the Championship, they posed little attacking threat all afternoon. With the score at 0-0 after 45 minutes, the record was within reach. Charlie Austin put the gloss on a productive day. Firstly, when he turned Junior Hoilett's cross into the net. Austin then converted a penalty for a second goal in the 87th minute, after he was brought down by Barnsley's Martin Cranie. Just a few minutes later, the final whistle was blown and this Rangers team had done something that no other had done, with a historic eighth successive clean sheets.

When you look at the Super hoops back four that faced Barnsley that afternoon, it was certainly made up of a motley crew. It was no surprise to see a character like Clint Hill there. A man who gave six years of outstanding service to the club, and always epitomised what was good about Queens Park Rangers. He was joined at the centre of defence by Richard Dunne. Signed on a free transfer from Aston Villa, he was injured at the start of that long run of matches in which QPR did not concede a goal. After just a couple of outings in the side, Dunne and Hill looked like they had played together for years.

At right-back was Danny Simpson. Signed from Newcastle United in the summer, Simpson was never a great attacking threat, in the way Dave Clement and David Bardsley so often were. But with regards to his defensive duties, he would be as reliable as any Rangers right-back of the 21st century. Despite this, Harry Redknapp would later offload Danny Simpson after just one year, because he did not think there was a future for him in a defence built around Rio Ferdinand for the 2013/14 season. The Ferdinand plan lasted just a handful of matches, and the former Manchester United and England defender was soon dropped and the team reverted to a more familiar 4-4-2 formation. Only by then, Simpson had left for Leicester City. He would go on to enjoy five years of

Premiership football with the Foxes and was their first choice right back when they sensationally won the Premiership in 2016. Getting rid of Danny Simpson represented one of the biggest transfer blunders by any Queens Park Rangers manager, in the history of the club. Meanwhile at left-back, was loanee Benoit Assou-Ekoto. The French-born Cameroon international was one of the most unusual and complex characters ever to turn out for QPR. A talented enough defender, he never shied away from expressing the view that he did not particularly like football and saw playing as nothing more than a well-paid job. On separate occasions that season, he got into blazing rows on the pitch with teammates Charlie Austin and Richard Dunne. At least with Joey Barton, we only had to worry about him fighting with the opposition. When Assou-Ekoto head-butted Cameroon teammate Benjamin Moukandjo at the 2014 World Cup, every supporter was relieved to see the back of this somewhat unstable individual.

And the man whose name was linked with this record even more than the four defenders in front of him, was goalkeeper Rob Green. A year earlier, he arrived at the club, with everyone expecting him to be first-choice keeper for the rest of the season. Yet within a matter of matches, Brazil's first choice stopper Julio Cesar became a Queens Park Rangers player to the surprise of everyone. Green was unceremoniously dumped, whilst many supporters were shocked to see Mark Hughes sign two high profile international goalkeepers within a matter of weeks. Under Hughes, Rob Green clearly had no future. But the Welsh manager's time with Rangers would not last long, and the former England keeper would get a second chance under Redknapp. In many ways, the run of eight consecutive clean sheets, represented redemption for a player who unfairly took much of the blame for the terrible start to the 2012/13 season. His treatment at the hands of Hughes, represented an appalling low point with regards to handling new signings.

The record run of shutouts holds a curious place in our modern history. On the one hand, the excellent start to the season helped ensure Rangers were ever present in the top six and the subsequent promotion happening. And cutting as many links as possible with the appalling 12/13 season, would have been most welcome. Yet despite the run of victories and clean sheets that were recorded, a large section of our support found the football being played, was devoid of memorable or entertaining matches. Not helped by the fact that Harry Redknapp was never universally popular. Also, the sight of Joey Barton back in the team after his disgraceful behaviour at the Etihad Stadium on the final day of the 2011/12 season, was another issue that divided our fans. Yet regardless of the fact that the team that got promoted in 2014 failed to capture the imagination of the overwhelming majority of supporters, they can always claim that they made history. All Queens Park Rangers club records (well, the good ones, at least) deserve due credit, and the eight successive clean sheets was no different.

45 *The Second Coming of Zamora*
Derby County 0 Queens Park Rangers 1
2013/14

There were two Bobby Zamora stories when it comes to his Queens Park Rangers career, and the second one happened slightly sooner than you might think. Zamora joined QPR at the end of January 2014, for a fee of around £4 million. He scored on his debut in a 2-1 home defeat to Wolverhampton Wanderers and got his second for the club four weeks later when QPR drew 1-1 against Everton. But they were his only goals for Rangers in 14 appearances in the 2011/12 season. There were already a couple of questions marks regarding his signing. He was 31 years old and had a long history of injury problems. The former England striker failed to find the back of the net in any of the five successive home wins that ensured Premiership survival. He was already beginning to look like a peripheral figure in the squad, within a couple of months of coming to Loftus Road.

In the summer of 2012, Mark Hughes also signed Bobby

Zamora's former Fulham teammate and strike partner, Andrew Johnson, which completed the trio of forwards the Welshman brought to West London, to go with Djibril Cisse, who arrived around the same time as Zamora. It looked like an accident waiting to happen. All three had long since blown out the candles on their 30th birthday cake, and like Bobby Zamora, Johnson and Cisse had previously suffered with numerous injury problems. Sure enough, in the first half of a thoroughly miserable season, the two former England internationals succumbed to further long-term injuries. Be under no illusion, this was not bad luck, it was bad management. The trio managed just seven Premiership goals between them (Zamora 4, Cisse 3) as Rangers recorded the worst league tally in their history, with a paltry 30 in the 2012/13 campaign. Upon his return to the team later in the season, Bobby Zamora got a needless red card for a dangerous challenge in a 1-1 home draw against Wigan, when the visitors equalised with a free-kick in the final minute. It seemed like his Rangers career was spiralling downwards at an alarming rate.

Though he was hardly on his own, in that respect. Being signed by Mark Hughes was beginning to resemble a 'badge of dishonour' for numerous individuals. Captain and recruiting figurehead for a new breed of overseas supporters, Park Ji-sung was a busted flush whose departure to former club PSV Eindhoven just 12 months into his two-year contract, must have been as much a relief for the South Korean international, as it was for the QPR support. Jose Boswinga took player conduct to an all-time low, putting in a series of lazy performances, refusing to sit on the bench, and finding it amusing that Rangers were relegated, moments after a goalless draw at Reading. Spaniard Esteban Granero and Cameroon international Stephane M'bia arrived with fine reputations, but were square pegs in a round hole, miserably failing to fit into English football. And the signing of Brazilian Julio Cesar, whose preparation for the 2014 World Cup would later involve being the third-choice goalkeeper at Loftus Road, meant that Zamora was not found wanting for candidates if he needed to look around for signings that had been as ineffective as his own.

With Rangers dropping down to the Championship, Bobby Zamora was back in the starting line-up as the new campaign got underway. But with no goals in the early part of the season, and a longstanding hip problem causing yet another injury, he would be out of action for a while as an operation was required. There was no getting away from the fact that Zamora had been a flop. He was injured for as long as he was available to play, and the goals were not exactly flying in, when his name was on the team sheet. In his absence during the 2013/14 season, Rangers were doing just fine without Bobby Zamora, as they never left the top six, meaning that the Play-Offs were very much in the thoughts of the entire fanbase. It was hard to see the experienced forward taking any part in what remained of the campaign. But Zamora had two strokes of luck. Firstly, the loan strikers that Harry Redknapp bought to the club in the January 2014, had made little impact, which meant that the door was now ajar, with regards to a possible return to the side. And upon Bobby Zamora's return to fitness, Redknapp spoke out in support of the forgotten forward, stating that he could still have a role in the final part of the season.

Sure enough, in a comfortable 3-0 win over Yeovil in March 2014, Zamora came off the bench to score his first goal for Queens Park Rangers in 13 months. A nice moment for the big striker, although Ravel Morrison took most of the headlines, as he recorded his second brace for QPR, in the space of a week. Seven days later, Bobby Zamora scored his second of the season at Middlesbrough, thanks to one of the all-time great blunders, ever gifted to

Rangers. Once again, he came off the bench, replacing the hapless Manchester United loanee Will Keane. With the score at 1-1, one of the Boro' defenders gave a routine back pass to keeper Dimi Konstantopoulos. Bobby Zamora ran towards the Greek keeper, fully expecting him to boot the ball back over his head. Only that never happened. Konstantopoulos took what is popularly known as a 'fresh-air shot' completely missing the ball. All of a sudden, Zamora found himself with no defender within 30 yards of him, which meant that he was actually able to 'walk the ball' into the net. For perhaps the only time in the history of Queens Park Rangers, someone looked embarrassed to score for us. By now, Bobby Zamora was beginning to make regular contributions to the team, and he had also started to earn the acceptance and respect of the QPR support. Especially when he was involved in the build-up of both goals in the Play-Off semi-final victory over Wigan Athletic.

On 24th May 2014, Queens Park Rangers faced Derby County in the final of the Championship Play-Off. It was 28 years since the club last visited Wembley Stadium. Even then, Wembley was a very different venue back in 1986. Most supporters have done their upmost to try and forget the Milk Cup Final defeat to Oxford United. At the very least, the huge support on the day hoped that whatever the outcome, we would at least be able to leave with our heads held high, rather than shaking them in disbelief which was the case last time round. With tens of thousands of blue and white flags placed on the seats occupied by QPR supporters, Rangers won the first battle of the afternoon, by bringing more colour to the occasion. But would that help inspire the team, once the game kicked off?

What little of the opportunities there were in the first half, went the way of Derby County, with the Rangers cause not being helped by the fact that they had to make a 33rd minute substitution, when Redknapp favourite Nico Kranjcar got injured and was replaced by Armand Traore. Which by definition meant that an attacking player was removed and a defensive one, took his place. Almost from the start, this game never looked like a classic, and it felt a bit like both sets of players on the pitch knew that tens of millions of pounds were riding on the outcome of this game. On the hour, 87,348 spectators witnessed what looked like the moment that would define this game. QPR's Gary O'Neil brought down Derby's Johnny Russell when he was through on goal. Everyone knew that the midfielder had somehow both saved Rangers yet at the same time, probably cost them the game. Sure enough, referee Lee Mason showed him the red card. For the next 30 minutes, Harry Redknapp's team had to withstand an onslaught, yet a number of players were rising to the occasion in fine style. In particular, Nedum Onuoha and Richard Dunne were immense at the heart of the back four, and on the rare occasions when they were beaten, Rob Green stopped whatever came his way.

By now, Bobby Zamora had replaced the ineffectual Kevin Doyle, just as he had done in the second leg of the Play-Offs. His knack of being able to hold the ball up to bring teammates into the game, made this the perfect scenario for Zamora, if only they were able to get possession to him in the first place. With the final whistle not far away, it looked like Rangers would somehow take the game into injury time, though the likelihood of holding out for a further 30 minutes with a man light in order to force a penalty shootout, was a big ask. Then with just moments of the 90 minutes remaining, Rangers got what was a rare sight of the Derby goal since O'Neil was dismissed. From a throw-in, Junior Hoilett chased down County defender Craig Forsyth and tackled him. Despite having two more defenders trying to block his path, Hoilett did manage to get a cross into the area, but only as far as the Derby skipper Richard Keogh. But rather than clear his lines properly, the Irish international only managed to place the ball in the path of Bobby Zamora, who then wrote his name into Queens Park Rangers folklore with a curling shot from 15 yards that found the left corner of the net. Cue the pandemonium and delight from tens of thousands of supporters that had rarely been seen in the long history of the club. It was too late for Derby County to respond, and at the first time of asking, QPR were returning to the Premiership. And it had happened thanks to a man whose standing at the club had reached rock-bottom, just months earlier. Zamora's contract was actually up at the end of the 2013/14 season, but his Rangers story had a couple more chapters to it.

Perhaps off the back of his Wembley winner, he was given a new one-year deal. Not a single fan begrudged him of that. There would be a couple of further surprises in his last year. Like the fact that he managed to get through the entire 14/15 campaign without any further injuries, and would even get to wear the captain's armband when Queens Park Rangers hosted Liverpool. Unfortunately, Harry Redknapp also happened to be asking too much of the striker who would turn 34 during the season. All of his fine work towards the end of the promotion year, was as a result of him coming off the bench. With just himself and Charlie Austin as the only recognised strikers for almost all of 2014/15, the lack of attacking options meant he had to start most matches. In reality, he would have been more effective had he still being coming off the bench, to make an impact late on in games. Predictably, Bobby Zamora was no more prolific in front of goal, than he had been in any of his three previous years at the club, with just three goals in 31 appearances-none of which came at Loftus Road. Which was a great shame given that it would have been nice to serenade him one more time with the chant "Oh, Bobby Zamora"! Although his overall performances were generally pretty good given his advanced age and what was being expected of him. And on the plus side, he did get one of the best QPR goals of the 21st century, with that outrageous chip over the keeper from a ridiculous angle, in the 4-1 win at West Bromwich Albion.

With Rangers relegated again in 2015, Bobby Zamora was one of many experienced players to leave the club. Taking a closer look at his time at Loftus Road, the statistics don't necessarily make great reading. He never scored more than five goals in any of his four seasons with us. He got a meagre 14 goals in 92 appearances. Whereas most strikers would like to be scoring at a rate of at least one goal every three matches, Zamora's record reads one in less than every six and a half appearances. There is no argument to claim he was an outstanding striker, when it came to the small matter of scoring goals for Queens Park Rangers. Yet at the same time, this was the man who got one of the most important, valuable, watched, and celebrated QPR goals ever. He well and truly repaid the £4 million transfer, thanks to that moment. And it came from a player most supporters had given up on, just months earlier. In a generation from now, most people will have forgotten his overall scoring record, and numerous injury problems. In comparison, Bobby Zamora's goal against Derby County will never be forgotten by those who were at Wembley, back in May 2014.

46 *A Win Away*
Sunderland 0 Queens Park Rangers 2
2014/15

There have been a few miserable runs of away results, in the modern history of QPR. Chapter 30 which looked at Ray Harford's time in charge, was a good example of that. It was a similar story under Mark Hughes. Rangers won 3-2 at Stoke City on 19 November 2011 and didn't get another victory on the road, until that 1-0 win at Stamford Bridge, on 2 January 2013. Hughes had come and gone as Queens Park Rangers manager, in between both of those wins taking place. The 2000/01 season was one of the most miserable in living memory, and only one away win was recorded, with that coming in the form of a 1-0 victory at Gillingham in February, thanks to a goal from Chris Kiwomya. But with wins in the last away game of 99/00 and the first of the 01/02 campaigns, at least there was no lengthy overlap from other seasons, to add to that. Even Ian Holloway was not immune to getting dragged into the mire that was a lengthy winless away run. Rangers memorably won 4-1 away to Birmingham City in February

2016, yet did not record another win on the road, until their next visit to St Andrew's, in December of the same year, thanks to a brace from Jack Robinson in a 2-1 victory. Yet a different miserable run away from Loftus Road was just as disheartening as those mentioned, and was potentially the most embarrassing of the lot.

Following the euphoria of beating Derby County in the Play-Off Final in Wembley 2014, now we all had to face the reality of playing Premiership football on a weekly basis. Harry Redknapp would need to make some shrewd decisions if Queens Park Rangers were to survive for more than one season. Unfortunately, they would be few and far between. Redknapp oversaw a number of poor signings when he attempted to strengthen the squad. Brazilian Sandro, midfielder Jordan Mutch, Croat Nico Krancjar and keeper Alex McCarthy all had failed spells at Loftus Road. But none of them were as damaging as Rio Ferdinand. Harry Redknapp was so desperate to bring the former Manchester United and England defender to the club, he built the defence, and by definition, the entire team around the man who would turn 36 a couple of months into the 2014/15 campaign. After a handful of poor performances and equally bad results, the five-man defensive system with Ferdinand at the heart of it, was unceremoniously ditched. And Rio Ferdinand whom the manager had placed so much faith in, would only appear sporadically in the side, thereafter. Other signings like the Chilean pair of Mauricio Isla and Eduardo Vargas, along with Dutch midfielder Leroy Fer, did bring more to the party, so to speak. But as a result of a return to a 4-4-2 formation, the trio were now playing in roles that they were not originally brought in for.

Rangers had become somewhat predictable and were even failing to make what good use of the strengths this team had. It was probably the tallest ever QPR side, and on occasions, ten of this team were six foot or over. Yet it was depressing to see Joey Barton monopolising the set-pieces. Given that there was so much height in this team, returns with regards to the number of goals scored from free-kicks and corners, was very poor. But week in, week out, it was the same old routine from our captain. A better leader would have given up the role for the good of the team. Or at the very least, shared responsibility with others, in an attempt to make the most of the one key element that should have frightened opponents. Alas, we simply had more of the same from Barton. And speaking of being predictable, too many other teams 'worked out' Rangers pretty quickly and knew that if you stopped Charlie Austin from scoring, there was not much threat from elsewhere on the pitch. For a fair amount of the season, own goals were officially the club's second highest scorer, after Austin.

To be fair to Redknapp, results were for a while fairly respectable at Loftus Road. And Queens Park Rangers probably produced a couple of their finest performances under him, in the form of the 2-2 draw at home to Manchester City and the 3-2 defeat against Liverpool. Unfortunately, some dubious decisions on the part of referee Mike Dean in the former, and a pair of own goals in the latter of those two games, meant that Rangers picked up just one point, when they could easily have gotten six. But if there was a hard luck story or two when it came to matches at Loftus Road, there were no such 'crumbs of comforts' when it came to away matches. QPR lost 4-0 to both Tottenham Hotspur and Manchester United in the first two trips on the road. Results were slightly less embarrassing, thereafter. But the common denominator was that Rangers kept losing. By the time Stoke City beat Queens Park Rangers on 31 January 2015, it was their eleventh consecutive away defeat since the Premiership season started. Shortly after that loss, Harry Redknapp quit as QPR manager, citing the urgent need for a knee operation.

With a battle to stay in the Premiership still to be fought, there was huge interest as to who would succeed him. As it happened, that man would be Chris Ramsey. Already at Loftus Road in a coaching role, Ramsey was not part of Redknapp's inner circle, in the same way that Joe Jordan and Kevin Bond were. Indeed, so unknown was he to many fans, many of them would probably have been more familiar with the stand-up comedian who is also called Chris Ramsey. Yet while it was unusual for Queens Park Rangers to appoint a manager who was so unfamiliar to Loftus Road regulars, rarely has the new boss being burdened with the weight of such high expectations. Just days after Harry Redknapp departed, owner Tony Fernandes publicly announced that he was close to signing his *'dream manager'*. Those comments unsurprisingly caused plenty of ripples among fans wondering who on earth Fernandes was referring to. As it happened, Ramsey was appointed as caretaker manager before getting the role on a permanent basis in the summer. In the absence of Arsene Wenger, Pep Guardiola or Jurgen Klopp stepping out of a taxi in South Africa Road, the new man in charge was in the eyes of some people, the person whom Fernandes might have been referring to all along.

Ramsey had enough on his plate to worry about, without having to deal with the ridiculous build-up on the part of our owner. Following a 1-0 home defeat to Southampton, Rangers went to Sunderland for a key relegation battle. This was the club's twelfth of nineteen away matches in the Premiership. There was now a possibility that QPR could go through an entire league campaign, and lose every single away match in the process. It would be a humiliation that would take a generation to live down, and a fact that would have turned up at pub quizzes and on TV quiz shows, like a bad penny. Among the trips still ahead were

Manchester City, Liverpool, and Leicester City who would be surprise Premiership winners a year later. There was little likelihood of getting anything from those games. So, to avoid making unwanted history, this match away to Sunderland represented one of QPR's best opportunities to stop the rot. Rangers beat them earlier in the season thanks to a 1-0 home win, courtesy of a Charlie Austin goal. Trouble is, he was injured for this game so that made Chris Ramsey's task all the harder. But if others could finally step up, then perhaps this losing run could finally come to an end. Thankfully, that is exactly what happened.

The first goal of the evening came on 17 minutes when Matt Phillips swung a cross in from the right, and it was met with a powerful header by Dutch international Leroy Fer, who outjumped his marker in the process. Phillips had a rather strange career of highs and lows, while he was at Queens Park Rangers. For all of Harry Redknapp's time in charge during the 14/15 season, the Scottish international winger was out of favour whilst Fer and Vargas were regularly selected ahead of him, in those wide roles. Yet, off the back of a long period out of the team, Matt Phillips returned to the starting line-up under Chris Ramsey and racked up no fewer than eight assists for the latter part of the season. For a while, he was responsible for setting up more goals than any other player in the Premiership. if it was a mistake on Redknapp's part to overlook Phillips, it was simply the latest in a long line of them. Leroy Fer almost made it 2-0 with a cleverly struck shot with the outside of his left foot from the edge of the area, that hit the inside of the post, before rolling along the goal line. None of his teammates were able to tap in the rebound. It was one of five occasions Fer hit the woodwork in the Premiership in his one top-flight campaign with the R's.

Speaking of which, a few minutes later, Rangers keeper Rob Green pulled off a spectacular save to parry Connor

Wickham's header on to the bar, then scooped the ball clear as it bounced behind him. On the stroke of half-time, Rangers had another attack on the right side of the pitch. With plenty of time to deliver a cross, Matt Phillips placed a low ball into the penalty area that was met by a superb volley with the weaker right foot of Bobby Zamora, who found the top right corner of the net. Sunderland's six foot eight-inch-tall Romanian keeper Costel Pantilimon did not even attempt a save, as it was in the back of the net, before he realised what had just happened. Once again it showed that although Zamora did not get many goals for Queens Park Rangers, the ones that he did score tended to be significant for one reason or another.

Sunderland were unable to muster much in the way of goalscoring chances, so the victory was pretty comfortable. But there was huge disappointment for Ramsey as Leroy Fer had to be stretchered off after 75 minutes, and was replaced by the now forgotten Mauro Zarate-an Argentinian who was Harry Redknapp's last signing for QPR. Zarate was supposed to help share the burden with an otherwise threadbare attack, to contribute goals alongside Charlie Austin. But his only notable achievement with Rangers was to get a two-week ban, after he threw a tantrum after been left out of the team, for the visit to Liverpool. He would make just four brief appearances for Queens Park Rangers, and failed to score in the process. But on a more positive note, this horrible run of away defeats finally came to an end. The travelling support that had become used to seeing one defeat after another, were able to celebrate by singing;

"A win away, a win away, a win away, a win away, a win away, a win away, a win away, a win away.
We're the Rangers, the Mighty Rangers, we're gonna win away.
We're the Rangers, the Mighty Rangers, we're gonna win

away!"

The chant, which had previously been sung at Wigan in the goalless first leg of the Play Off Semi Final in 2014, was based on the 1982 UK number one single 'The Lion Sleeps Tonight', by Tight Fit. And that in turn, was a cover of a South African song dating all the way back to the late 1930's. Temporarily at least, that win at the Stadium of Light, took Rangers out of the relegation places. But not for long. QPR lost their next five Premiership matches, among them a 3-1 defeat at Crystal Palace where fans chanted the same song, except they removed the word 'gonna' and replaced it with 'never'. At least supporters kept their sense of humour. Despite a memorable 4-1 away to West Bromwich Albion, the home form fell apart in spectacular fashion and that ensured relegation came the end of the season. Ramsey was not popular among some Rangers fans and could do no right, in the eyes of many of them. He would only last until November 2015, before getting the sack. Weeks later, Chris Ramsey returned as Technical Director and has rebuilt his reputation overseeing a youth system that has finally started to produce players who are integral figures in the first team.

During his time as manager, that win at Sunderland remains one of the highlights while he was in charge. Had the visit to the Stadium of Light ended in defeat, that would have been twelve in a row. And with each passing away defeat, more panic would have set in among the players, and on a wider scale, the club would have been a cross between a freak show and a laughing stock, as the rest of football would have looked on to see if Queens Park Rangers would have made an unwanted piece of English football history. Ultimately, it is always a relief when such long run without an away win, comes to an end. And perhaps the relief that greeted the victory at the Stadium of Light, was greater than that of the other numerous examples of this unwanted QPR genre.

47 *The Gift Outright*
Queens Park Rangers 1 Sheffield United 0
2017/18

Over the years, Rangers have been the recipient of so many opposition blunders, you could devote an entire DVD to the subject. Thanks to Jamie Pollock, Queens Park Rangers were on the right end of perhaps the most famous own goal in the history of English club football. And if you go back to 1968, 1983 and 2004, the history of the club was influenced by opposing own goals which contributed to promotion in one form or another, in all of those years. And speaking of historical dates from the past, the 1986 Milk Cup semi-final second leg at Anfield also finished victorious as a result of two Liverpool own goals on the night.

With own goals and blunders coming at the rate of sometimes a couple, and occasionally, a few of them in any given season, the amount that can be found on film, would easily come in at three figures. A startling number which goes to prove that it is one area in which QPR have never been short of good fortune, over recent decades. Long-standing supporters must have thought that they had seen everything regarding farcical goals for Rangers, by the time Sheffield United visited Loftus Road in October 2017. But thanks to the Blades goalkeeper, this match was proof that it is a genre that never stops evolving.

Early on in the game, a punt upfield looked like it could find the QPR striker Idrissa Sylla, who in turn would have a decent goalscoring opportunity. Ironically, the big Guinea international looked somewhat disinterested, as his defensive marker Cameron Carter-Vickers seemed to easily cover the danger, about the time the goalkeeper came out to claim the ball. The stopper in question was Jamal Blackman. Blackman was one of the army of footballers on loan from Chelsea at the time. At six foot six inches tall, the giant stopper should in theory have had no trouble collecting this innocuous ball forward. Sylla was even getting out of his way to let him collect it. On the basis of what followed, perhaps Carter-Vickers would have been advised to do likewise.

Jamal Blackman tried to climb on top of his teammate. Which was okay initially, as he grabbed the ball comfortably enough, which you would expect from such a tall keeper. But when he went to ground as a result of the contact made with the defender, the ball fumbled out of his hands as he took a heavy landing on the Loftus Road pitch. And the moment got even more bizarre as it rolled gently in the direction of Sylla, who initially never saw what had just happened. He quickly realised that a rare gift had just come his way, and promptly tucked home a left-footed shot with the minimal of interference from the rest of the United defence. As if this incident couldn't get any dafter, Blackman initially tried to scramble back to retrieve the ball, but then rolled around in agony, when he saw Idrissa Sylla tap home. Jamal Blackman went off with a head injury, before the game restarted.

With no further goals, Queens Park Rangers comfortably held on for the win, although the next most memorable incident of the evening, involved Sylla almost making a fool out of a second United keeper in the same game. The Blades substitute stopper Simon Moore-who is one of the few professional footballers to hail from the Isle of Wight-was almost beaten by the most audacious of chips from almost 40 yards out. In trying to stop the lob, Moore finished up in his own net. But unfortunately, from an R's point of view, his hands and the ball were on the other side of the goal line, which resulted in one of the more unorthodox saves Loftus Road has ever seen. As a result of the two incidents involving QPR's Guinea international forward, it was certainly one of the more unusual one-nil wins.

Although Rangers finished that season in 16th place and Ian Holloway would get the sack at the end of it, this was actually the second time in four days, they beat the team at the top of the Championship-following on from a 2-1 home win over Wolverhampton Wanderers. Different things might be said in the privacy of the dressing room, but it is rare for a manager to publicly berate one of his own players for such a significant blunder. Blades manager Chris Wilder was no different. He was more concerned about the health of his keeper, and went on record to thank the QPR support for applauding the keeper, as he was stretchered off. 'It was a proper gesture from a proper football club', said a grateful Wilder. Whilst such praise from visiting managers and players is always nice, it is probably wise not to ask would the injured keeper have gotten the same round of applause, if all of the home support knew which parent club he hailed from.

And what of Jamal Blackman? Having gone off with a

head injury, it was a relief to hear that there were no serious repercussions as a result of the tumble he took that evening, and less than three weeks later, he was back in the Sheffield United starting line-up. All of which lead to a few people cruelly suggesting that the most painful blow that he suffered that night, was the one to his pride. Watching the highlights again, it would be easy to miss an important incident that took place in the lead-up to that goal. If you look at it in slow motion, you can see that the punt upfield that lead to Sylla's goal, actually hit the back of Cameron Carter-Vickers heel and bounce upwards, prior to Blackman's doomed attempt to collect the ball. Whether it had any effect on the events that followed, we shall never know. So, in the pantheon of own goals and blunders that have come the way of Queens Park Rangers, where exactly does this one feature?

The likelihood is that nothing will ever top what Jamie Pollock did back in 1998. But Jamal Blackman's nightmare moment would undoubtedly feature in any top ten most ridiculous of goals. As a genre, it has continued to add bizarre, humorous, lucky, unusual, freakish and painful additions, with each passing season. And long may that continue. No doubt the future will see further unexpected gifts come the way of QPR.

48 *35ᵗʰ Time Lucky*
Nottingham Forest 0 Queens Park Rangers 1
2018/19

Rangers have long-standing poor records at Old Trafford and Anfield. Although in the space of less than twelve months in the early 1990s, they were the scenes of two of the greatest victories in the history of QPR. They being the 3-1 win over Liverpool in March 1991 and of course, the legendary 4-1 thrashing of Manchester United on New Year's Day 1992. Even if this has meant a few miserable visits to these two famous venues ever since, supporters can always look back fondly at those truly wonderful away days. But whilst long-awaited victories were finally recorded at those grounds many years ago, there remained one football ground that Queens Park Rangers just could not win at.

The City Ground in Nottingham had pretty much been the scene of one disappointment after another for QPR, ever since the home side thumped the R's 4-0 in a FA Cup 3rd Round tie, in January 1934. It was understandable that

Forest was a difficult place to get anything, during the Brian Clough years, when they were undoubtedly one of the powerhouses of English football but their glory days are long since gone. As was featured in Chapter 39, they have also suffered the ignominy of falling down to the third tier of English football. But in both the good times and the bad, QPR just could never win at Forest.

The 2018/19 fixture between the two clubs had a little bit of spice added to it. After four years in West London, Jack Robinson left Loftus Road for Nottingham Forest on a free transfer. It was a source of much disappointment to Rangers fans. Robinson had been spent most of the first three seasons with Rangers being injured. Yet throughout that time, Loftus Road regulars were never judgemental towards him. Indeed, with what little we saw of him prior to the 2017/18 season, there was much to be admired, with his commitment on the field showing that all of the time that he missed from playing, wasn't something he was prepared to let hold him back. He had the look of a player who could slot into a number of positions when fit, and also possessed a monster throw-in, that surprised many people, as he had quite a slim build. Which was in stark contrast to muscular physiques of Andy Gray and Jay Emmanuel-Thomas, who would probably have been the only Queens Park Rangers players of the modern era, who could match the distance Robinson was achieving regularly from throw-ins.

With the fit-again defender very much part of the Rangers first team squad having surprised many people by playing so many matches in the centre of the defence, it felt disheartening to see him turn down the opportunity to sign a new contract with the club. This meant that he would have to face his old side, when Forest hosted QPR in December. Many players might have felt a bit anxious about facing their old side. If Jack Robinson did, he certainly made a good job of disguising that fact. In the build-up to this game, Robinson stated that if Nottingham Forest played at their best against Rangers, they would *'blow them the out of the water'*. Little did he know that those words would come back to haunt him, by the end of this encounter.

On the stroke of half-time, Luke Freeman took a free-kick which he curled in with his left-foot. Rising highest was Toni Leistner. Much to the delight of every Rangers supporter regardless of whether you attended the match or not, failing to stop the QPR captain heading home was none other than Jack Robinson. One photo that was taken at the very moment the big German was about to score, memorably showed Robinson pulling the shirt of Leistner as he headed the winner. This just a moment before the Nottingham Forest defender finished up a dishevelled heap on the floor. It was now more a case of 'eating dirt' than 'blowing anyone out of the water'.

There was an onslaught from the home team in the second half. Albeit one with very few genuine efforts on target. The best of their chances was a superb 35-yard shot from Adlene Guedioura, which Joe Lumley tipped onto the crossbar. After seeing off some more Forest pressure, Queens Park Rangers had finally recorded a first ever victory at Nottingham Forest's City Ground. It was a relief, as much as it had been a momentous day. In recent years, even the rest of English football was looking at this fixture with a combination of bemusement and shock that QPR had visited this ground on so many occasions, and never won. After so many years of disappointment and failure, the burden of failing to win there couldn't come to an end, quick enough. And Jack Robinson's foolhardy attempt to talk up an inevitable big win for Forest, felt like an extra present, coming as it did just three days before Christmas.

Steve McClaren's time as Queens Park Rangers manager is not remembered with any great fondness. A large percentage of the R's fanbase never wanted him in charge in the first place. He did little to persuade the doubters wrong during a largely miserable eleven months. McClaren lost his first four consecutive league matches and failed to get the best out of any of the young players who were trying to establish themselves in the side, ironically he was brought in because the club hierarchy claimed Steve McClaren was the best man to oversee their development. Fans were stuck with dreary tactics that generally meant that every side that visited Loftus Road, dominated possession. And if that wasn't bad enough, he was largely responsible for the worst season in our history, in terms of home defeats. But he can always claim to be the Rangers manager who finally oversaw a win at the City Ground. And this having once been Nottingham Forest manager for a period of just ten matches, before resigning in 2010.

49 *When Rangers Declared War on Wales*
Queens Park Rangers 5 Swansea City 1
2019/20

It does not happen very often but from time to time, QPR will scale the heights by following one brilliant performance, with another that is even better. Let us look at a couple of examples. In the 1991/92 season, Manchester City were dispatched 4-0 and a few days later, an even better performance saw Gerry Francis' side thump Leeds United 4-1. In the following campaign, Easter 1993 was memorable for Rangers beating Nottingham Forest 4-3, as the visitors belied their status as the Premiership's whipping boys, with a totally committed performance in defeat. 48 hours later, Queens Park Rangers won 5-3 at Goodison Park. Only a couple of late goals from Everton brought some respectability to the score line. To this day, supporters still recall this magical period when Les Ferdinand scored back-to-back hat tricks. The new decade was only days old when fans would see a repeat of this most welcome example of the club soaring the heights in successive games.

On New Year's Day, Cardiff City came to Loftus Road and were thrashed 6-1. Bright Osayi-Samuel terrorised the Bluebirds defence all afternoon, Nahki Wells scored only the second QPR league hat trick in fifteen years, and even goalkeeper Joe Lumley got an assist to his name when he cleverly picked out Osayi-Samuel who scored twice, himself. We even had the scenario of Alex Smithies who left Queens Park Rangers in the summer of 2018 to further his career with Cardiff in the Premiership, having to sit on the bench on his first trip back. Though given the events of this Bank Holiday cracker, it may well have been the first time that Smithies was delighted that Neil Etheridge was ahead of him in goal, in the pecking order. An outstanding afternoon over one Welsh side, was followed by the visit of another, just four days later, with Mark Warburton's side hosting Swansea City in the FA Cup Third Round.

The club's showing in the FA Cup since the turn of the 21st century, had been a source of shame and humiliation to Rangers supporters. Most years have seen Queens Park Rangers depart the competition at the first time of asking and the long list of defeats, featured numerous embarrassing lows over the past 20 years. Among them, Paul Hart who can boast one of the shortest ever tenures as QPR boss lasting just 29 days, hastening his own departure with a team selection disaster, for the defeat at home to Sheffield United in January 2010. Harry Redknapp oversaw three successive ignominious exits from the FA Cup. In two spells as Rangers manager, Ian Holloway failed to win a single tie in no fewer than six attempts.

When Steve McClaren oversaw a 2-1 win at home to Leeds United in January 2019, it was the first time since Trevor Sinclair scored that overhead kick against Barnsley in

January 1997, that Queens Park Rangers had actually won an FA Cup tie, at the first time of asking. The 2018/19 side made it to the Fifth Round of the competition, yet ahead of the Swansea City tie in January, there was another unusual statistic that needed banishing. With three goals coming from corners, one from a free-kick and the other from the penalty spot in the cup run under Steve McClaren, Rangers hadn't actually scored a goal from open play in the competition since January 2013. The scorer of that goal incidentally, was the now-forgotten figure of one-time Manchester United loanee Fabio. The Brazilian scored late on in a 4-2 home defeat to MK Dons, on a day Harry Redknapp made nine changes to the starting line-up, and then bandied about terms like 'diabolical' and 'disgusted', off the back of a loss with what was effectively a second-string side. Little wonder then that there is so much apathy from supporters, towards the FA Cup.

Moving on to January 2020, Rangers came into this FA Cup match, off the back of that outstanding league victory. Though not surprisingly, only a handful of players who started the Cardiff match, would do likewise against Swansea. Only Geoff Cameron, Lee Wallace, Dominic Ball, Bright Osayi-Samuel and Ilias Chair were on the pitch at the beginning of both games. But with the likes of Josh Scowen, Mark Pugh and Jordan Hugill coming in for the cup match, there was still plenty of experience in the QPR side. After the Swans hit the crossbar in the opening minutes, it was Hugill who would make the breakthrough for Rangers. A cross from Todd Kane on the right, picked out the Rangers striker who chested the ball which allowed him the opportunity to take it away from his marker. Then he followed that up with a superb volley from just inside the penalty area that gave the goalkeeper no chance as it found the bottom left-hand corner of the net. After the small matter of seven years, we finally had a goal that took from Fabio, the status of being the last one scored in the

FA Cup from open play. It was a superb finish from Jordan Hugill, but as it happened, there would be much better Queens Park Rangers goals later on in the game.

In the 29th minute, former R's defender Jake Bidwell was caught flat-footed by Osayi-Samuel, and the lightning fast winger took the ball off him before beating another defender, and tapping home from eight yards out. It was his third goal in two games. The same amount that he managed in the whole of the 2018/19 campaign, incidentally. The same player very nearly made it four goals in 2020, but was denied by keeper Kristoffer Nordfeldt. After that, Hugill was quickest to react to a Chair free-kick and poked home from close range. With no further goals in the first half, it looked like the cup tie was already won. Just shy of the hour mark, substitute George Byers pulled a goal back for the visitors, when he was allowed a free run outside the penalty area, and scored with a well-placed shot from 25 yards. But that would be as good as it would get for Swansea City.

Fifteen minutes later, a right-wing cross from Bright Osayi-Samuel was drilled towards Hugill at the far post. He was only able to head it towards the edge of the area, where it looked like City's French midfielder Aldo Kalulu would comfortably clear the ball. But in his attempt to be clever by flicking the ball clear with his heel, completely mistimed the clearance and Lee Wallace picked up possession. The experienced Scottish defender headed the ball to allow himself a shooting chance. Despite the attention of Kalulu who quickly recovered from his initial error, Wallace hit a stunning right-footed volley from 25 yards which found the left corner of the net. It was all the more impressive given that the former Scottish international is actually left-footed. It also brought back memories of a couple of former QPR defenders who rose to the occasion in the FA Cup. David Pizanti and Kenny

Sansom never managed a league goal for Rangers, between them. But in 1988 and 1990 respectively, both could boast fantastic goals in the cup. Brilliant strikes by Queens Park Rangers players in the FA Cup had almost become a thing of the past, and when Lee Wallace scored, it was undoubtedly the finest from a player in blue and white hoops, in the 21st century. Minutes later however, it wasn't even the best goal of the afternoon.

With such a commanding lead, confidence among the Rangers players was sky high, and Todd Kane, Josh Scowen and Osayi Bright-Samuel were exchanging passes for fun, whilst the Swansea defence could not get a look in. Eventually, Scowen timed his run into the penalty area, as Kane flicked the ball to the QPR midfielder. With that, Josh Scowen chested the ball down and on the turn, hit an amazing volley from a very narrow angle that found the opposite corner of the net. A stunning conclusion to such a memorable match. Unfortunately, it was something of a bittersweet moment for Scowen. Earlier in the season, he had been subjected to considerable online abuse from a minority of so-called fans. A few weeks later, he joined Sunderland. Hopefully in time, he will come to appreciate what a special moment that was.

As has often been the case, when Queens Park Rangers scale such heights, what follows is often a 'damp squib'. The following league match saw Rangers lose 3-1 at Brentford, and in the next round of the FA Cup, Sheffield Wednesday won 2-1 at Loftus Road. Not the long-awaited cup run, supporters were hoping for. But off the back of a generation of failures in the competition, QPR had their first truly memorable FA Cup match, in this millennium. Unfortunately, not that many people turned up to see it.

Legacy is an underused word when it comes to Rangers, and although it can be used to describe a positive effect on the club, it can equally apply to a negative scenario. Even off the back of hammering Cardiff City, the attendance was just 6,712. If any Queens Park Rangers supporter had asked the fan sitting next to them during the 6-1 win if they were coming watch the game against Swansea, there was probably only a 50 percent chance of them responding in the affirmative. But can you really blame those that couldn't be bothered to come along and watch this cup tie? Any supporter under the age of 30, has only ever really known failure. And even some of those who are old enough to remember the 1982 FA Cup Final, or the marathon run in the 1989/90 season, had simply tired of weakened teams being put out, that lame old excuse about "concentrating on the league", or one shambolic exit too many. Truth be told, it will require a lot more than this superb win over Swansea City, to win over what is a sizeable proportion of the Rangers fanbase, who believe that the FA Cup is simply not worth bothering with.

Whilst QPR do not have a proud record in the competition, there have been a few great cup games in days gone by. But with each passing failure, those golden moments were becoming more and more of a distant memory. And younger fans who have long since become 'conditioned' to accepting such a dismal showing on an annual basis, accept failure as a rite-of-passage during the course of a given season. The thrashing of Swansea offered a long-awaited alternative way to how supporters might view the FA Cup, for different reasons. The manner in which the win came, the spectacular goals from Wallace and Scowen and the fact that it came off the back of beating Cardiff City four days earlier. It doesn't get much more entertaining than eleven goals scored with just two conceded, in successive matches at Loftus Road. There are some matches you know are still going to be remembered in years to come. No wonder there was a humorous one-liner making the rounds of some of the R's online forums with the declaration that this was when 'Queens Park Rangers Declared War on Wales'.

50 *A Fair Wind*
Nottingham Forest 0 Queens Park Rangers 0
2019/20

The weather has generally never had the same influence over a game of football, like it does with other sports. Let us look at a couple such examples. When the captain of a cricket team goes out for the toss just before the start of a Test match, he will be well aware of what the weather forecast is like. If he wins the aforementioned toss, and knows that there are a couple of hot sunny days ahead, he will inevitably choose to bat with the aim of building a significant innings. Alternatively, if the weather is much cooler and there is significant cloud cover along with the prospect of rain later in the day, he will more than likely insert the opposition into bat, and let his pace bowlers try to fill their boots. Equally, the weather can play an influential role in the sport of athletics. In long distance events like the 10,000 metres and the marathon, milder temperatures and even a bit of rain would be welcomed by competitors taking part in those endurance events. Conditions can play a key part in the more explosive events, too. Wind readings can have a major bearing on times recorded in the 100 metres. A more favourable following wind can ensure significantly quicker performances from sprinters. But equally, any wind readings over two metres per second, will make whatever times were recorded-no matter how impressive they are-ineligible for the record books. In comparison, the elements have never played as important a role, when it comes to football matches. Or at least that was the case until Rangers visited the City Ground in January 2020.

Having suffered two home Championship defeats to Nottingham Forest since that historic win there, thirteen months earlier, it did not feel like QPR suddenly held the Indian sign over the team from the East Midlands. Though there was another coincidence to go with the previous visit, as in the case of Steve McClaren, Mark Warburton was another former Forest manager. The match was played at a time when the weather all over Britain was appalling. Whilst this did not pose a threat with regards to the game going ahead, little did we know that it would have an influence over the result.

After just twelve minutes of the game, a first half corner from Joe Lolley was floated into the penalty area via his left foot. Centre-half Joe Worrall got his head to the ball first, as it looped over all-comers and into the back of the net. Straight away, a couple of the Queens Park Rangers players started protesting to the match officials about the goal. Initially you would have wondered what on earth they had to complain about? A foul on one of the QPR players? No. An obstruction on the keeper Liam Kelly perhaps? No. A Forest hand ball? No. Ungentlemanly conduct? Well, by the time you eliminated all of the other options, you may well have thought that this was the sole straw that some of our players were now clinging to. As it turned out, there was a completely different issue that the

R's defenders had a problem with.

Around a second before Lolley was about to take the corner, the excessive wind conditions caused the ball to move. A close up reveals that the gusts were so strong, not only was the football in motion, it looked like the corner flag was about to be uprooted at any moment. The match ball was not stationery when it was struck by the Forest winger, and a couple of sharp-eyed defenders were quick to raise that point to the officials. By definition, free-kicks, corners, and penalties, are collectively referred to as 'dead ball situations'. And as the television footage showed, the ball was moving at the crucial moment. Thankfully, the referee Rob Jones and his linesman noticed it as well, and the Worrall's goal was disallowed.

The reaction of the big Forest defender was one of disbelief. He had already celebrated with teammates and supporters alike, before learning that the goal would not stand. Joe Warrall's look of horror when the goal was disallowed, was matched by that of his manager, Sabri Lamouchi. This led to a long discussion with the officials, which no doubt included a chat about the more obscure rules of the game. After the match, the Frenchman admitted to feeling hugely disappointed about the goal being disallowed but also conceded, somewhat reluctantly, that it was the right decision.

After the drama of that disallowed goal, Nottingham Forest were in control for much of the rest of the match, but managed just a couple of efforts on targets. Perhaps the best of them saw Kelly pull off a brilliant save from a 30-yard shot from Sammy Ameobi. On an afternoon destined to be remembered for one particular corner, another one later in the game saw Tiago Silva hit the crossbar. Once again, that moment was as a result of the wind playing havoc all afternoon.

Meanwhile QPR could only muster a few half chances all afternoon, like when early in the second half, Ryan Manning had a shot from a narrow angle which tested Forest's Congolese keeper Brice Samba. The visiting defence held firm all afternoon, blocking most shots that they faced. Most memorably when Angel Rangel twice cleared off the goal line in a matter of seconds, whilst other chances went wide. Subsequently, Queens Park Rangers collected a well-earned point in the most unusual of circumstances. From a Nottingham Forest point of view, long-standing supporters have probably had many reasons to blame for failing to win a match, over the years. A goalkeeping howler, defensive mistake, wasted opportunities from a striker, or glaring errors from either the referee or linesman. On that afternoon in February 2020, they could add the weather to that lengthy list.

As with a few other chapters in this book, the key incident in this game is something of a one-off and is not likely to be something that will be repeated in a Rangers match. And for that reason alone, it begs one very interesting question. And that is 'would supporters have felt hard done by if Mark Warburton's side been on the wrong end of this occurrence'? The likelihood is that we would initially have felt that the goal should have been given, just as our opponents did. But after the initial phase of disbelief, would have come the realisation that the match officials had made the right decision. It is doubtful however, that we will one day find Queens Park Rangers robbed of a goal because it came at the exact moment that the weather intervened. Chances are, it is one of those once-in-a-lifetime occurrences that comes from following QPR. Which is exactly the reason why it forms the final chapter of this book.

Rangers would play only a further three matches, before

the Covid-19 crisis caused the lengthy cancellation to the season, along with all sporting events. With no football for three full months, it gave me time to reflect on so many memorable moments and matches in the history of this football club. Seeing Rangers earn a point off the back of the intervention of the weather, was the latest in a long list of matches that were memorable, unique or unusual. Sometimes for the wrong reasons, but often for the right ones. And in many ways, they have all formed their own little part in our colourful history. Whether they are games that you recall attending from your own lifetime of supporting Queens Park Rangers or learned about them for the first time, I hope you have enjoyed reading about them, as much as I did, when I watched, read, or discovered them for myself. From a personal point of view, it was a pleasure to take so many strolls down Memory Lane.

Come on You R's!

ABOUT THE AUTHOR

Ray Eaton saw his first Queens Park Rangers match in the 1980/81 season and has followed the club ever since. For many years, he has been a contributor to the long-running fanzine A Kick Up The R's. Away from QPR, Ray has worked for the Royal Mail for over 30 years. A fan of most sports, he follows the England and Middlesex Cricket teams and British Athletics. A keen quiz enthusiast, his other interests include music, cinema, swimming and overseas travel.

Printed in Great Britain
by Amazon